T0194654

THE
BROTHERS
OF
ST. JOSEPH

THE BROTHERS OF ST. JOSEPH

GEORGE KLAWITTER

THE BROTHERS OF ST. JOSEPH

iUniverse books may be ordered through booksellers or by contacting:

iUniverse
1663 Liberty Drive
Bloomington, IN 47403
www.iuniverse.com
1-800-Authors (1-800-288-4677)

ISBN: 978-1-5320-8069-2 (sc)
ISBN: 978-1-5320-8070-8 (hc)
ISBN: 978-1-5320-8068-5 (e)

Library of Congress Control Number: 2019912497

Print information available on the last page.

iUniverse rev. date: 08/24/2019

Also by George Klawitter, CSC

Adapted to the Lake: Letters by the Brother Founders of Notre Dame

Boys to Men: Holy Cross School in New Orleans

The Life and Letters of Brother Andre Mottais

After Holy Cross, Only Notre Dame: The Life of Urbain Monsimer

Holy Cross in Algeria

The Poems of Charles O'Donnell, CSC

Early Men of Holy Cross

for

Thomas Maddix, CSC

"The originating vision came more from what some now call 'laboratory theology' vs lived experience. In other words, the vision Moreau talks about as a professor does not have any roots in a lived experience especially in the world in which he lived. Thus, for all his words, his congregation came to resemble many of the other groups founded or in existence with priests in charge and brothers in a subservient position. The Brothers' vocation from Dujarie came about from a lived experience with a commitment to be educators and equality and grounded in the example of the Christian Brothers. Two very different visions shaped our founding story."

CONTENTS

INTRODUCTION

When Brother Rémi Mérianne sat down in 1878 to write his recollections of Holy Cross, he did not begin with 1837, the year that religious brothers in Le Mans, France, joined with priests to form a single community. He began rather with the year 1820 when a simple country priest started to gather around him young men willing to leave their homes in northwest France and learn the rudiments of teaching. People today who know the men's Congregation of Holy Cross experience it as a religious community of Brothers and priests who live together and serve the Church on an equal basis—there is no discrimination among members based on their ministries. But for Rémi Mérianne Holy Cross began with one type of religious—the brother.

In a letter to his provincial superior Louis Champeau, Brother Rémi wrote that he would "show that the addition of priests joined to Brothers [in 1837] was not a new foundation but only the complement of the congregation in the plan conceived by its first founder, [James] Dujarié, who tried to do it [amalgamate brothers and priests] several times" (qtd. Vanier 542). So Holy Cross did not begin in 1837, not in the eyes of one of its most venerable chroniclers. This book will therefore explore what happened in the little town of Ruillé two hundred years ago when good-willed men banded together to teach French children the basics of math, reading, penmanship, and catechism.

Received opinion is that the Brothers of St. Joseph were a group of well-intentioned young men who rallied in the 1820s to Ruillé-sur-Loir in order to serve as religious teachers in little French towns near their headquarters. Some attention has been given to their premier Brother, Andre Mottais, but little has been written about most of them. Their priest founder has been honored for his zeal and bravery while hundreds of them have slipped into the silence of historical oblivion. They remain only as names in a French *matricule* (list), young men who arrived with promising virtue and who remained faithful to their religious calling for twenty, thirty, forty years or more.

This book will look to post-1802 France when the Spirit began Her work to revitalize religion in a country both devastated and enlightened by revolution and blood. Good things can begin with violence, especially when power has become disdainful of ordinary people. The nightmare of rulers is that ordinary folk (England in 1642, Massachusetts in 1776, France in 1789) will revolt and rebel, fed up at last with senseless law and structure. Such upheavals can be healthy, resulting in new methods of governance which, of course, eventually themselves may rot and have to be replaced.

Because they were not founded until 1820, the Brothers of St. Joseph did not witness the tug of war that the Sisters of Providence (also founded at Ruillé) had to watch between Napoleon and Pius VII. The literal captivity of the pope and his sequestration in France would not have affected the Brothers because all of that tussle between emperor and pontiff was over by 1812. The Restoration brought with it, however, new challenges as bishops and clergy worked to assume a comfortable place in the new France. Persecution of priests was over, but pockets of irreligion among leftover revolutionaries had yet to be faced. While the mobs of the 1790's had ridiculed the Church and religious practice, the ordinary people of the Empire and Restoration began to assert a reverence for the religion of their forefathers. The Brothers of St. Joseph sprang from those ordinary people, whose search for religious truth was genuine. Hundreds of their sons would find peace and fulfillment as Brothers of St. Joseph.

Because there had been little recruitment to the clergy during the Revolution and few ordinations during the Empire (Dansette 1.174), the duty for religious instruction of the young fell on the shoulders of the family during the Restoration until gradually religious women and men set up schools across the country. It was into this religious renaissance that the Brothers of St. Joseph would take their first steps.

This book on the Brothers of St. Joseph covers the years 1820 to 1840. Are the dates arbitrary? The first year is not because we know exactly when the first recruit came to Ruillé to become a Brother of St. Joseph. The second number, however, is more fluid. One could say the twenty years (1820 to 1840) cover a generation of Brothers. That is as good as any explanation for the *terminus ad quem.* Two years I want to avoid as beginnings for Holy Cross are 1835 and 1837. In the former the Brothers moved their headquarters from Ruillé to Le Mans, but they were still officially the Brothers of St. Joseph. Most Brothers at the annual retreat in the summer of 1835 did not even know they were being transferred to Le Mans. In 1837 the merger of a small group of clerics with the Brothers in a "Fundamental

Act of Union" might seem a logical endpoint for the Brothers of St. Joseph, but in 1837 the Brothers did not stop calling themselves the Brothers of St. Joseph.

Between 1820 and 2020 there is an unbroken continuity of the community today known as Holy Cross. There was no end to the Brothers of St. Joseph in 1835 when they changed the location of their motherhouse and accepted direction from a new superior, and there was no end to the Brothers of St. Joseph in 1837 when they accepted merger with priests. What began in 1820 as a unity of hearts remains to this day a oneness of spirit, sharpened by the "Fundamental Act" of March 1, 1837, but not begun by that "Act."

What, after all, is a "community"? It is a unity of like-minded people living together, sharing a common cause. The Brothers of St. Joseph achieved this beautiful sense of living because they lived together as much as was possible. One good indication of their sense of community is obvious from their longing to be back with their community when they were separated one from another. We have letters from the early Brothers expressive of such longing:

> I can no longer continue the subject. I'm too weak to tell you more. What I can tell you in truth is that they don't take as much care of me here as a human being would of a sick dog. I can't stop crying in telling you this, my well loved Father, but it's the truth. I take God as my witness: during the two and a half days I was so sick, no one came to ask "Do you want anything," except Tourneux, who came three times after work. (Anselm to Sorin, August 4, 1844, in Klawitter, *Adapted* 69)

So if the early Brothers did indeed miss being with each other, a genuine community did exist early on.

The "mix" of Brothers and priests did not actually begin with the 1837 "Act." The Brothers of St. Joseph were a mixed community from Day One. When the first young men arrived at Ruillé, they lived with the pastor-founder. They ate at his table with him, listened to his counsel, studied what he told them to study. They all lived together in his rectory, and when he sent them one by one out to the little French towns to run grade schools, they wrote to him their concerns, and they looked forward mightily to the annual September retreat when they could all troop back to little Ruillé for two weeks of close comradeship with their father-founder. Today we tend to isolate this gentle pastor-founder from the men he gathered together around his vision, but in reality they were one community—one priest, multiple Brothers of St. Joseph. And when the Community was moved lock, stock, and barrel from Ruillé up to Le Mans by a new priest-leader in 1835, the Ruillé pastor missed them so much that Brother Andre Mottais moved his priest-mentor up to Le Mans where he lived happily for one year until he died among his Brothers of St. Joseph.

So there they are—the priest-visionary sitting down to breakfast in 1820 with Ignatius and Louis. They talk of the gospel, and they plan the day's work—one young man will study his math tables and practice long division, and the other will study French vocabulary and practice his penmanship. All three come together again for a lunch of bread and fruit in the rectory's dining room. They pray together as the priest-founder solders them slowly into a semi-monastic lifestyle, and they talk over the mundane news of the morning: the barn needs cleaning, the weeds along the path to the church need trimming, the apples have to be gathered into the fruit cellar. They separate for afternoon chores. The priest may walk over to the Grand Providence to discuss matters with the irascible mother-superior. Ignatius and Louis go about their work. In late afternoon they gather for study, the priest leading them through the psalms and some Church history or rudimentary theology. They pray. They sit down to a modest supper. They chat before an evening prayer. They go to bed as the sun sets. They are a mixed community.

Prior to the 1837 "Fundamental Act," which joined hearts (and finances), the two groups (Brothers and priests) lived for two years in proximity after the Brothers had been moved up from Ruillé, a small town twenty-eight miles south of Le Mans. The group of clerical men had begun their own community in 1835 at Le Mans when an energetic and charismatic priest, who was assistant rector at the local seminary, gathered a few priests to live together and minister in outreach to parishes in the diocese. They were called simply "auxiliary priests," auxiliary to the diocese where the bishop saw them as useful for preaching parish retreats and occasionally spelling overworked pastors. Interestingly, as early as 1823 the pastor of Ruillé was himself thinking about organizing five or six auxiliary priests to preach parish missions and to help him in guiding the Brothers of St. Joseph, but his plans never coalesced (Catta, *Moreau* 1.322). We will see more about this plan later in this book.

There are two problems with dating the Congregation of Holy Cross to the 1837 amalgamation of the Brothers of St. Joseph and the "auxiliary priests." First of all, as I have noted, the Brothers continued to refer to themselves as the "Brothers of St. Joseph." Secondly, the bulk of the newly combined community was composed overwhelmingly of men who had lived as Brothers, some of them (e.g., Andre, Stephen) for seventeen years. If the "Fundamental Act" was an official recognition of merger into a new community, what about the unofficial realities? There was, for example, the psychological unity within the men who transferred up from Ruillé: their lives changed very little. They continued to spend fifty weeks of the year out in parishes around the diocese, returning to Le Mans only for a retreat before a new school year would begin. They had the same commitment to education, and they pursued the same religious life, with all of the obligations they had had when they were attached to the initial foundation at Ruillé. It is true that their new superior in Le Mans was younger, more vital, and more "connected" ecclesiastically than their Ruillé founder had been, but their Church-related obligations remained the same.

For example, one of the Brothers of St. Joseph who made the transition from Ruillé to Le Mans with no fanfare was Vincent Pieau. Twenty-five years old when he entered the religious formation program, he was eventually to become a bedrock of stability, not only at Ruillé and Le Mans, but also in Indiana where he would serve as the patriarch of the 1841 mission group, revered from his arrival at Vincennes right up to his death in 1890 at Notre Dame, a much beloved teacher, formator, and confidant. Brother Vincent had thrived in Ruillé where the founder-priest named him one of the four Brother-Directors to guide the fledgling community. Becoming a novice in 1823, the same year that he received his teaching license, he would be entrusted with the direction of novices many times during his life. The Brother Vincent of Ruillé did not morph suddenly into a new Brother Vincent in his transition to Le Mans or to Indiana: he remained the same integral person in all three places, his personality and his religious commitment entwined.

There is danger in thinking that the Brothers of St. Joseph would not have survived if they had not come under the capable and exemplary direction of their new priest-director in Le Mans in 1835. There was at the time, unfortunately more than not, a tight sense of priestly superiority evident in post-revolutionary France. It had not always been so. Before the sixteenth century, the education of priests had been cursory, sloppy, and quite unlike anything we expect today in seminary training. Then came Pierre de Bércelle (1575-1629) who, as the best of the "French School" of new theologians, formulated new expectations for priestly education. By insisting on God as the center of life and emphasizing the "divinized humanity" of Jesus (Deville 139), Bércelle focused on the need for perfection in priests. What he began so providentially was followed up by three disciples: Charles de Condren, the mystic (1588-1641), Jean-Jacques Olier (1608-1657), and John Eudes (1601-1680). It was the last of these who stressed the need for well-kept and well-regulated seminaries. So by the eighteenth-century, seminary formation was rigorous and fruitful. Unfortunately along with "select education" can come a sense of empowerment and entitlement, especially as one moves up the hierarchy of command. It took a revolution in France to move priesthood back toward servanthood with, sadly, the execution or exile of hundreds of well-educated priests.

As the nineteenth century inched forward after the Concordat of 1802, priesthood gradually regained prestige for the non-juring clergy, who had gone underground for a decade to avoid swearing fealty to the Revolution and who emerged as heroes from their hideaways. The Brothers of St. Joseph had the good fortune to be started by a member of this non-juring clergy and to be guided later by a member of the post-revolutionary clergy. But the latter priest would prove to be more hierarchy-inclined than the earlier Ruillé priest ever was. It was partially a matter of age: the one born in 1767 suffered as a young man during the Revolution, the other, born in 1799 and aged three at the Concordat, knew nothing first-hand of the Revolution's atrocities.

When did the Brothers of St. Joseph become the Brothers of Holy Cross? The answer may lie in a French preposition: "de" can be translated as either "of" or "from." In its original use, the phrase "Les Frères de Sainte-Croix" meant "Brothers *from* Holy Cross," an indication that their home base after 1835 was a section of the city of Le Mans known as "Sainte-Croix" ("Holy Cross"). Over time, however, the English translation of "Les Frères de Sainte-Croix" came to be "Brothers *of* Holy Cross" connoting in the minds of some that this religious group had a special devotion and dedication to Christ's cross, a devotion that may exist/have existed in some members but has never been codified as such.

So to be specific about an answer to the question "When did the Brothers of St. Joseph become the Brothers of Holy Cross?" one can only say the answer depends upon several factors. Literally, once the Brothers moved their headquarters from Ruillé to Sainte-Croix in Le Mans, one could say they were then the "Brothers *from* Sainte-Croix." But historically they actually continued to refer to themselves as "Brothers of St. Joseph," even on the 1842 deed for the property today known as the University of

Notre Dame, a property officially contracted in their name. So the literal answer to the question of the name change is obviously fluid. A canon lawyer might argue that the change came seventeen years after the first recruits arrived, when in 1837 the Brothers were amalgamated with a small group of diocesan priests at the signing of the "Fundamental Act," by which the Brothers of St. Joseph merged governing authority and finances into one unit, one new "congregation."

A third answer to the question might also come from a canon lawyer who could argue that the Brothers of St. Joseph became the Brothers of Holy Cross on August 25, 1836, when the first Brother embraced the "evangelical counsels" of poverty, celibacy, and obedience in a public setting with a vow formula document signed in public. That Brother was the great Brother Andre Mottais. Before that time the Brothers took only an annual promise of obedience to their priest-founder at Ruillé.

A fourth answer to the question is more interesting than the first three answers: it could be that the Brothers of St. Joseph never really ceased to exist but simply became recognized under two different perspectives: one title refers to their devotion to a particular saint (humble St. Joseph), and the other title refers to their physical location (a section of Le Mans). Thus in one way the Brothers of St. Joseph never ceased to exist but remain somehow inherent within the men known in the Catholic Church as "Brothers from Holy Cross."

At Le Mans did the Brothers become secondary to priests by the 1837 "Fundamental Act of Union"? This is a difficult question to answer. The originating founder differed from the 1835 "founder" in several ways. For example, the Brothers' Le Mans director wrote a life of the Brothers' Ruillé priest-founder, a short biography that today prefaces the Le Mans director's collected circular letters. We should expect that in this piece, no matter how short it is, there be some mention of individual Brothers. After all, the earliest of them lived in their founder's rectory and for fifteen years that priest was their inspiration. However, not a single Brother is named in this mini-biography (Maddix 75), not even Brother Andre Mottais, who has been hailed as "the second founder" of the Brothers and who lived with the priest-founder at Ruillé for seventeen years. This priest-focused mini-biography of James Dujarié notes that usually a Brother was sent out to check on Brothers teaching in the schools. Basil Moreau, the author of the mini-biography, calls this man the "Brother Visitor." No name. Today of course we know that this "visitor" was Brother Andre, who for a dozen years did most of the work in training and supervising the Brother-teachers. To write an entire biography of the Brothers' founder without naming a single Brother is an accomplishment. Thus in 1837 was furthered the danger of hierarchy within Holy Cross.

Some Brothers ignore hierarchy. Some Brothers like hierarchy. Others disdain it. I do not know how the latter deal with the gospels' select Twelve, but since 1837, the "ordained" members of Holy Cross have received deference. The new director of the Brothers in 1837 articulated it in a circular letter:

> I have not the slightest intention to subject the Brothers to the priests in such a way that any priest would have the right to give orders to any Brother, or that the Brothers would be obliged to obey all the priests indiscriminately. Even though the Brothers owe respect and deference to all the priests without exception, because of their sacerdotal character, still the priests cannot give orders to the Brothers unless they have been elected to an office or employment to which this right is attached. In addition, both priests and Brothers shall always show themselves grateful for the least favors which they receive from one another. (Moreau, *Circular Letters* 1.44)

But Basil Moreau had already codified hierarchy in the 1837 "Fundamental Act" itself: "Abbé Moreau will present later the principles by which he desires to establish the government of the members of the Congregation of the Brothers of Saint Joseph, which direction is to be confided to the Auxiliary Priests" (*Fundamental Act of Union*, Article IX). If the "ordained" members were the only members allowed to be major superiors (provincials, superior general) and thus govern the non-ordained Brothers, as Moreau wished, where was equality of membership?

We need a new approach to the origin of "Holy Cross." An apostolic way of looking at its genesis is to consider its evolution over a period of twenty years (1820 to 1840) as a work in progress. Thus the Brothers of St. Joseph in 1820 were an inchoate group heading toward fusion with a group of auxiliary priests in 1837. Evolution of a community makes more sense than a second birth. After all, it really was the Ruillé founder's wish to bring priests into his community of Brothers, a vision later articulated by Brother Andre Mottais in a November 14, 1834, letter to Bishop Bouvier. Thus we should see Holy Cross as a gradual movement from 1820 to 1837 and beyond, rather than a *fait accompli* brought about by the "Fundamental Act" of March 1, 1837.

In his monograph "Brothers and Priests in Holy Cross," Gerard Dionne explains the Holy Cross origin in this way:

> As a congregation, Holy Cross was not born of a personal revelation or even of an absolutely clear gospel imperative. Holy Cross did not come into being all at once through an inner vision carried out by one person alone. Rather it was progressively, over a number of years, through an insight that took root and began to grow in the mind and heart of several different people that the congregation acquired its specific external traits. This incarnation, progressive and unique, of the reality of Holy Cross sheds meaningful light for understanding the diverse ways of living out the same vocation to religious life, that is, as brothers and as priests (as baptized and as ordained to the ministry of the Word and sacraments). ("Brothers" 1)

Dionne's explanation of the Holy Cross origin makes good Darwinian sense, and we can only add (and hope) that Holy Cross will continue to refine and polish the plans of its three earliest visionaries: Dujarié, Mottais, Moreau. Later transformations through the sensitive work of superiors general and chapters (both provincial and general) will continue the work of the Spirit in the evolution of Holy Cross.

Brother Andre Mottais letters between 1825 and 1843 (Appendix XX) can be found in my casebook on him (2001). The translations are my own. Translations of letters by Brothers Vincent, Leonard, and Rémi are also mine. Manuscripts of all the letters can be found in the Holy Cross General Archives held at the University of Notre Dame. Parts of some chapters in this book are adapted from *Early Men of Holy Cross*.

For this book I thank the Brothers of Holy Cross at Columba Hall who have encouraged its writing. I thank the Superior General Robert Epping, CSC, and the Provincial Superior Kenneth Haders, CSC, for their trust and support. Librarian Tom Cashore was kind and helpful by opening up to me the Moreau Seminary Library, and the rector of the seminary, John Herman, CSC, endorsed my use of the collections there. My primary research was done under the kind supervision of Kevin Cawley and Joseph Smith, both of the University of Notre Dame Archives, where the General Archives of

Holy Cross are now held. I thank Richard Critz, CSC, for the photograph which appears on the cover of this book. I thank Robert Mosher, CSC, and Thomas Maddix, CSC, for reading the manuscript and offering valuable suggestions for revision.

CHAPTER ONE

Beginnings, 1820 to 1824

It may be difficult to appreciate the disastrous effect that the French Revolution had on French children in the first generation of the nineteenth-century, but Lacordaire in a contemporary report estimated that only about eight percent of the students in Parisian secondary schools made their Easter duty and only one percent retained their religious practices after graduation (Dansette 1.191). Napoleon wanted young men to be soldiers: his tolerance of and outreach to religion was meant only to pacify the Church at large. But gradually matters changed so that in the Restoration a third of all students were being educated in church supervised schools, and gradually religious practice crept back into the lives of ordinary people. No small part in this revitalization was brought about by the "Missions de France," originating in 1814 and attempting to reignite the practices of the seventeenth-century Redemptorists and Passionists (Dansette 1.194), but the effects of their hell-fire-and-brimstone parish retreats were often short-lived. The people appreciated occasional bouts with evangelical rant, but little perdured with lasting effect.

After the Concordat, the reverence with which the Church honored Napoleon cannot be underestimated. In fact Cardinal Caprara made the Assumption (August 15) into the feast of "St. Napoleon" and fabricated a fourth-century martyr named Neopolis to give credibility to this new holy day (Dansette 1.143). July 14 (the fall of the Bastille) and December 2 (Napoleon's coronation day) were also instituted as official holy days in the French Church. The bishops did all they could to respect the man who had brought stability to the ravaged country. The enthusiasm with which individual parishes celebrated these days is yet to be established, but ordinary people undoubtedly enjoyed added breaks in their work cycles. Meanwhile, religious communities began to flower.

The founding of the Sisters of Providence at Ruillé in 1806 was not an isolated endeavor on the part of one priest in France. It was rather one of a dozen such foundations around France. 1802 saw the beginnings of the Sisters of Christian Schools of Mercy as well as the Langres Sisters of Providence. 1804 brought the Sisters of Mercy of Montauban, and 1805 saw arise the Sisters of the Sacred Heart. In addition to the Sisters of Providence at Ruillé in 1806, France in that same year also saw founded the Sisters of St. Regis and the Sisters of Notre Dame de Bon Secours. In 1807 the Sisters of Christian Teaching and Nursing began, in 1808 the Sisters of the Blessed Virgin Mary, and in 1810 the Sisters of St. Joseph of Vaur, the Sister Hospitallers of Rennes, and the Sisters of St. Joseph of Cluny. The curé at Ruillé was not working in a religious vacuum when he founded his Sisters— he was working within a wave of religious good-will that France had not enjoyed since the Revolution. He would have been well steeped, therefore, in the dynamics of religious foundations when, fourteen years later, he would start a parallel group to be known as the Brothers of St. Joseph.

So the Brothers of St. Joseph did not arise in a vacuum. One source names several contemporary male communities: the Brothers of Christian Doctrine, the Little Brothers of Mary, the Marianist Brothers, and the Lamennais Brothers (Catta, *Dujarié* 106). All these arose before the Brothers of St. Joseph. Rather than the wasteland we may have thought Ruillé was part of in 1818, France was actually in a wonderful rejuvenation of religious fervor among the young. Naturally preeminent among all the new communities of men were the de La Salle Brothers, first to enjoy the blessings of the government under Napoleon, who singled them out and invited them back into France.

What exactly did the Brothers of St. Joseph inherit from the de La Salle Brothers? One naturally would look for some kind of effect because the Christian Brothers had been founded a century before the Brothers of St. Joseph. In fact, the Ruillé priest-founder sent his prize Brother (Andre Mottais) off to study with the Christian Brothers in Paris before that Brother took over the day-to-day management of the Brothers of St. Joseph in 1822. John-Baptist de La Salle (1651 – 1719) brought four innovations into French education: "simultaneous teaching," free schools, elimination of Latin for the youngest students, and no compulsory manual labor for the Brothers (Deville 172). "Simultaneous teaching" meant that one teacher could instruct multiple students at the same time in one room, something we take for granted today but was not the practice in post-Renaissance France where education had been one teacher with one student, reminiscent of ancient Greek education. Sadly, "simultaneous teaching" fell into abuse as teachers often faced fifty or more young people in one classroom, even well into the twentieth century.

Accustomed as we are today to the flourishing of public, religious, and private schools, it is difficult to imagine an entire country as large as France devoid of schools. But the French Revolution in its zeal to break the power of the Church, which had controlled all primary schools, simply eliminated all schools, letting parents find ways as best they could to have their children educated. Religious houses (except hospitals) were suppressed in August 1792, and in the same month all religious congregations were suppressed. Then in March 1808 when Napoleon invited the Christian Brothers back into France, their influence was limited because their religious rules required houses of no fewer than three Brothers. Most communes could not afford three Brothers—providing for one teacher was hardship enough. In 1816 a law permitted the opening of schools by individuals, and by 1824, schools were turned over to bishops.

When the priests in the diocese of Le Mans gathered for their annual summer retreat in 1818, the pastor of Ruillé was pressed to consider forming a community of religious men as he had already done fourteen years earlier in forming a community of religious women, the Sisters of Providence, who were thriving in their work educating young women. The pastor of Ruillé agreed that a group of young men trained by him would be feasible. And so the idea for the Brothers of St. Joseph began to form in his brain. That idea took two years to germinate. The Le Mans bishop wanted a community of brothers to teach in his diocese, a desire undoubtedly prompted by the growing number of men's religious communities in France, one of which was a group in nearby Brittany at Ploërmel.

The Brothers of Christian Instruction at Ploërmel were not an old group. They were founded on June 16, 1819, just one year before the Brothers of St. Joseph. Their ties to the de La Salle Christian Brothers, however, were strong enough to ensure that their basic training, originally taken at the Christian Brothers' novitiate, was quite solid. Their rule as well showed heavy reliance on the de la Salle Brothers. The result of collaboration between a pastor in Auray (Gabriel Deschayes) and a vicar-general (Jean-Marie de Lamennais), the Ploërmel group did not receive papal approval until 1891, almost forty years after the Brothers of St. Joseph had received their own approval. The earlier approbation of the Brothers of St. Joseph may have been due to three factors in 1857: linkage to priests, a tenacious director, and an opportunity to please the Vatican by accepting a foreign mission (Bengal) that other communities would not or could not staff. The Brothers of Christian Instruction had established their headquarters well at Ploërmel by the end of 1824 so when the Ruillé Brother Leonard Guittoger stayed there to observe and learn from them in 1835, they were a respected part of the Church's movement to further primary education as an ecclesiastical priority. Today the Brothers of Christian Instruction number about 1300 men.

Interestingly, de Lamennais' irascible brother Félicité had organized a community of priests (Mission Priests of the Immaculate Conception) before the Revolution at the family estate La Chênaie. This group, unlike the later Holy Cross auxiliary priests, never amalgamated with a group of religious Brothers, even though Félcité de Lamennais' saintly brother in nearby Ploërmel had that thriving community of Brothers. The Ploërmel Brothers were actually a remnant of an older order established by St. Louis de Montfort (1673-1716), a group (Brothers of St. Gabriel) who had joined with mission priests into one organization until the Revolution when they were suppressed and disbanded. Gabriel Deshayes and Jean-Marie de Lamennais never revived that idea of mission priests. It is good to know that such collaborative communities of Brothers including ordained priests had existed before the creation called Holy Cross formed at Le Mans in 1837.

So we start in 1820, just eighteen years after the end of the French Revolution and the Reign of Terror. France was devastated, its people demoralized, its government reconstituted, its royalty humbled, its institutions, including the Church, demoralized. In that year young men started to filter into a little French town called Ruillé, coming because they had heard in their parish churches in central France that young men were being recruited to work as teaching brothers in village schools. They came to Ruillé with great hope for a religious career. They came with generous hearts and noble ideals. Eighteen years after Napoleon's Concordat, which reconciled Church and State, the educational system in France was waiting for such teachers to help resurrect its broken school system.

When Pierre Hureau came to Ruillé-sur-Loir on July 15, 1820, the Brothers of St. Joseph began. Before his arrival, the Brothers were just a dream, a hope, a plan, but once he got to the little town, the Community started. He was twenty-four years old. Born on December 18, 1795, in Sainte-Colombe near La Flèche, thirty-four miles from Ruillé, he settled into the Ruillé parish rectory with the pastor at the height of the summer. He was not the solitary recruit for very long: a month later Louis Duchêne also moved into the rectory. He was nineteen years old, born in Ruillé, a nephew of the Ruillé pastor. A few months passed and a third young man arrived—from Larchamp came Andre Pierre Mottais, twenty years old. And a final candidate that year came in November—Stephen Gauffre from St. Loup du Gast. Of these original four, two came from the Sarthe Department and two from the Mayenne Department. The town of Ruillé itself nestles in Sarthe.

For Louis, Andre, and Stephen we have dates on which they began their novitiate training: Andre and Stephen on November 25, 1821, and Louis on December 24, 1821. For Pierre we have no early novitiate entry date although we do know that his novitiate experience began four years later on August 16, 1824, after he had left the group in June 1821 and returned to the group on April 15, 1824. The hiatus of three years did not affect his status as the first Brother of St. Joseph: a recruit's rank was established as soon as he entered the Ruillé Community for the first time.

For these dates we are indebted to the *Matricule Générale* compiled by Brother Bernard Gervais, who worked in 1944 from a matricule assembled in 1860. During his tenure as General Steward and member of the Holy Cross Congregation's General Council (1926 to 1950), Brother Bernard Gervais assembled this *Matricule Générale* as a list of every man who entered the Brothers of St. Joseph. The list begins in 1820 with Pierre Hureau. For each man, the *Matricule Générale* generally gives a date of entry, a date for the beginning of novitiate training, and the date of either departure or death (Appendix I). The departures, of course, greatly outnumber the deaths of those who persevered in the Community. In the matricule departures are noted as either "sorti" ("left") or "renvoyé" ("dismissed").

We know from which sources Bernard compiled this matricule because he tells us in a cover letter for his *Matricule*, and it is obvious that he did not use the "accounts" volumes that Brother Andre Mottais kept in the 1820s and 1830s. For example, Bernard's entry #250 reads:

> Jacques, Brother II (Jacques Nourry), later Brother Ambroise IV, born April 25, 1800, at Gorron (Mayenne): entered August 27, 1833, novice March 19, 1836, left January 31, 1838.

The "II" after Brother Jacques' name means he was the second man in the Community to be named "Jacques." (The first was dismissed in 1825.) It was customary for the Brothers of St. Joseph to have only one Brother at a time named for a saint: for example, there were never two "Brother Jacques" in the Community at the same time. Brother Andre in the second volume of his ledger book gives the August, 1833, date as the day that Jacques was accepted into the novitiate. Quite naturally the thirty-three-year-old man would be given a new name when he received the novice garb, and for Jacques that name would have been "Ambroise," as noted by Brother Andre (2.84). The novitiate date given by Bernard in his *Matricule Générale* is March 19, 1836, three years after Jacques had come to Ruillé. The novitiate had been transferred to Le Mans by that time.

A similar inconsistency in dating occurs for *Matricule Générale* #251:

> Barnabé, Brother II (Louis Grangé), born April 2, 1815, at New-Brissach (Haut Rhin), entered August 28, 1833, novice (?), dismissed October 9, 1833.

Andre gives the August 28 date as the novitiate entry date, but he also gives the names of the parents of this eighteen-year old: François Grangé and Marie Geller. Had Bernard used Andre's data he would have included the names of Brother Barnabé's parents.

Entry #252 in the *Matricule Générale* is scanty and contains similar misinformation, if we rather trust Brother Andre's on-site ledger, which I think we should since it was contemporary to the events recorded. Consider *Matricule Générale* #252:

> Brother Alphonse II (Jacques-Félix Perrin), born February 11, 1814, at Courcité (Mayenne), entered September 11, 1833, became a novice March 31, 1834, dismissed July 26, 1836.

Now consider Brother Andre's entry for this man:

> Brother Alphonse arrived September 11. Born at Courcité February 11, 1814, to Jean Perrin and Julienne Voiteau. Novitiate September 11, 1833. Spent seven and a half months at the Esclimont novitiate, sent to Choisel, then to St. James, came back to the novitiate of Holy Cross [in Le Mans] July 1836 and was dismissed July 26.

We have some important information in this Andre entry. First of all we learn that the nineteen-year-old young man spent time at the novitiate in Ruillé because he came to the Community before the move to Le Mans. He then taught in the town of Choisel and after that in the town of St. James.

After the Brothers under a new director moved their novitiate to the Sainte-Croix (Holy Cross) suburb of Le Mans, Brother Alphonse came to the new novitiate location to continue (or complete) his novitiate training. But he was dismissed from the Community the same month he showed up in Le Mans. Brother Bernard Gervais did not have access to this information or he would have at least included the names of the young man's parents.

Just how fluid the religious formation system was in the earliest years of the Brothers can be seen from any number of profiles. Brother Isidore (Pierre Verdier, #259) later became known as "Victorin" because he probably started his novitiate twice. When he arrived in 1833, he was given the name "Isidore." He left (or was dismissed) and assumed the name "Victorin" when he received the religious habit in 1836. He was, sadly, dismissed two months later.

Information is curious for another young man: Jacques-Charles Flequin (#258). In both the *Matricule Générale* and Andre's 1830-1837 accounts/records book he is noted as having entered twice, once in 1833 and again in 1835. The first time he received the name "Charles," the second time the name "Philémon." His second attempt at community life lasted less than a year. The *Matricule Générale* lists him as leaving on his own both times, but the 1830 accounts/records book notes he was dismissed both times. He was probably a man of good will and his second dismissal may have been the result of the general upheaval that attended the transfer of the novitiate headquarters from Ruillé to Le Mans in 1835. He was fourteen-years old when he entered the first time and was dismissed at age fifteen. He re-entered at age sixteen and was dismissed fewer than two months later, still at age sixteen.

Earlier in the *Matricule Générale* we meet Brother Joseph de Jésus (Gentien-Julien Faucheuse, #239). His last name in Andre's book is "Faucheux," the masculine form of the family name. The *Matricule Générale* gives his birth date as April 25, 1808, but Andre gives April 17. Bernard questions if he were ever a novice, but Andre gives his novitiate entry date as March 17, 1830. Bernard notes that he left January 14, 1831, but Andre gives January 1. Andre also notes that "Brother Léonard made an offering of 5 francs for this postulant, but this postulant returned 3 francs that he had received back home from his brother." Andre also notes the young man got all his things back by February 14, once he had paid 250 francs. This sum was probably due for boarding expenses incurred during the novitiate.

The first entry for a recruit in Brother Andre's second volume (2.1) is for Pierre Jean Marchenoir, who was born at Mézeugé on October 22, 1803.

The entry curiously also gives this young man's birthday as "30 vendermaire in the 11th of the French Republic." This is the only entry in the entire accounts/record book to give the double entry for a birth date, indicating perhaps the reluctance of the writer to abandon the form instituted during the Revolution over a generation before. This young man's parents are named Pierre Marchenoir and Marie Agathe Aubert. The young man entered the Ruillé novitiate program on Jaunary 1, 1830, but was dismissed on February 23 "for thoughtlessness and disability." Andre adds, "We gave him back everything that belonged to him." The *Matricule Générale* does not list this person at all.

Brother Julien (Guillaume-Victor Glaume) is listed as #236 in the *Matricule Générale*, the son of Joseph Glaume and Marie Cabouet. The *Matricule Générale* gives his entry date as February 16, 1930, a date which Andre's book gives as his date of entry to the novitiate. The *Matricule Générale* uses a question mark for his novitiate entry date and notes he left in 1830. Similarly the *Matricule Générale* data on Brother Prudence (Joseph Loiseau) gives as his entry date what the accounts/records book lists as his entry to the novitiate. This man left in 1832. Brother Basilde (Justin Renault) gets similar treatment with the *Matricule Générale* listing his novitiate entry date (February 27, 1830) as his arrival date at Ruillé. This man also left in 1830.

In the *Matricule Générale* what exactly does the "entry date" mean? Does it mean the day a young man showed up at Ruillé? Or does it mean the day he was admitted to the novitiate? We can take for example the case of Brother Narcisse. The *Matricule* lists him as #280 and notes he entered on December 14, 1835. It notes he is a novice as of February 2, 1836. So the two acts are distinct. But Brother Andre's note on Narcisse (page 128 in his 1830's accounts book) gives the December 14 date as the day the young man went to the novitiate, the February date as the occasion of Narcisse's receiving the religious habit and the name "Narcisse." So for a period of a month and a half, the young man would have lived at the novitiate as Jean François Hulot, not Brother Narcisse. He entered at Le Mans, the fourth recruit in the new site of the Brothers' novitiate under new administration. This Brother persevered, dying at Angers in 1887 at age 70. Only eleven of the earlier Brothers outlived him.

One very important fact we should learn from the *Matricule Générale* is that the Brothers of St. Joseph were not a mere blip on the radar screens of nineteenth-century France—there were hundreds of these Brothers teaching in scores of schools. They were not an insignificant little group of young men intent on doing good. They were a religious army of energetic young men determined to keep alive the religious faith of rural France. But they did not teach in cities like Paris or Lyons or Orleans. They were educators dedicated to small schools in small towns.

Although acceptance into the Community became more formal after 1835 (as far as entry dates are concerned) at Le Mans, exceptions were still made. For example, by 1836 it seems February 2 was one of two dates in the year when groups of men were given the religious habit and a new name, but Nicolas Pierre Drouin came to Le Mans twelve days after Jean François Hulot and was not given a habit or a new name until March 19, the feast of St. Joseph. Why the delay? Had the new administration put in place a minimum time of adjustment to religious life before a recruit would be given a habit and name? Or was it simply that Nicolas needed more time than Jean-François needed, in the judgment of the novice-master, to settle into the religious routine? It could be that the novice-master had some concerns over Nicolas' health because he died at St-Aignan on June 28, 1837, just a little over a year after receiving the name "François d'Assise." He was nineteen years old and probably teaching there at the time of his death, it not being uncommon that novices were sent out on assignment before completing a full year of canonical novitiate. In fact some recruits spliced together summer months spent in Ruillé as their novitiate "year."

Some recruits waited less than a month to be given a habit and religious name. François Joseph Bodinier arrived at the novitiate on January 12, 1836, and was received as a novice on February 2 and given the name Brother Auguste. He was nineteen at the time and received his teaching license in September 1837. Unfortunately he left the Community the following July.

Some who analyze the early beginnings of the Brothers do not use the *Matricule Générale*. For example, Catta, who has written the most definitive biography of Jacques Dujarié, does not seem to have used the *Matricule Générale*. To the first four recruits (in 1820), Catta (112) adds a fifth (René Ménard), who does not appear in the *Matricule Générale*. Catta then shuffles the arrangement of the 1821 recruits and omits one (Charles Faribault). His recruits, if he had used the *Matricule* listing, would be numbered 8, 6, 11, 7, 10. For 1822 he notes there were twenty recruits, but the *Matricule* gives only fifteen. Evidently Catta worked from some source that he does not identify. We would be better off today if historians had used Andre's two ledger volumes faithfully. We owe much to Andre.

Readers may wonder what would prompt a healthy young twenty-year old to leave his family's farm and embrace a lifestyle of evangelical poverty.

Part of the answer may very well lie in the scores of pastors who dotted the French countryside around Ruillé, men who could have moved through an incipient capitalism to make their fortune in farming or in a cottage industry but followed instead a call to minister to God's people. Selfless men, like the pastor of Ruillé, men who managed to escape the bloodiest days of the Revolution, saw in their own pastoral sacrifices a way to help heal France's soul, which had survived the necessary horrors of its Revolution and limped into the modern world longing for the old comforts of religion.

We can see, for example, why Andre Mottais would have found in the Ruillé pastor a paragon of simple virtue, hard work, and vision, with the emphasis on hard work. Here was a pastor who not only attracted young women to devote their futures to the education of local girls but who built a house and chapel himself for his new Sisters of Providence, stone by stone, with the sometime help of neighborhood boys. So when did the Brothers of St. Joseph actually begin? Was it when that pastor made his decision in 1818 to found a community for men? Or was it rather in 1820 when the first recruit showed up at his doorstep? I think the latter because all the plans in the world are of little use if there is no physical, tangible proof that the idea has merit. So on July 15, 1820, Pierre Hureau came to Ruillé, took the religious name "Brother Ignatius," and the Brothers of St. Joseph began.

We can try to imagine that first day of the Brothers of St. Joseph when Pierre arrived in Ruillé, ready to undertake the challenge of religious dedication and abnegation. Did he take the formal vows of poverty, celibacy, and obedience? No, but he may already have been poor, and he was probably celibate, so now all he needed to do was to put his will under a promise of obedience to the priest-founder of the Brothers, a priest he had never met before but who was intent on getting children in northwest France educated. Here was Pierre Hureau—the first to bring this dream into reality.

We can try to imagine the weather that summer day in Ruillé. France is cradled by water—on the northwest side by the Atlantic and on the southeast side by the Mediterranean. The northwest coast can be rugged. If we think of the beaches at Normandy, or if we think of Chaucer's *Franklin's Tale*, we remember the turbulence that the Atlantic waters can bring to the northern coast. We know, on the other hand, how gentle southeast France is. The Mediterranean pampers Avignon and beach houses. Most of France enjoys a temperate climate, and no more so than in the center of the country. Ruillé rests in the heart of agriculture, in the heart of flax and lavender fields, in the heart of fields teeming with wheat and barley. Ruillé does not sit on the Atlantic or on the Mediterranean. It is neither rugged nor pampered. It is temperate. Summers are warm but not oppressively so. Pierre Hureau showed up before the harvest began in earnest on local farms.

On that first day of the Brothers of St. Joseph, Pierre came with all of his belongings, probably not much, in a bag or sack. He may have walked all the way from Ste. Colombe, his hometown, or he may have been brought to his new home, to his new life, in a horse-drawn cart driven by his father or a brother or a cousin. No matter. He arrived, and the pastor welcomed him into the rectory where the two would live together, the one the founder, the other the originating Brother of St. Joseph. They would rise early in the morning for Mass in the parish church next door to the rectory, and they would take a simple meal of bread and porridge. Instruction would follow their little meal because Pierre, now known as Brother Ignatius, would have to learn educational basics. Eventually the daily schedule would become more formal as more young men showed up:

> The signal for rising was given at 5 a.m...At 5:20 the Brothers came down from the dormitory, made their meditation on their knees, and then assisted at Holy Mass, which was sung and served by the Brothers or the postulants. At 6:45 there was a period of study devoted to catechism, which was interrupted for breakfast, and then continued until 8:00. The morning was taken up with classes in group reading, writing, arithmetic, grammatical analysis, and plain chant until 11:40. Then the community made particular examen...Dinner was at noon, followed by recreation. Classes resumed at 1:30: reading, writing, and catechism. They stopped at 4:30 to give time, as at the beginning, for the visit to the Blessed Sacrament or the recitation of the Rosary, and sometimes for the Way of the Cross. At 5:00 there was a study period for grammar, after which came spiritual reading, most often given by Brother Andre. He also presided at the Chapter of Accusation... Supper was served at 7:00. It was followed by recreation and prayers, at the end of which the subject of the next morning's meditation was announced. At 9:00 p.m. the community retired to the dormitory. (Catta, *Dujarié* 115-116)

As if this were not a busy enough schedule, the young men were also used next door to help in building the motherhouse of the Sisters of Providence.

They worked in the garden, made wine, hauled stones, and slaked lime (Catta, *Dujarié* 114).

The pastor, of course, had a parish to run with scores of parishioners to father, and he had a growing community of Sisters next door with an irascible mother-superior whom he had to placate, so this priest-pastor hired a young local man, Céleste Ferre, a rather silly youth, to bring the young Brothers around to mathematics, French grammar, penmanship, and catechetics—the major disciplines that they would carry with them when they ventured out on their first teaching assignments.

On August 20 when Louis Duchêne arrived, the community of two (Brother Ignatius and the pastor) became a community of three (Brother Ignatius, Brother Louis, and the pastor). This second recruit kept his baptismal name (Louis) as his religious name. Then on October 22 a great recruit, Andre Mottais, showed up. On November 16, a fourth recruit, Stephen Gauffre, came. The community was thickening. There may also have been another priest in the rectory—Jean Samson, sent to assist the pastor on August 10, 1819. This would increase the rectory population to six.

Out of these early Brothers of St. Joseph one giant remains fixed in the history of Holy Cross: Brother Andre Mottais. Born Andre Pierre Mottais in Larchamp, fifty miles northwest of Le Mans, the man who was destined to help forge Holy Cross came of solid farming stock. His parents were Jean Mottais and Jeanne Blot, who were married May 14, 1793, seven years before Andre's birth. The father was born in 1768 and the mother in 1773 making them 24 and 20 at the time of their marriage in the bloodiest year of the French Revolution. Jeanne Blot and Jean Mottais had four children: Jean François (born September 16, 1794), Andre Pierre (born February 21, 1800), Jeanne Julienne (born August 10, 1805), and Joseph (born June 17, 1811). For generations the Mottais family had lived at Pontperrin, a farm-estate in Mayenne near the town of Larchamp, fifteen miles east of Fougères. The property had been in the family since the sixteenth century. Before the French Revolution it comprised over two hundred and fifty acres. Today it has a single manor house owned by the de Blic family, who also own four surrounding farms. The Mottais farm-estate is located just southeast of Larchamp, off the intersection of Route 799 and Route 523, and its name "Pontperrin" suggests that the family property may have been named for a bridge over a small river on the eastern edge of the property.

The Mottais home, standing today, is three stories tall, with chimneys at either end of the building. Its brick is fine weathered and indicates a family of some wealth. Stone steps lead up to an entrance on the second level, suggesting that originally the lowest level was probably used for storage. The living quarters would then be confined to the two upper levels, and the orderly placement of the windows suggests two or four rooms per floor, the middle level for living and dining, the top floor for sleeping. A barn next to the house is equally old and is still used by the de Blic family. Its walls are twenty feet high, and its roof peaks to thirty feet. At one end a high shuttered window indicates a grain loft. The other end appends a smaller building still used as living quarters.

Andre Pierre Mottais came from a family with deep roots in the area going back several hundred years. As a second son, he was not christened with the name of his father, grandfather, and great-grandfather, nor would he have inherited the family farm. Born in the winter of 1800, Andre was welcomed into a country chronicled by a new calendar: revolutionary France records Andre's birth as 2 Ventose in the year 8 (February 21, 1800). His birth announcement in the Larchamp parish records begins, "Today, the second Ventose," indicating that the Revolutionary Calendar was duly regarded as official in small French towns. In its fourteenth year (1805), however, the calendar would revert to the Gregorian style. The parish church in Larchamp dominates the town and remains much as Andre would have known it. The bell tower is the highest structure in the area, its old dark stone already hundreds of years old when Andre was first carried into the church. The baptistery, where the Mottais family had their son baptized in February 1800, is a separate little room at the back right of the church, a small room that can accommodate a dozen people. The stone font in which he was ritually brought into the Larchamp faith community is still used today to welcome infants of the parish into their ancient religion. The interior of the church is dark, although some stained-glass windows let in welcome light. The foot-thick walls would give a little boy the sense of a fortress, affording him security in his religion, albeit tinged with gloom.

The school Andre attended in Larchamp has only recently been torn down, but Andre, like the sons of other farm owners, would have learned the basics of reading, writing, and numbers before giving himself full time to work on the family farm, awaiting whatever destiny would come his way. Did he enjoy farm work? We have no record left of his early life on the farm, but later letters written from Africa demonstrate a keen sense of farming. We presume that this virtuous young man worked with a willing back and a cheerful heart, but at some point there resonated in him a call at the age of twenty to leave his family and travel south to the little town of Ruillé where

Dujarié was beginning to gather young men into his Brothers of St. Joseph. Andre would have walked, or perhaps ridden in a cart, south to Ernée, then further south to Laval, the largest city he would have seen in his life so far. Then he probably would have headed southeast to Sablé and farther down to La Flèche where he would have encountered the Loir River—not the mighty Loire of famed chateaux, but the little Loir that runs east-west joining the Sarthe River (from Le Mans) just north of Angers. From La Flèche, Andre would simply have headed east, following the little Loir as it rambled with him, past Le Lude, Château-du-Loir, and La Chartre-sur-le-Loir to little Ruillé-sur-Loir, where the pastor of the parish either expected him (possibly apprised of his arrival by letter) or was pleasantly surprised by the young farmer's appearance.

Three months after Andre arrived, Dujarié told him to start a school at Ruillé. Such was Dujarié's impression of Andre's promise and talents. The young man had just come from a farm and had no training as a teacher. Then, since Dujarié felt he himself did not know how to train male religious, in spite of his successful guidance of the Providence women, the priest consulted Abbé de Lamennais, who advised him to study the spiritual practices of the Christian Brothers. Thus a few months after Andre had started his little school in Ruillé, Dujarié sent him north to Le Mans where the young man had to be reviewed for military conscription, was exempted, then lived for five months in 1821 with a priest named Lamare while taking classes with the Christian Brothers. He also took classes at the major seminary there.

The books that Lamare gave Andre to read in that five-month period tell us much about what Andre valued. First there was the life of Vincent de Paul and a history of his foundations. Here Andre would have seen witness of the great charitable works of the hospitalers. Secondly, Alphonsus Ligouri's book on the love of God which Andre characterizes as the work of a "faithful soul." Thirdly, that bedrock of religious meditation right up into the twentieth century, Thomas à Kempis' *Imitation of Christ*. Fourthly, the New Testament. And finally the *Exercises of the Presence of God*. Most of Andre's reading, therefore, was of the quieting kind, just the sort of material he needed to balance the intellectual foot race he was running with the Christian Brothers, learning all he could to help him return credibly to Ruillé as a master-teacher of the young men, many of them teenagers, who would be sent out to teach in schools with even less of the rushed preparation than Andre had received in Le Mans. The practice among religious communities in the nineteenth and twentieth centuries of sending out young men and women with astonishingly little formal preparation to run a classroom endured for over a hundred years, yet many of these religious did surprisingly fine educational work. Many, of course, failed themselves and their students, who were sometimes almost as old as their teachers. Andre later questioned the wisdom of this practice, but under the protection of Lamare, he was well prepared to assimilate a hasty education from the Christian Brothers, and Andre recalls with great appreciation Lamare's "wise counsels during my critical troubles" (Andre to Lamare, Feb. 4, 1833). Andre does not specify what these troubles were, nor does he specify when they occurred. They may have arisen while he lived with Lamare, but as he kept in contact with the old man for another dozen years until Lamare's death in 1833, he may be referring to any number of crises that arose in the little community at Ruillé.

When Andre returned to Ruillé at the end of November 1821, with Brother Stephen, who had apparently been sent to Le Mans to retrieve Andre, the two men were met by Dujarié outside of Ruillé at the foot of a cross and vested with a religious habit designed by the bishop. The habit was simple:

> It was decided that they would wear a kind of black robe or soutane without a train, buttoning down to the waist and buttoned inside from the waist to the bottom, of ordinary cloth, and descending to six inches from the ground; a hat flat in the middle, that is, five and a half inches, and the edge three and a half inches; a small black and white collar, a cloth skullcap, and short pants. Several weeks after, a white band was added to the collar with two branches, resting on the top of the chest, and sewn together halfway. Each branch was about two inches wide, and the length from the neck to the end was about four inches. (*Chronicles*, qtd. Klawitter, *Early* 8)

At this time in Ruillé there were five Brothers, the first recruit (Pierre Hureau) having left in June. Only two, Andre and Stephen, were given the habit, possibly because they were considered "novices." In December four more recruits would arrive, the same month that Dujarié sent Andre away for a second time, this time to Paris to live for six months (until June, 1822) at the Christian Brothers' novitiate in Paris. In all, Andre spent almost a year in training (five months in Le Mans for teacher training and six months in

Paris for spirituality training), not a bad educational experience when one compares it to what was afforded most of the Brothers of St. Joseph.

Andre Mottais became the backbone of the Brothers of St. Joseph, and the priest pastor recognized the potential in him. Catta lists Andre's strengths:

> He was an unusual young man, gifted with tender piety, animated with persevering zeal and admirable generosity... He never abandoned his Founder, having vowed to him, as well as to his foundation, a loyalty which nothing could discourage. In moments of greatest difficulty, he gave evidence of a quick and penetrating intelligence. (Catta, *Dujarie* 116)

Within two years of his arrival at Ruillé, Andre was made responsible for the spiritual direction of all the Brothers (Catta, *Dujarie* 116). It was Andre who formed the new recruits, served as their novice master, taught them educational rudiments, and visited them yearly out in their little French schools. The Brothers of St. Joseph did not wait long to start their apostolic work. Already in 1821 Brother Andre was teaching in Ruillé, Louis in Larchamp, and Stephen in St. Denis d'Orques (where he taught until 1833).

Fortunately, Andre was writing letters. Andre's first letter home was posted a little over a month after leaving Larchamp. In it he assures his family that he is in good health and that he has good companions to live with. In his second letter home, he tells his family that he has everything he needs. He also notes that he cannot send them anything because his superior has impressed upon him that his primary responsibility now lies with his religious community, but he will continue to support his Larchamp family with prayers—he is not forgetting them and will visit them from time to time. If he gets sick, his Ruillé brothers will take care of him. It is a new life not just for him, but for his Larchamp family as well. Andre's reaction to separation from his family is a refreshing change from what Alphonsus Liguori had counseled religious: "He who wishes to enter religion must detach himself from his parents and forget them altogether" (3.403). Today this advice sounds cruel. Alphonsus Liguori continues: "Let him know that he cannot go to visit his parents in their own house, except in the case of some dangerous illness of his father or mother" (3.404). Today we rejoice that Andre ignored such counsel, if he even knew about it.

It is comforting to read in Brother Andre's first two letters his conviction that he has chosen the right path for himself, that he is fulfilling what it is that God set in front of him to help the boys of Ruillé and the surrounding towns. He did not know, of course, in 1820 what terrific work he would do with the Brothers of St. Joseph for the next twenty-four years until his death at age forty-four.

Brother Andre's fifth letter home is full of sadness—he has learned that his sister-in-law Marie has died. He consoles his parents as best he can from Ruillé, but they also have another upset in their lives—their son John has left farming to become a carpenter. Andre then lectures his brother that the new trade his brother has chosen may throw him in with bad companions so he will have to be on his guard. Brother Andre did not rush back to Larchamp to be with his parents, but they knew that his solid spirituality would help them accept the death in their family and the career change for one of their three sons. In one sense Andre was still with them. In 1825 Andre has good news for his parents—he will soon be visiting them in Larchamp and will have a chance first-hand to be with his brother Francis, the brother who had lost his young wife.

Andre was a busy man. Within two years of his arrival at Ruillé, Andre was put in charge of all the day-to-day operations of the Brothers of St. Joseph. Not only was he the novice-master and had to train the new arrivals in spirituality, he was director also of teacher training so there were daily lessons to give in reading, math, religion, penmanship, and bookkeeping. He had to process the newly arrived and on occasion dismiss those who were not suited to the religious community. Annually he had to visit every little school where the Brothers were teaching (over thirty of them in some years) and assess the Brothers' teaching abilities. For each school he also had to elicit an inventory down to the last dish in the kitchen. And the Brothers respected him. Of the four Brother Directors at Ruillé, he was always named as the Chief Director, the man-in-charge, the man with the final word.

As noted earlier, since the Christian Brothers insisted that their men live in groups, they did not staff small country schools but worked only in cities. The Brothers of St. Joseph did not, for the most part, live in groups. They labored singly or in some cases with another Brother or two. Only once a year (for two weeks at the end of summer) did they gather for an annual retreat in Ruillé. However, they thrived, rewarded by the thought of that annual community event, for them all the more sweet because they had been separated from each other for most of the year. During the year they may have visited each other between towns, but usually they lived alone.

It is difficult to establish precisely how many men came and went at Ruillé in the early years. Record keeping was good but not precise. For example, the *Chronicles* note that in 1822 twenty men arrived and three left, but the *Matricule Générale* lists for that year only fifteen arrivals and no departures. It could be that men who stayed for only a few days were not officially recorded. If a young man came, for example, just to test the waters, so to speak, he may have been regarded as an overnight visitor rather than as someone serious about devoting his life to religion. In 1823 one man is listed as arriving in April and leaving sometime that same year, but we do not know how long he stayed. It is not until 1824 that the *Matricule Générale* lists a young man (Jean-Pierre Chabrun) who arrives at age fifteen, takes the name Brother Alexis, and leaves two days later. We must remember that for the last half of 1821 and the first half of 1822, Andre was not in Ruillé and record keeping was probably in the hands of the over-extended Dujarié. When Andre did get back to Ruillé, he was totally responsible for the instruction of the young men who came, one as young as twelve, to be Brothers of St. Joseph. As for those men who went into the field, the *Chronicles* note: "Those of these novices who had grace of state studied in their establishments and little by little they made themselves useful teachers" (qtd. Klawitter, *Mottais* 39).

The loose federation of men that constituted the Brothers of St. Joseph was united by a single promise (obedience), which they would take annually. The formula was simple and read in part: "I submit fully to the rules and statues of the said Congregation, promising to observe them exactly; and consequently I renew for one year the vow of obedience to the superior of the said Congregation." Simple as it was, this promise was enough to hold the group together: departures in the first decade of the Brothers of St. Joseph numbered 171 out of a membership of 241. There were, of course, never 241 members at any one time in those first ten years. The peak enrollment was 106 in 1827. Perseverance from 1820 to 1835 was 19% (Appendix XIII), not bad for a young community.

Loss in membership was unusually low for this fledgling community, but such loss had to be expected: when young people decide to change the course of their lives, they often have second thoughts. Andre himself was not without temptations to leave, not at Ruillé where Dujarié kept him busy and important, but rather in Le Mans in 1821 where he was studying. A note by Andre in the *Chronicles* maintains that without the encouragement of Lamare, he may have abandoned the Brothers of St. Joseph. One incident in particular is very important. A seminarian Andre counted as a friend came to the carriage which was about to carry Andre back to Ruillé. The seminarian "made the last efforts to make him lose his vocation in forcing him to change his determination, but Brother Andre saw the snare which the demon held out to him, rejected his perfidious advice, and entered the cart on the field, detesting the conduct of this pretended friend" (*Chronicles*, qtd. Klawitter, *Early* 18). What exactly was the friend's advice? It was apparently not the first time he had attempted to influence Andre's vocation. Did he want Andre to become a seminarian in Le Mans? Andre's strong reaction and references to "the snare which the devil held out to him" and "perfidious advice" and "pretended friend" suggest something stronger because, after all, the temptation to enter a seminary is not "perfidious." It is a rather noble calling. The last minute appeal, the dramatic appearance at the carriage, all suggest that the friend did not want to lose Andre's company and, suspect or not, he wanted whatever bonds they had to continue.

Of the fifty-one letters and memos we have by Andre Mottais, all but two of the first thirty were written at Ruillé, and most of them concern business relating to administration of the Brothers of St. Joseph. In one letter, to Brother Adrian at Hardanges, Andre gives sparse directions for settling in: the Brother's belongings will soon be sent to him, and the pastor there owes the community for books and supplies. The Brother is to bring the money to Ruillé in one week. Apparently to assuage Adrian's fear of being separated from the community, Andre tells him that Hardanges is not far away from the town where Brother Francis teaches: "You can see each other from time to time" (Oct. 11, 1825). What little affection we can discern here is cradled in business. Eight months later, in another letter to Adrian, the formality is still evident: "I'm obliging you, my dear brother, to follow as much as possible the Rule Book for the schools, because those of our brothers who use most of what it prescribes are also those who succeed the most in their classes" (June 22, 1826). The advice is almost formulaic, and one wonders what comfort it would have brought to a young man living with a parish priest who is, we are told, in bad health. Adrian was only three years younger than Andre and had been sent out to teach within seven months of his arrival at Ruillé. He received a teaching license one month before Andre's first letter to him, one of the fortunate young men sent out to teach with an actual license (Appendix IX). Such a license, easily obtainable by simply showing the local authorities a letter of obedience from Dujarié, would have been a sign of willingness to teach more than an ability to teach.

These first years of the Brothers of St. Joseph were vibrant times. The number of Brothers grew year by year. The Ruillé novices moved into a wonderful new building, the Grand St. Joseph, in 1824. New schools were opened year after year (Appendix V). By 1824 the Brothers were operating twenty-seven schools, apparently much to the satisfaction of parents because only three schools were vacated by the Brothers in that same four-year period (Appendix VI). Beginnings are exciting. Living on the edge brings challenges to young people who often thrive on new turns in their lives, and wherever a Brother of St. Joseph was working, he always knew that his religious roots at Ruillé with Brother Andre were secure and healthy.

CHAPTER TWO

Development and Flourishing, 1825 to 1829

Appointed by Dujarié to serve the little group as novice master, spiritual director, and supervisor of instruction, Brother Andre must have been disheartened at times both in Ruillé and out visiting parish schools by the rate of turnover among his young Brothers. Of the first fifty men to come to Ruillé, thirty-eight eventually left or were dismissed (Appendix II). Only twelve died as Brothers of St. Joseph. But as is still true today, the work that Andre did in affording young men an opportunity to live a prayerful life and acquire the rudiments of a teaching career must have at times convinced him that parishes were much enriched by the men who returned to their homes better for their having lived in a religious community for however short a time. In the first of Andre's circular letters (dated July 17, 1826), Andre reminds all the Brothers to think somberly of the coming retreat as it may be the last for some of them: two men have died since the previous year's retreat, the first two men lost to death within a community which already had over eighty-five members. As early as 1825, Andre each year visited all the schools, even the most remote ones, scattered across fifteen "departments," sections set up by the Revolution. Dujarié thought the visitations would be a good thing, but he himself attempted to make the visits only twice and gave up both times soon after he left Ruillé because of his health, delegating the trips to Andre who travelled on foot because most of the roads could not be used by carriages.

Andre was a careful supervisor and very particular in what he expected of his young teachers. Among his early letters is an inventory of goods for the school at Milly. Every door, window, and stick of furniture is inventoried. Even the number of bolts and hooks in the shutters is set down. Linens are inventoried down to dishrags. In the dormitory are four little beds for the Brothers. The library has fifty-five books. The date of the inventory is May

1829, near the end of the first year the Brothers ran the school. Two years later Milly is thriving and Andre pronounces it "the best and most agreeable in our Congregation" (April 21, 1831). One can imagine the joy and pride the men and students must have felt when the Brother supervisor made a visit: since he would inquire after every imaginable detail pertinent to good teaching, everyone would be on his best behavior.

The establishment at Milly was not founded without problems, however. In a letter dated November 11, 1929, Andre indicates step by step what had to be done via the mayor and the local prefect in order to get the Brothers sanctioned for the Milly school. The process began in September 1828 with a request from the mayor to the local prefect. Five months later the project was approved by the commune and three copies of the contract were requested. They were sent within three days to the mayor who signed them and forwarded them to the prefect, who refused the documents because they were written on the wrong kind of paper. Two months later the Community still waited for approval to teach at Milly, but the Brothers were already working there: a letter from Andre to Brother Stanislaus in September, 1830, indicates Brothers had been in Milly for a year teaching 110 students (Klawitter, *Mottais* 7).

The Brothers of St. Joseph enjoyed rich apostolic years between 1825 and 1830. Their schools proliferated, the Brothers staffing forty schools in 1825, forty-four in 1826, fifty-two in 1827, fifty-one in 1828, and forty-eight in 1829 (Appendix V). These are amazing numbers for a Community less than a decade old. They did not wait for a long time to build their apostolic commitments. The first year after their founding, they already were responsible for three schools: at Larchamp, St. Denis d'Orques, and Ruillé. At Larchamp (Brother Andre Mottais' home town) they remained only eight years and only twelve years at St. Denis d'Orques, but at Ruillé they ran the school for forty-nine years, probably because Ruillé was their town of origin and devotion to their priest-founder ran high.

Of the ten schools staffed in 1822, only one (St. Pierre de Chevillé) failed to hold on for more than a year. Marçon had a Brother teacher for fourteen years and Montourtier for thirteen. In 1823 ten schools were added to the list for a total of nineteen, the one closure being St. Pierre de Chevillé. Of the new schools in 1823, Aigné would last under the Brothers' care for twenty-seven years and Marcillé-la-Ville for eighteen. In 1824 eight primary schools were added and one boarding school. This latter foundation was at Ruillé and would last twelve years, closing only one year after the Brothers transferred their motherhouse out of Ruillé to Le Mans. Of the new primary schools added in 1824, Daon would last twenty-eight years (until 1852).

In 1825 the number of schools jumped from twenty-five to forty. With the addition of fifteen new schools, the presence of the Brothers in northwest France was becoming significant, and we must remember the contact would involve between thirty and sixty boys for every Brother—the impact on the rejuvenating French Church would have been appreciable. In 1826 the schools numbered forty-four with one (at Bouère) destined to last sixty-two years (until 1888). Abondant would last forty-four years (until 1870).

In 1827 the jump in number of locations was almost as spectacular as what 1826 had enjoyed. Thirteen new schools were added in 1827. St. Denis d'Anjou would stay under the Brothers' care for fifty-one years (until 1878). Fifty-two schools in 1827 were under the care of the Brothers of St. Joseph, and one (at Craon) would stay under the Brothers for seventy-six years, until 1903 when all religious were expelled from France. In 1828 the Brothers taught in fifty-one towns, and the new school in Milly-la-Forêt would stay in their care for thirty-seven years. Milly seems to have had a special place in the hearts of the Brothers, and it enjoyed more than one Brother assigned to it at a time. 1829 added only one new school to the Brothers' list, and it (at Rouessé-Vassé) lasted only six years under the Brothers' supervision.

Thus in the first nine years of its existence as a religious community, the Brothers of St. Joseph would undertake responsibility for teaching in seventy-five schools, pulling out of only twenty-six of them during the same time period. For a fledgling community with abbreviated training for its teachers, this commitment to the children of France was remarkable indeed, a witness not only to the generosity of young religious men, but also witness to the welcome they received by pastors and grateful parents. That the schools would retain Brothers year after year showed a real attempt by the rural French to bring back their revered Catholic faith that had been so challenged and persecuted during the Revolution. That the Brothers of St. Joseph were part of this admirable *resorgimento* reminds us today how proud they must have been of their accomplishments, working as they did with rudimentary teaching supplies and often in less than acceptable educational conditions.

But the Angers rector could be rather blunt about Brothers of St. Joseph. On July 9, 1829, he wrote to Dujarié:

> One of the inspectors visited the school at Mamers that
> is run by three Brothers from Ruillé. Led by Brother
> Philip they met 112 children in two classes. This

establishment, the inspector said, is very badly maintained and is disgustingly filthy. There is no order, calmness or subordination in the class. The Brothers strike the children at times; the inspector said he was a witness to this...The students know poorly their catechism; reading and writing are not any better; the cleverest of the students do not know subtraction...It appears, M. le Supérieur, that your Brothers do not stay long enough in the novitiate. In the interest of the common good and for the good of your congregation you should send out only subjects who are well tested. If public confidence is lost, it will never be recovered, or only by infinite struggle. If means are lacking, it is better to have only ten good establishments in place of twenty. (Smith 112)

Obviously local authorities at Mamers were concerned enough about the school that they reported abuses to Angers. There were three Brothers teaching at Mamers in 1829, but another letter of complaint (July 10, 1829) does not name the offending Brothers. When Dujarié replied (July 23, 1829) to these letters, he blamed the untidiness on the configuration of classrooms and the kitchen.

If we had to pick one early Brother of St. Joseph who epitomized the purpose of the new Community out in the schools, it could very well be Brother Stephen Gauffre. The fourth young man to show up in the first year of the Brothers (1820), he had a long tenure at his assigned school, Denis d'Orques, the foundation credited as the first established by the Brothers (CSCG 1 A 71). The school at Ruillé for some reason either was not the first or was not considered an outreach apostolate. Go to Denis d'Orques Stephen did, and he taught there for twelve years, until the Community pulled out of the school in 1833. Obviously Stephen liked his work there and the parishioners must have liked him. His tenure did not set a record for the Brothers, but he certainly must have been exemplary to his fellow Brothers for his length of service in one school. Vincent moved around, and Andre did not have a regular teaching position until the 1835 move to Le Mans, unless, of course, he was teaching in the school at Ruillé while he managed the training of the novices and supervision of the men out in schools. Double duty could have been possible (teaching and supervising), but the workload would be oppressively heavy and unfair to Andre, the children, and the novices.

Studying the list of the Brothers' schools that opened between 1821 and 1840 (Appendix V), one can easily conclude that the period of greatest growth and, we presume, greatest influence lasted from 1822 until 1828. In that seven-year period the Brothers opened seventy-one schools, with the highest number of openings occurring in 1825 (fifteen schools). It is true, of course, that during the same period they withdrew from a number of schools (twenty), but the total remaining in their care (fifty-one)during that time is amazing. Five of the seventy-one schools were under the Brothers for only one year, but many enjoyed staying open for multiple years. Meslay, for example, stayed under the Brothers' direction for forty-seven years, and Craon, as we have noted, seventy-six years (1827 to 1903). Nineteen of the seventy-one schools stayed open for at least a decade, and seven stayed with the Brothers for twenty-five or more years.

One wonders, of course, why many schools would lose their Brother (or Brothers) after three or four years, and the answers are many. Sometimes the pastor was unable to pay the Brother's annual salary, or he became upset with the quality of instruction being given to the children. Veteran teachers like Vincent Pieau, Rémi Mérianne, Leonard Guittoger, and Vital Breton were much appreciated in their schools, but other Brothers were not successful in their pedagogy and precipitated their own withdrawal. Brother Andre Mottais had his hands full not only with supplying Brothers to parish schools but also ensuring that teaching quality was good and stayed good.

Why did the number of schools drop drastically from 1829 to 1835? We will look at this matter in the next chapter, but we should note here that civil unrest, e.g., the 1830 July Revolution, cannot account totally for the drop because the drop began a full year before the outbreak of unrest and lasted five years after it concluded. Only in 1836 did the number of schools begin to pick up (four openings in 1836, five in 1837, nine in 1838). The drop between 1829 and 1835 may have been due in part to a crisis in management: the founding father was aging, and the four Brother-Directors needed recycling. And it may also have been true that the base for vocations had been drying up—there are only a limited number of young people available within any geographic area, and the Brothers of St. Joseph may have started to exhaust the available young men by 1828, thus limiting the number of new schools the Brothers could open. Moreover, some of the forty-eight schools they did run in 1829 employed more than one Brother, and as a school proved excellent, the local pastor would naturally request additional Brothers for the parish school.

Would that we had exact personnel lists for these early years, but with the loss of Brother Andre's first volume of accounts (1822 to 1829), we have very scant information on placement. Records could be gleaned, of course, from parish records here and there, but an accurate list of assignments from the early years may be next to impossible to create. Even with the second Andre volume of accounts (1830-1836) intact in the University of Notre Dame Hesburgh Library, we find various pieces of information but nothing like a precise register that we could appreciate today.

At the heart of this wonderful resurgence in French education was a special Brother of St. Joseph, Vincent Pieau, born Jean Pieau on February 15, 1797, in Courbeveille, France, three years before Andre Mottais was born. The town, located ten miles southwest of Laval in the district of Mayenne, is one of a number of small towns that contributed its young men to a resurgence of religious life after the atrocities of the French Revolution and rampant anti-clericalism had died down. Though volatile sentiments against church workers had never been as strong in the Laval area as they were in Paris, there was enough hostility in the outlying districts forcing clergy to hide during the notorious Reign of Terror. How the French Revolution affected the young boy named Jean Pieau we do not know. He was born near the waning of its worst violence so his own schooling was not nearly as troubled as that of those who came before him. He was orphaned early, and in 1822, at the age of 26, he traveled to Ruillé-sur-Loir to join Dujarié's young band of Brothers, organized a little over two years earlier.

Thirty miles southwest of Le Mans, Ruillé is a gentle town, its most prominent structure today being the chapel of the Grand Providence, the motherhouse of the Sisters of Providence. By 1824 the town contained the "Grand Saint-Joseph," a large building used for Dujarié's Brothers of Saint Joseph. Today this building is an apartment house. The only buildings left original from the Brothers' first years are the church and the rectory, which has been incorporated into one of the side buildings sitting on the front road thirty yards from the church.

Jean Pieau, when he arrived in Ruillé, would not have lived at the Grand Saint-Joseph because it was not purchased until 1824. He would have lived in the rectory, sleeping in either the rat-infested attic with other Brothers, or in the laundry room, barn, or stable where young men had to bunk because of the numbers arriving to join the group. The pastor housed twenty-five to thirty recruits in the early years. How spacious the Grand Saint-Joseph must eventually have seemed to the men—it had a large refectory, classrooms, and ample sleeping quarters. The property also had a garden, a pond, and a small brook.

There is something exciting about a new venture that cannot be repeated in later years, no matter how successful an institution becomes. Neither of the first two recruits persevered in their religious vocation, Pierre leaving a year after he arrived and therefore not at Ruillé when Jean Pieau arrived in 1822. The other, Louis, did not leave the Brothers until 1825 and would thus have known Jean Pieau. Brother Vincent, of course, knew Brother Andre very well—they became close friends as several of their last letters prove:

> Good-by then, my very dear Brother Vincent. Good-by for eternity undoubtedly, because you are for America, we for Africa. Good-by—I embrace you with all my heart. (Andre to Vincent, May 18, 1840)

At the time Andre was waiting in a religious residence in Lyons before he shipped out of France to go to Algeria with the first Holy Cross missionary colony. Broken in health years later at Holy Cross, he wrote to his friend Vincent in America:

> When I came [back] to Holy Cross, Reverend Father honored me with the title of Assistant and made me a member of all the councils: although much inferior in virtues and merit to you, my very dear Brother, I am replacing you for the time being. (Andre to Vincent, May 26, 1843)

Even allowing for nineteenth-century sentiments, the letters came from a genuine heart much on fire with love for the Community and reflect as well on Vincent.

When Jean Pieau joined the Brothers on October 9, 1822, the group numbered sixteen, including Pieau himself. Three of the four who joined in 1820 had persevered, as did all six who joined in 1821 and six who joined in 1822 before Jean Pieau arrived. Few of them, of course, would have been on hand in the fall when Jean Pieau arrived since the school year would have begun already at the beginning of October. He began his novitiate training on August 17, 1823, and he was awarded his teaching diploma on November 2 of the same year, so he may very well have begun teaching while he was still a novice. Religious rules were fluid at the time, and a young man was often called on to fill a need. Since the Brothers of Saint Joseph took no vows of poverty, celibacy, obedience, and made only a yearly "promise" of obedience, without the canonical force of the evangelical counsels, it is a wonder that any members of the early group endured. During the next seven years, Vincent rose to a position of respect and authority among the Brothers.

Vincent's position among the Brothers of Saint Joseph should be recognized for what it was: he is repeatedly named as one of the four "Brother Directors" resident at Ruillé, guiding the Community as Dujarié's health worsened. His living at Ruillé, while most of the Brothers were farmed out to small towns, indicated just how much Dujarié relied on his local presence. It was an earned respect that Vincent enjoyed throughout his religious life. Of the other three Brother-Directors, we know much about Andre and Leonard. We know next to nothing about Henry Taupin. Since he was dismissed from the Community in 1834, his correspondence, if any existed, would probably have been destroyed. In the Holy Cross General Archives no letters remain to or from him. He was dismissed under a cloud, and we know little about the circumstances of his being sent away. He was not young: thirty-one when he came to the Brothers in 1823, he lived his prime years as a Brother of St. Joseph and was probably a fine teacher as his selection to be one of the four Directors shows that both Dujarié and Andre had respect for and confidence in him. He is an enigma. Even his occasional signature is an enigma: he signs himself as "Henry" instead of "Henri." Was he affecting English affiliation? Or was he simply being singular? He remains a mystery waiting to be solved. We can only hope he found happiness after he left the Community at age forty-two.

From 1823 until 1841, Brother Vincent taught in Ruillé and in Le Mans, steadily building a reputation for being a highly effective educator, a reputation that stayed with him throughout his almost seventy years as a religious Brother. We can surmise that he was content with the move of headquarters from Ruillé to Le Mans and that he was elated at the Community's growth under the firm direction of Basil Moreau. Since the two men were almost the same age, Vincent two years older than Moreau, we can understand the warmth and respect the two shared for each other, evidenced on every page of the letters extant from Vincent to Moreau. Unfortunately we have no letters remaining from Dujarié to Vincent. Early Brothers did not keep many of the letters sent to them. Teaching out in small towns and moving with as little baggage as possible, there would be no reason (or file cabinet) to retain correspondence, unlike in the more stable situation of either the Ruillé or Le Mans motherhouse.

In America by 1841, Brother Vincent eventually settled into an active routine. He was in charge of the novices, and he was, as the only certified teacher, in charge of teacher training. In addition, he undoubtedly taught courses to the students who were beginning to show up at the new secondary school at Notre Dame. There were, of course, breaks in his routine. In April of 1844 he watched at the deathbed of Brother Joachim, the first of the French missionaries to die in America. One month later, in May, 1844, he set out for France in order to escort a third colony of missionaries to Indiana. Vincent traveled to New York by way of Detroit and Buffalo, using a steamboat on Lake Erie. The steamboat trip for Vincent and his companion Brother Augustine (Jeremy O'Leary), who was heading to Le Mans in order to teach English at Sainte-Croix, cost five dollars for the pair, semi-private cabin and food included. The boat ride took them three hundred miles to Buffalo in two days. From Buffalo to Albany they traveled by canal, a three and a half day trip. Finally on June 6, after a two-day stay in a town where Augustine had relatives, they arrived in New York City. They were booked on the *Duchess of Orleans* bound for France.

One month later, Vincent writes from France to his superior in Indiana Edward Sorin telling him that he has paid a visit to Sorin's elderly father:

> Your father, who was in bed, jumped up when he saw me.
> We chatted, but he stopped so that he'd get to morning
> Mass. Following that, we had lunch together at his place. I
> stayed there until 10 o'clock, and before leaving I received
> 20 francs from your brother (he's generous). Your father
> gave me 10 also, and the Curé of La Brulcatte 5. (July 14,
> 1844, in Klawitter, *Adapted* 67)

Not on a pleasure junket, Vincent was under orders from Sorin to solicit money for Notre Dame, so he canvassed in Laval and various towns, including Ruillé. Apparently the trip was a success, and Vincent was able to meet scores of old friends. He had hopes to bring Basil Moreau back to America for a visit, but the priest decided that a visit to a planned foundation in North Africa should come first.

Back in America, the death of a young Brother in southern Indiana must have touched Vincent profoundly—the drowning of Anselm in Madison, Indiana, on July 12, 1845, at the age of twenty. Anselm's pastor, Julian Delaune, reported the loss to Moreau:

I have sad news for you. Sudden death has taken Brother
Anselm away from us. He came to see me Saturday
afternoon, July 12, to tell me he was going swimming.
After hesitating a bit, I agreed to accompany him. He went
into the water about seven or eight hundred feet away from
me, in a place which did not seem the least bit dangerous.
He went out more than five hundred feet without finding
water deep enough for swimming. I was in water about
three or four feet deep, a little distance off the bank. All of a
sudden, while he was swimming, I noticed an expression of
suffering on his face. He went down, but I thought he was
doing it on purpose. He came up, then went down again,
while uttering a cry for help. What a moment for me! I
was more than three hundred feet away from him and did
not know how to swim. We were two miles from the city,
with no houses nearby. He came up again and then sank.
A moment later he lifted his arms and I saw him no more.

All aghast, I hastened to give him absolution. He had
probably received it that morning for, as usual, he had gone
to confession, and he went to Communion at least every
Sunday. I ran to a cabin. A child told me that there was an
old man not far away. I ran to him and brought him with
me and pointed out from afar the place where the Brother
disappeared. "He is lost for good," he told me. "Right there
is a drop-off at least twenty feet deep, and the current
all around is very swift. Anything I could do would be
useless." I went home, got some good swimmers together,
and procured boats and nets.

All our efforts proved useless. It was ten o'clock in the
evening before he was found, five hours after he had
drowned. An inquest was held by the civil authorities,
and then we brought him back to the church at one-
thirty yesterday morning. He was laid out in the basement
chapel. Some of the Irish settlers watched beside the coffin
until daybreak. I clothed him in his religious habit and he
remained exposed in the Chapel until yesterday afternoon
at four. Everyone was dismayed by the event. Thank
God for having borne me up throughout this trial and

its accompanying fatigue. Sleepless, and almost without having tasted food, broken-hearted and yet forced to stifle my grief in order to look after all the details, I suffered more yesterday than I ever thought I could.

At four in the afternoon we brought him to the church. The coffin was uncovered, and the calmness of his features made him look as though he were only asleep. Protestants and Catholics alike gathered to the number of more than a thousand. The choir sang the Vespers of the Dead. With painful effort I preached on Chapter Four of the Book of Wisdom, beginning with verse seven. ["But the just man, if he be overtaken by death, shall be in rest. For venerable old age is not that of long time, nor counted by the number of years...He was taken away lest wickedness should alter his understanding, or deceit beguile his soul."]

I had the thirteenth verse written in English on a black banner: "Being made perfect in a short space, he fulfilled a long time." After the Libera, the children from his school kissed his forehead; then the coffin was closed and covered with the funeral drape. The two schools led the funeral procession with the banner and the cross. The hearse followed, and then the people, two by two. I marched between the school children and the carriages. We crossed the city to the cemetery, which is a mile from here. (Moreau, *Circular* 100-102)

Vincent does not document his own grief for the young man, but he had visited Madison in the previous October on one of his supervisory trips, and he must have felt the loss as if it were the loss of a son. He had known Anselm in Le Mans when the sixteen-year old boy was a novice under Brother Andre Mottais' care at la Charbonnière. Vincent had traveled the Atlantic with him, lived with him in the episcopal residence in Vincennes when Brother Gatian, Brother Francis Xavier, and Edward Sorin had moved north to Notre Dame. Vincent taught next to the young man in the Vincennes cathedral school and guided him in the first years of his profession.

In spring of 1849 at the age of fifty-two, Vincent was presented with a challenge: he was sent to New Orleans with four Brothers and three Sisters to assume direction of St. Mary's Orphanage, an institution founded in

1835 by a young diocesan priest who died in 1837 of typhoid incurred from his heroic efforts to save his orphans during a hurricane. St. Mary's had languished for a decade under inadequate supervision, and the prelate of New Orleans (Anthony Blanc) was very anxious to have a religious community take the children under its wing. The orphanage sat on Chartres Street right on the Mississippi River levee, down river from the heart of the city. When Vincent arrived on May 1, 1949, he found ninety-eight boys in pitiable condition. The miserable blankets they had were quickly burned by the Sisters who had come with him. Thanks to the generosity of the Ursuline Sisters and the Sisters of Charity, Vincent and his staff were able to turn things around for the good.

Of the seven Holy Cross men who came to America in 1841, Vincent, eldest of the missionary colony, outlived most of them. Joachim died in 1844, Anselm in 1845. Gatian left the community in 1850 and died on his family's farm in France in 1860. Lawrence died in 1873, much lauded for his contributions to the success of Notre Dame. Only Sorin and Francis Xavier outlived the patriarch Vincent. Francis Xavier was the last to die (1896), his grave dug by a novice named Bernard Gervais.

We should appreciate that the Brothers of St. Joseph did not stay a religious group localized to a small section of France—by 1840 the Brothers had ventured to Algeria, by 1841 to Indiana, and by 1847 to Canada. Wherever they went in those early years, however, they retained their vigorous commitment to teaching young boys. Their pedagogy improved as they aged, and their reverence for their earliest guides, Jacques Dujarié and Andre Mottais, remained rooted in their hearts. What was planted in the earliest years, 1820 to 1829, grew strong and healthy, a wonder to the Church and to themselves. They never worked for applause or craved recognition. Theirs was a quiet life, quiet but forceful in the impact they made with their educational outreach.

CHAPTER THREE

Revolution and Dismay, 1830-1834

To call the 1830 uprising in Paris a revolution rather than a riot may be to give it a sobriquet it does not deserve. Charles X had made several no-compromise decisions that led to his overthrow as the last of the Bourbon kings. The "July Ordinance" as promulgated on Sunday, July 25, did away with freedom of the press and fanned the flames that growing unemployment had started. On Monday, the first day of the insurrection, mobs gathered to harass royalists, and on Tuesday, twenty-one citizens were killed in skirmishes by French soldiers. On Wednesday, the king ordered the Garde Royale into action, and that, coupled with bad advice from Polignac, his chief minister, compounded the tension. Mobs seized the Tuilleries Palace, the Louvre, and the Hôtel de Ville. Those acts brought the riots to a finale with the king abdicating by August 2 and his cousin Louis Philippe being awarded the throne. Charles had ruled for fifteen years. Louis Philippe would last eighteen.

The emotional rant of media can do much to fuel revolution, and so it was in the months leading up to the 1830 turmoil in France, turmoil due in no small part to the hysterical rhetoric of two anti-clerical voices, the pamphleteer Paul Louis Courier and the balladeer Béranger (Dansette 1.199). Revolutions are ever carried on emotion, firing the hearts of the oppressed (i.e., *Common Sense* in 1776) or the marginalized (i.e., *Declaration of the Rights of Woman and the Female Citizen* in 1791). Then came 1830. A mini-revolution in France sent the Brothers of St. Joseph into a tailspin. One-third of them left the Community. Others were dispirited. Their founding priest was sickly and old.

Over the years there has been much speculation on the decline in numbers for the Brothers of St. Joseph post-1830. In general, blame falls on the mini-revolution in July of 1830 when three days of unrest rippled across

Paris and affected the entire country by inducing the king to abdicate. It is true that at the end of the 1830 school year there were forty-two schools operated by the Brothers of St. Joseph, and that at the end of the 1831 school year there were only thirty-two schools under their care. But eleven schools closed in 1830 (before the July Revolution) and another eleven in 1831 so the mini-revolution could not have been fully responsible for the closing of all twenty-two schools unless, of course, the build-up to revolution had already affected the morale of the Brothers.

We should, therefore, look to other causes for the decline in membership and the decline in the number of schools under operation. It might very well have been that the Brothers were looking for new leadership. After all, for ten years they had been under the titular care of an aging priest who relegated most of his supervisory duties to four Brother-Directors, and the Brother-Directors may have been a source of unease as well. It is no secret that term limits are good for organizations: presidents and prime ministers need to be changed regularly. By 1830 Brother Andre Mottais had been in effect making all decisions for the Brothers for half a dozen years, not only in regard to pedagogical training but also their spiritual direction.

What militates against such a conclusion, however, are two things. First of all there is no indication of any dissatisfaction with Brother Andre from any of the Brothers. Secondly, after the dreadful closing of twenty-two schools in two years, 1830 and 1831, such closings level off: only two in 1832, five in 1833, two in 1834, and five in 1835. At the same time seven new schools were opened by the Brothers so the net fall for the period 1832 to 1835 was only seven, compared to seventeen for 1830 to 1831.

So civil unrest might be the primary culprit, but not the only culprit, for the decline in the Brothers of St. Joseph Community. Most young people want stability when they choose a career. Very few are life-long agitators. The excitement of challenging a government is heady for the young, but once the cause has served its purpose, most rioters return to business as usual. After the Brothers of St. Joseph suffered a two-year hit in their apostolic endeavors, they were ready as a group to settle down into their religious lives. There is no significant decline in the number of schools operated between 1832 and 1837. School count begins to rise: thirty-seven in operation in 1838, forty-one in 1839, forty in 1840, a count possibly influenced by the major change in both leadership and location of the motherhouse.

Watching the political rollercoaster in the early 1830s were the four Brother-Directors—Andre, Leonard, Henry, and Vincent. Of them Leonard

is best known for the role he began to play in the transition from Ruillé
to Le Mans. He was born Pierre-François to Pierre Guittoger and Marie-
Scholastique Poussin at Terrehaut (Sarthe) on July 13, 1802, the year of
Napoleon's much needed and much welcomed Concordat. Thus he arrived
when France was settling down into a relative peace following the terrible
dozen years of the Revolution and its bloody aftermath, the Reign of
Terror. Robespierre, Danton, and Marat would still, of course, be names
on everyone's lips, even in remote provinces, but the country by and large
began to enjoy the calm of Napoleonic dictatorship, a calm that would last
until the next upheaval, the petit revolution of 1830. In the Guittoger family,
Leonard would have spent his early years getting a rudimentary education
at the local elementary school and thereafter being employed on the family
farm or in the family business, but we know nothing precise about his youth
until, at the age of 23, he went to Ruillé-sur-Loir in the autumn of 1825 to
enter Dujarié's Brothers of St. Joseph. By the time of his arrival, the little
band of Brothers, begun only five years earlier, had swelled in number and
was serving as teachers in a dozen towns around the diocese. Over one
hundred men had come to Ruillé before Leonard, and over seventy of them
had remained with the Community.

At Ruillé in these early days, life was regulated by the talented Brother
Andre Mottais who served as Dujarié's right-hand man and more or less ran
the community on a day by day basis. Andre was not only novice master, but
he was also supervisor for all the schools making him totally responsible
for the academic development and expertise of all the Brothers. Since he
was also responsible for the spiritual direction of all the men at Ruillé, one
wonders what exactly Dujarié had to do with the little community, aside
from the daily Mass, weekly confessions, and correspondence with priests
regarding placement of his men in the parishes. Of course Dujarié, a saintly
man himself but never a vowed religious, remained throughout his life a
guide to those within the Brothers of St. Joseph. Dujarié, with whimsical
respect, would on occasion refer to Andre as "his Holiness" (Rémi Mérianne,
qtd. Vanier 552). Having had a formal novitiate and scholastic training with
the Christian Brothers in Paris, Andre shouldered quite properly the daily
shaping of the amorphous group at Ruillé into the vigorous community it
would eventually become. He and Dujarié made a superb team, although
he has been overlooked more often than not, or simply dismissed by Holy
Cross historians as Dujarié's secretary. He is named, in fact, in one legal
document as "secretary" to the priest-director. The document concerns

Brothers exempt from military service because they are members of a religious institute.

Three months after arriving at Ruillé, Leonard began his novitiate, or rather became a novice since the term "novitiate" implies a limited time (a year or two) in a semi-cloistered atmosphere. In Dujarié's community, however, the Brothers could remain "novices" for ten years or more, until they felt impelled to take a simple promise of obedience, a step some of them never took. We know, however, that Leonard renewed his vow of obedience on September 11, 1830. We have no record of when he first took the vow. One year later he signed the "Pact of Fidelity," the touching document that, following the political turmoil of 1830, the remnants of Dujarié's band of Brothers created and signed as an endorsement of their wish to remain faithful to Dujarié's vision. In the document Leonard is named "Second Director," right after the First Director Andre Mottais, and before both the Third Director Henri-Michel Taupin, and the Fourth Director Vincent-Ferier Pieau. Thus at the age of twenty-nine, just six years after his arrival, Leonard had already risen to a position of prominence and authority, so evident were his talents and his promise as an administrator and leader. He had been, in fact, one of the four directors since 1826 and would remain so named until 1833 when he would be assigned to teach for one year at the school in Esclimont.

As an administrator, Leonard was entrusted with significant responsibility as can be deduced from his January 1833 letter to a priest concerning the ability of the Brothers to acquire property in their own names without legalizing the purchase under Dujarié's name alone. The problem on which Leonard was seeking the priest's advice was the matter of obligation that the community had or did not have to consult ex-members on the matter of property disposal. Leonard argues, and we presume he is arguing as a voice of all four Brother Directors, that consultation with ex-members would be difficult if not impossible in the matter of property the community enjoyed while those members were still legally members of the community. Leonard is trying to argue for an institution's ability to buy and sell property in its own name, not in the name of a specific individual, a matter of intense debate in France at the time. Moreover, five of the ex-Brothers in question are dead, and consultation with their relatives would be pointless since the latter would have little or no knowledge of or interest in the affairs of the Ruillé Brothers. The addressee of this letter is not known, but he obviously was a canon lawyer since Leonard requests that the priest's decision on the matter be communicated to a notary for legal approbation.

Leonard writes an intelligent letter in impeccable French. He writes with authority, deferential but authoritative nonetheless.

Leonard's name surfaces often in Andre Mottais' ledger—one of the most valuable records we have for the Brothers of St. Joseph, a large folio volume of 366 lined pages giving information on new recruits, assignments, and finances between 1830 and 1837. It is mostly in Brother Andre's handwriting. As First Director, he would naturally have been responsible for data keeping on both personnel and finances. The 1830 to 1837 volume is actually one of two volumes chronicling the early Brothers. It is tagged as "Vol. 2" and in several places refers to a "volume one," an earlier volume presumably covering the years 1820 to 1829. The earlier volume, if ever found, would be immensely valuable to Holy Cross historians. Volume two of Brother Andre's massive ledger also contains valuable information about yearly assignments to various schools. For anyone who has the inclination to trace the openings (and closings) of all the little parish schools run by the Brothers of St. Joseph, volume 2 is a source that must be consulted.

In 1831 as foundations increased and money matters grew complicated, Bishop Carron of Le Mans thought it necessary to disentangle the finances of the Sisters of Providence and the Brothers of St. Joseph. The Sisters, established by Dujarié a generation before the Brothers, were solid financially and legally, but the Brothers continued to struggle for the legal recognition that would facilitate their financial health. To understand the dynamics of this separation, one needs to appreciate the character of Marie Lecor, the mother superior of the Sisters of Providence at the time. The Sisters began their history more amorphously than the Brothers, as a group of a half dozen pious girls living two miles from Dujarié in a small house he had built for them on the outskirts of Ruillé. Financed in part by a loan from Marie Lair, the first woman Dujarié asked to teach the local children in 1804, the establishment encountered problems when Lair proved to be mentally unstable (Catta, *Dujarié* 59). It took years to get rid of her. Meanwhile, Dujarié's pious women saw to the needs of the local poor and trudged into Ruillé every Sunday to receive spiritual guidance from their director. By 1811 they numbered ten, and Dujarié relied on a superior named Sister Félicité (her family name is lost) who lasted but a short time before she left the group. In 1813 more stability came with the arrival of Madeleine Beucher who directed the group for seven years, until Zoé du Roscoät was elected first Superior General (1820). When Zoé arrived, the Sisters numbered eighteen. Four years later she died, having been with the Providence Sisters only a short time but leaving an indelible mark on their history. A woman of great virtue and sweet personality, she came from an aristocratic background that heightened the generosity of her selfless dedication to Dujarié and his little community.

Her successor was decidedly different: Perrine Lecor was a Breton peasant who grew up on an isolated peninsula in northern France and spoke only Breton, no French, until the age of twenty. Madame du Roscoät had hired her as a teaching aide back in Brittany, and Perrine followed Madame to Ruillé, succeeding her as Mother General in 1822. Where Mother Marie-Madeleine was diplomatic, Mother Marie Lecor was brusque. Where the former venerated Dujarié, the latter confronted and circumvented him, not afraid to recognize that the aging priest was losing his ability to direct. Marie-Madeleine had put the person of the founder primary in her concerns, but Marie Lecor barged ahead with Providence as her single concern. Before being elected Mother General, Marie Lecor judged herself to have "a cold temperament" (Catta, *Dujarié* 202) to be undereducated, and to be without virtue. The Cattas dub her predecessor, Mother Marie-Madeleine, the "Angel of Providence." Mother Marie Lecor, on the other hand, was anything but an angel.

Thus when the separation of finances between the Brothers of St. Joseph and the Sisters of Providence surfaced in 1831 as a necessity in the eyes of Bishop Carron, it is against the backdrop of a tough Mother General, the only one that most of the Brothers would have known because the gentle one had died in the second year of the Brothers' foundation. Andre would have known Mother Marie-Madeleine, but she died when there were but a dozen Brothers in Dujarié's new little religious group of men. What the Brothers therefore had to deal with for most of their religious lives was the strong minded Breton Mother Marie Lecor. If the separation of finances was effected in an atmosphere of paranoia and gloom, the onus lies on Marie Lecor who wanted what was best for her Sisters and was not particularly concerned with the future of the Brothers, whose future was darkened by more departures than arrivals in the three years previous to this financial separation. Some of the bad feelings must, of course, be traced to Dujarié himself. He alienated himself from Marie Lecor by refusing to deal with her. On one occasion when she visited his rectory to see him, half a block from the Providence motherhouse he had built for the Sisters, he refused to see her, and when she then wrote him a letter, he sent it back unopened (Catta, *Dujarié* 202). The pettiness that grew over several years between two very strong personalities nowhere reflects itself in Andre Mottais who, as primary director of the Brothers, was in a position to become as rancorous as the other two players in the scenario but who remained, like Bishop Carron, fair and above the fray.

Andre was no match for Marie Lecor's grit, and Dujarié, plagued by gout, often confined to bed, no longer enjoyed the deference of the mother general, her council, or the Sisters in the hinterlands who barely knew him. If anything good can be said for Marie Lecor, it is that she exerted a tremendous amount of power at a time when women were quite powerless both in the church and in society generally. Once she found her foothold, there was no stopping her, and the last thing she wanted was any financial co-dependence with a group of men who had declined in numbers for two years and showed no signs of any restructuring. A new director for the Brothers was waiting in the wings at Le Mans, but Dujarié was still in charge, and Marie Lecor wanted less and less to do with him. She should be admired surely for her tenacity in promoting the Sisters, but the bad chemistry between her and Dujarié was as much her fault as his. The old man expected things to go on as they always had under his kind and generous eye: she looked to the future and saw a wonderful opportunity for women to assume their own direction. What she thought of Andre Mottais we do not know. She probably considered him well intentioned and harmless, linked by gender and domicile more inextricably to Dujarié than she was. Her energies were employed to cut off Dujarié: Andre was simply one of his adjuncts. Enjoying the ear of the bishop, she was unstoppable.

The document in Andre's handwriting for the financial separation of the two communities is dated April 21, 1831, which would be the final day of the bishop's three- day visit to Ruillé. Andre sets out in detail the Brothers' financial status from November 1826 up to the day of the document. He notes that peak membership came at the annual August retreat in 1829 (almost 105 men by his count) from sixty-six foundations, but "since that happy time the number of Brothers, and establishments, has declined a lot" (April 21, 1831). He does not here specify reasons for the decline, but various historians have attributed the decline to two reasons: the political unrest leading up to the July, 1830, mini-revolution when old embers from 1789 were rekindled for another revolutionary outburst, as we have noted, and the lack of a solid formation for the young Brothers before they were sent out to teach in parish schools. Andre then lists twenty-five schools taken on since 1826 (some of which were operated by the Brothers for only one school year) and fifty-three schools which have paid or failed to pay annual salaries. Some items include benefactors who bankrolled the schools: e.g., the Duchess of Tourzelle who gave 900 francs a year for the Larchamp school and M. de la Porte who gave 10,000 francs to construct classrooms at Sablé and repair the Brothers' house. One of the most poignant entries is the one for the Ruillé boarding school that was under Andre's direct supervision and existed legally under his name, not Dujarié's, so the Brothers could count on some property: it was later sold for 7000 francs to a contractor employed by Basil Moreau to build Holy Cross in Le Mans. Although it has always been known that Moreau was involved in the spiritual guidance of the Brothers as preacher and confessor as early as 1823, that is, within three years of the first vocations at Ruillé, it has generally been assumed that Moreau's involvement with the Brothers' physical properties did not begin until 1835.

The Brothers were not exactly poor at the separation from the Sisters of Providence. They owned and enjoyed income from the Grand Saint-Joseph (eventually sold for 11,900 francs), the Ruillé boarding school, several vineyards, and some farm property. The *Chronicles* note that the boarding school brought in revenue from its twenty boarders, and the salaries of Brother carpenters were significant. Moreover, various benefactors continued to be generous. The Sisters, of course, had developed their Ruillé motherhouse rather grandly, some of the work being done by the Brothers. The women were, however, established sixteen years earlier than the Brothers and had had as their leader for nine years that intrepid mother general who fought aggressively for her Sisters.

About this time someone, probably Andre, came up with an idea for the Brothers to swear an oath of allegiance to the community (and to Dujarié). The oath is mentioned by Andre in a letter to Brother Adrian dated July 20, 1831, and was conceived as a way to show support for the elderly priest, support much needed after his clashes with the mother general. It is dated September 1, 1831, indicating that it was administered and signed during the annual retreat, that one time of year when all the Brothers were expected to come to Ruillé (Appendix XIX). It is signed by only seventeen men, but some whose signatures do not appear on the document did sign a vow formula four days later binding them to a promise of obedience to Dujarié. Noting that they lacked the "hope of expanding or even continuing to exist for any length of time" (Klawitter, *Mottais* 12), seventeen Brothers wished to preserve what they had joined so faithfully, but should they have to disband, they wanted "to remain united in heart and affections, supporting and assisting one another." The "Pact of Fidelity" reads:

We pledge ourselves by the present act of the strictest obligation that we can make so that violations will constitute sin:

1) to live attached to our holy Institute
2) to sustain each other until death
3) to remain united in the body of the Congregation and the Community as long as possible, following the same practices and rules that we have practiced up to now
4) and in case we have to dissolve, to remain united in heart and affections, sustaining and assisting each other reciprocally
5) to assemble as a body in Community as time and place permit.
6) We Brothers of Saint Joseph will continue our submission to and dependence on Father Dujarié...
7) Conforming to the dispositions of the preceding article, he will be able to innovate and abrogate in our rules and customs everything he judges necessary for the time and circumstances.
8) Near our superior we have our rallying point
9) and if we have the misfortune to lose him, we will rally around the bishop of Le Mans. (Klawitter, *Mottais* 12)

This "Pact of Fidelity" or oath of allegiance is striking for several reasons. First of all, it is in Andre's hand and therefore indicates his primary workmanship. Secondly, it swears a fidelity to each other, even if the institute should dissolve. The bonds forged by many of these men over a decade were considered valuable enough and enriching enough that the men would want to stay supporters of each other even if they were no longer financially or organizationally a unit. Thirdly, the document lists the four directors (up from three of previous years). All but one would die in the community (Appendix XIX). Thus the Brothers did enjoy a modicum of self-governance even if Dujarié remained ostensibly their superior.

The vow formula for September 5, 1831, is also found in Brother Andre's ledger:

In the name of the Holy Trinity, in the presence of his Holy Virgin Mother of God, of St. Joseph and the holy angels, I Brother . . ., after being approved and having

asked God to consecrate me to the education of children
in the Congregation of the Brothers of St. Joseph, submit
publically to the rules and statutes of the said Congregation,
promising to observe them exactly, and consequently, I
make for one year the vow of obedience to the superior
of the said Congregation. So help me God and his Holy
Mother. (Klawitter, *Mottais* 13)

Whether each Brother said the formula or whether the group said it all
together we do not know. We presume that each man recited the formula
out loud before affixing his name beneath it—that at least is the tradition
that has come down to this day. It is, after all, a very personal contract
between one and a community.

We should not be surprised to see that these two major documents,
the "Pact of Fidelity" and the promise formula, differ rather obviously in
the signatures affixed. After the beautiful "Declaration," written out of love
and desperation, seventeen signatures appear. Many of the names we would
expect: in addition to the four Brother-Directors there appear the signatures
of Rémi Mérianne and Stephen Gauffre, both significant contributors to the
early history of the Brothers of St. Joseph. One signature appears for a man
(Michel Coupin) who does not appear in the 1944 *Matricule Générale*. He
may have been present for the occasion as a new recruit who had not yet
been accepted into novitiate training and thus did not rate a ranking in the
Matricule. The "Pact of Fidelity" and the signatures appear on page 165 of
Andre's ledger.

Four days later eighteen Brothers made the promise of obedience
and signed their names. We would expect that most of these eighteen
signatures would correspond to the seventeen signatures on the "Pact of
Fidelity." They do not. The four Brother-Directors signed both documents,
but other signers of the "Pact" (Baptiste, Michel, Antonin, Vincent de Paul,
and Marie-Joseph) did not sign the promise of obedience formula. Men who
did not sign the "Pact" but did sign the promise of obedience document were
Vital, Augustin, Arsène, Louis de Gonzague, Gervais, and Irénée. We might
conclude that the "Pact" was an impromptu idea, but, as already mentioned,
we know that Brother Andre had announced the "Pact" months before (in
July 1831). It is hard to imagine how a stalwart teacher like Vital would not
sign the "Pact of Fidelity" unless, of course, he had not yet arrived for the
retreat. The "Pact" was, after all, a one-time thing. The promise formula,
on the other hand, was a ritual at the annual retreat, anticipated and no
doubt celebrated.

In 1833 Dujarié considered having his Brothers pronounce two perpetual vows: obedience and stability. Neither vow would blanket poverty and chastity, disciplines which Dujarié felt his men were not yet strong enough to pledge. Those who wished to take the vows of obedience and stability could so petition only if they had worked already ten years in his Community. The Brother candidates for final vows would also have to be approved by the six eldest Brothers (Smith 6). But Bishop Carron died in 1833 before his permission could be secured. Thus Dujarié in his failing years was already considering vows as a way to keep his flock together. He was not alone in his worries. Brother Andre Mottais had suggested in the late summer of 1834 that a meeting was needed in which Dujarié and three Brothers could discuss in detail with the bishop the financial and spiritual crises of the Brothers of St. Joseph. Brother Vincent was one of the three Brothers chosen for the task.

In the summer of 1834 Andre wrote the first of three remarkable letters that had enormous impact on the future of his Brothers. In a letter marked "private" to the bishop in Le Mans just before the beginning of the 1834 August retreat, Andre points out that the community is being demoralized by one of the four directors, Brother Henry, who does not follow the rules and gives permissions indiscriminately to those who wish to circumvent Andre. Secondly, the Community has been trying to sustain two novitiates, one at Ruillé and one at Esclimont, and the latter is draining them with little hope of attracting many recruits in that region. Thirdly, the matter of Dujarié's ability to direct is becoming problematic: the elderly priest weakens both physically and mentally. Andre closes with eleven points he would like the bishop to discuss face to face with three of the four Brother directors (omitting only Brother Henry from the interview). The eleven matters are substantial and include matters of property as well as matters of administration and formation. Recognizing that Dujarié's group of Brothers was disintegrating, in spite of all the effort that Dujarié and Andre had put into revitalizing the group at each summer retreat, Andre asked the bishop to push Dujarié for reforms (August 18, 1834).

Among the eleven points he makes to the bishop is the need for an administrative structure with specific attention given to the number of officers for the Brothers. More importantly, Andre asks for a chaplain for the Brothers at Ruillé, admitting for the first time in print that Dujarié was unable to minister to the spiritual needs of his own community. Andre closes his letter by saying "with these matters on the table for the Bishop, it will be impossible for our Father to refuse to deal with them." The implication is that Dujarié has been approached about the crisis, but the aged priest has been unwilling to face reality and deal with it. With this letter Andre puts two mechanisms in operation: the rescue of the Brothers and his own eventual replacement as a leader. There is no mention of Moreau in the letter, only a remark that a chaplain is needed for the Brothers at Ruillé.

A lengthier letter in November to the bishop has a more upbeat tone than Andre's previous letter. In fact, this November letter is downright jubilant. In the course of this letter he uses Moreau's name twice so even if the bishop had not already been thinking of Moreau as a replacement for Dujarié, he may very well have been nudged in that direction by this letter.

> The existence of the Brothers of Saint Joseph being quite precarious up to this time, I feel the need to set forth the means which my mind considers proper in order to consolidate, enlarge and make perfect its real end. These means involve the creation of three societies in one. The first would be the priests under the title of the Sacred Heart of Jesus; they would exercise the duties and tasks of the superiorship in the Congregation: thus the Brothers of Saint Joseph with that support would have clear and firm direction and government. The goal of the entire Society would be to be an asylum for people in all conditions, to put them at the service of God, to work for his glory, to work for their own salvation and that of their neighbor, while holding themselves away from the dangers of the world. The secondary goal would be to give a Christian education, one suitable under all conditions of our times, and for all classes of society.

> The Institute of three societies in one, or of the Holy Family, could establish houses everywhere in a manner that I am going to explain. The priests of the Sacred Heart would maintain houses where, at the same time, they would have a novitiate for the Brothers of Saint Joseph and a normal school in which to train lay school masters, these however living in separate quarters. The Brothers of Saint Joseph would continue to expand in the villages and countryside, several Brothers together or alone in the pastors' houses; they would live dependent on the Order or Institute. The lay teachers, once formed, would be free

to establish themselves and live as they wished, except that they would be given and ever receive protection, good advice and counsel, and any of them who found themselves closer to the spirit of the Order as a whole, by their zeal, good morals, piety or celibacy, could form a branch with a rule, one like or shortened from the rule of the Brothers of Saint Joseph or a short form of the rule of Sacred Heart priests. This rule of the priests of the Sacred Heart would be a reflection of the teachings and conduct of Jesus Christ, of Saint Joseph and the very holy Virgin. But since a while later they would have more extensive functions to fulfill (such as I will explain later), they would accept the rule of Saint Ignatius for the Jesuits, whatever is suited to their condition and perhaps even the same rule in its entirety. The priests of the Sacred Heart of Jesus, aside from the functions which have just been assigned, will themselves maintain boarding schools or colleges for the upper class. There they would teach Latin, rhetoric, etc. They would also do the work of diocesan missionaries; they would conduct annual retreats for the Brothers of Saint Joseph and the masters of the lay schools, in the houses of the novitiate and the normal schools during the vacations. They would be able to do the same for people in the outside world and even in their houses like the one in Brittany. The three societies in one would have to contribute to this, at least by their prayers and alms. To help the souls in Purgatory would always be the object of their zeal; to this end they would gain a number of indulgences each month; that is, every member would strive to gain such indulgences judged in harmony with the practice of their duties. Briefly put, saying everything in a few words: it is the Holy Family, the name the Congregation bears. (Nov. 14, 1834)

Andre elaborates a totally new idea for the Brothers: he suggests that they be amalgamated into a new tripartite community of priests, Brothers, and laymen. Andre obviously does not consider the Brothers to be "laymen" in the canonical sense and envisages them as ecclesiastically median to priests and laymen.

The new community will be named for the Holy Family, and there is ample evidence in the letter that Andre considers the priests as the elite members: he reserves to them the instruction of children of the "upper class" while the Brothers will continue to work with poor and ordinary children. He does allow for some fluidity among the priests, Brothers, and laymen in that "the two lesser societies would be able to rise into the society of the Sacred Heart," but the elevation, Andre cautions, would have to be watched carefully because few men would be capable of moving upward. As tasteless as this hierarchical reference to higher and lower vocations is today, what is remarkable in Andre's plan is that the vision for a mixed community of priests and Brothers of St. Joseph, a vision often attributed to Moreau, actually originated with Andre, who spun it off Dujarie's earlier attempts to amalgamate "auxiliary" priests with the Brothers of St. Joseph. We cannot say, however, that the plan was entirely Andre's since he mentions in the letter to the bishop that he has bounced his new idea off one other person: Moreau. If the two men had a conversation in which they probably reviewed the problems of Dujarié's Brothers, Moreau may have mentioned that he was starting a group of priests who would serve as auxiliaries to the diocese. Andre may then have mused in private on amalgamating Moreau's priests and Dujarié's Brothers, thus germinating the "Congregation of Holy Cross."

Such an explanation, however, leaves an important person out of the process: Dujarié himself, as we have seen, had planned on starting a group of priests devoted to parish missions as early as 1823, eleven years before Andre's letter to Bishop Bouvier. Dujarié even planned to dedicate his auxiliary priests to the Sacred Heart. Andre would have known about all of these plans since he was Dujarié's right-hand man during all the years that Dujarié dreamed of his association of auxiliary priests. Although Dujarié never founded such a group, his plans were intended to bind priests to his Brothers and Sisters. Once the Sisters were out of the picture (by 1831), Andre could dream of a different tripartite community, a dream he confided first to Moreau and then to Bouvier. Andre was not given credit for his plan, however, for over a hundred years. Finally in the 1940's, Philéas Vanier, CSC, archivist for the Congregation of Holy Cross, wrote a note to Albert F. Cousino, Superior General at the time:

> The confidential letter of Brother André (November 14, 1834) greatly influenced Father Moreau in the organization of the Community; this is a very important point to study, which can explain many things; it should be done without

taking sides, slowly, etc. Please excuse the candor of this
remark. (Vanier, qtd. Klawitter, *Mottais* 45)

It is obvious from this note by Vanier that Andre's plan had fallen into the
cracks of history. Was Andre's fifteen-year leadership enough to quality
him as a "founder" of the Brothers of St. Joseph? Vanier seemed to think
so, but what makes a "founder" a founder? Bernoville would not even grant
the title "founder" to Dujarié: "Dujarié is not a founder in the strict sense
of the term implying an original rule, a particular spirituality" (55). Catta
disagrees: "Both [Dujarié and Moreau] are founders, each in his own special
way, and each one's right to this title implies at the same time that of the
other" (Catta, *Moreau* 1.366). Studying the history of the early Brothers,
however, one can easily conclude that the Brothers were originated by three
men, not two: Dujarié, Andre Mottais, Moreau.

Andre's concern for the well-being of the Community flowered into
a letter tri-authored with Brother Vincent and Brother Leonard to Bishop
Bouvier in April of 1835. They suggested that a set of rules they had drawn
up (without Dujarié's help) be reviewed by the bishop, and they suggested
a face-to-face meeting to discuss the financial and spiritual crises. Brother
Leonard himself wrote another letter to Basil Moreau (in June) apprizing
him of continued problems and asking him to assume direction of the
Brothers. Brother Vincent was probably privy to this letter.

During the years, 1825 to 1834, after a decade of struggling for legal
recognition of his little group of Brothers, Dujarié faced harassment from
local officials over his ability to hold religious property in his own name.
By careful maneuvering in October 1834, he ceded ownership of the Ruillé
motherhouse to Brother Vincent and Brother Baptiste (Jean Verger). It is
significant of the great faith that Dujarié had in Vincent that Vincent was
chosen for this ruse, he and Baptiste being styled on the document "two
men of confidence who agreed to dedicate themselves to the teaching of
youth," as if Vincent had not already been so dedicated for a dozen years and
as if Dujarié himself were not devoted to the same apostolate. Significant
of the regard in which he was held in those early years, the following was
afforded Vincent in a letter to him from André Mottais: "I know only you
are capable of giving authentic testimony of what has been done since our
origin" (May 18, 1840).

Clearly the Brother-Directors were getting more and more concerned
about their religious community as the summer of 1835 approached, but
they never gave up their hope of regeneration because they knew that the
work they had done in parish schools over the previous fifteen years was

valuable—and they knew that there was a priest in Le Mans who was not only capable of directing their community but who was also energetic enough to effect a smooth transition in leadership. Andre, Leonard, and Vincent took it upon themselves to engineer this transfer of authority, and Andre had laid the groundwork for it by contacts with the bishop over the previous year. So the movement toward Le Mans was not abrupt but was anticipated and planned deliberately with simple honesty and, we presume, prayerful consideration. One page ready to be turned, the Brother-Directors looked to a new page in their short but eventful history.

CHAPTER FOUR

Transition and Amalgamation, 1835 to 1839

In his third and final letter to Bouvier, cosigned by Leonard and Vincent, Andre had begged the bishop for a secret meeting without Dujarié's being aware of it. Andre was concerned that the rules he had been designing for the Brothers would irk Dujarié because the old priest was not in on their making. This April 1835 letter makes no mention of Moreau and gives an indication that the Brothers were convinced they themselves could salvage the community. But four months later they were turned over to Moreau's control. Andre's final memo as head director is dated June 28, 1835. It is a simple notice that he has received fifty francs that the Sisters of Providence owed on a year of rent. His days as the central administrator were about to end.

As the Brothers began to look to Moreau to save their community, it is curious that we have no records of letters from Andre to Moreau. Brother Leonard, however, did write to Moreau in June, 1835, and Moreau responded with an offer of the house in Le Mans "which would be perfectly suited for you, and where I would gladly set you up, in preference to another foundation which I plan to get underway" (Catta, *Dujarié* 259). It is obvious that Moreau is eager not only to assume direction of the Brothers but also to move them to his own territory. He adds, "Nevertheless, I want to wait some time yet out of consideration for your own interests, and you can inform Brother Andre accordingly." A reader today wonders why Moreau was not communicating these very important sentiments to Andre himself who, as Primary Director, was really the person who should have been consulted. The tone of "you can inform Brother Andre accordingly" is slightly ominous, indicating that Moreau may have had little concern for the Primary Director's prerogative. Finally, Moreau delivers a coup: "If you speak to the Bishop, tell him only that I would consider to revive and develop you, provided that I am given full freedom of action" (Catta, *Dujarié* 259). By "full freedom of action," Moreau could mean freedom from restrictions by the bishop or diocesan authorities, but the phrase could also be the triumphant call of a victor. There is no deference in this letter to Andre, Dujarié, or even the bishop. Moreau knows what he wants to do, and he wants it on his terms. There is no room in his plans for a Primary Director who may be bringing old baggage with him into a new situation.

In Ruillé at the end of the 1835 summer retreat fifty-four Brothers learned that their headquarters and novitiate were to be moved north to Le Mans, twenty-six miles from Ruillé. They would be leaving the inspiration of their first founder behind and would find themselves under the wing of a new superior at Sainte-Croix. Andre, Vincent, Leonard, and Dujarié discussed with Moreau the details for the transfer of superiorship. On the final day of the retreat (August 31), all the Brothers gathered in the chapel at the Grand Saint-Joseph and waited. Dujarié struggled to reach the altar to address the bishop, formally asking Bouvier to entrust the Brothers to Moreau's care. The Brothers were swept up in the emotion of the moment as they witnessed the man they had worked alongside for many years give up his role to a younger, more energetic priest. The ceremony was captured in Andre's own hand:

> Father Dujarié saw his own inability to continue on with the Brothers and requested Fr. Moreau take over. The next day Moreau gathered the Brothers into a general assembly and made them elect a General Council of ten members, not counting himself. Then he named a Particular Council of four Brothers and made Fr. Hupier chaplain of the community. The two councils met and discussed the lack of training in the novitiate—a situation that could not be rectified in Ruillé. They decided to transfer the novitiate to Le Mans where the superior at the seminary volunteered to instruct them in geometry, penmanship, natural history, etc. It was in the chapel of the novitiate of the Brothers at the Grand St. Joseph the following night after honoring the Blessed Sacrament that Fr. Dujarié gave up his position as superior. He then spoke like a true patriarch. He could not hold back his tears when he heard the cries and groans from all the Brothers. Here are approximately the words he used: "Bishop, you see for a long time I haven't been able to handle the direction of the Brothers of St. Joseph

that Divine Providence put in my hands. You counseled me to undertake this project. Today I entrust it into your hands to put it under Fr. Moreau's care, to make him my successor. I've known him for a long time. He has my complete confidence"...

"Father Moreau, I ask you to accept the running of this little congregation of Brothers of St. Joseph because of my infirmity and inability to continue on as I confide them to you to be their father and protector." (*Mottais* 111-115)

Immediately, Moreau began to make changes: he dismissed some Brothers and insisted all teachers keep careful financial records. Older Brothers who were showing signs of ebbing academic fervor were shifted into manual labor (Catta, *Moreau* 1.343). Andre Mottais began to lose power. Many Brothers had, of course, suspected Basil Moreau would be their new superior and may have hoped it would be Moreau, but did none of those present ever think to wonder if the Brothers under Andre could have controlled their own destiny as successfully as the Sisters of Providence had controlled their own?

Basil Moreau's first "circular" letter to the Brothers of St. Joseph (November 8, 1835) was actually addressed to one Brother, not the total membership. This technique was a nice touch because as a "circular" letter it would move around ("circulate") Brother to Brother, one at a time reading it. The effect was to give an intimacy with the writer that the writer could not achieve with a letter addressed to multiple readers. In houses of more than one Brother, the letter was probably read aloud so all could get the benefit of the message at the same time. In this first letter, Moreau stressed unity: "We must be, first of all, so closely united in charity as to form but one mind and one soul; for, as you well know, 'In union there is strength'" (*Circular Letters* 1.2). So several years before he achieved a unity of ordained and non-ordained, he was already aware of the necessity that all in a community think as one. Then in the letter he sets out new regulations: recruits will be accepted only between the ages of 15 to 25, and they must arrive with a trousseau and be able to pay the room and board for a two-year novitiate. Gone are the days of a rather too fluid novitiate system whereby recruits had sometimes strung out their training by serving a few weeks every year in novitiate formation.

These regulations were meant to stabilize the group, tighten its expectations and requirements, but one wonders how rigorously these dicta were enforced because quite a few Brothers died after long years in the Community without ever taking final vows (Appendix XVIII). Moreau then notes in his circular letter that he has not yet formulated rules and constitutions for the Brothers—no need to rush, he writes. He ends with a plea that the Brothers send him candidates for the new boarding school he is establishing in Le Mans where young men will be able to study Greek and Latin in addition to standard secondary-school subjects. He obviously is already planning to use his auxiliary priests to teach in this new boarding school because no Brothers were trained in Greek and Latin. In fact, the first draft of his *Constitutions* forbid any Brother from studying Latin or teaching it, nor could a Brother "aspire to the ecclesiastical state" (Heston 56). La Salle was intent on keeping his Brothers also differentiated from clerics, but for a different reason: "Would such priests be humble enough to confine themselves to the limitations of a vocation which has nothing flamboyant about it in the world's eyes?...It must be admitted, therefore, that the priestly state is not compatible with that of a teaching Brother" (Blain 80, qtd. Koch 15). Here a negative onus and the definition of ministry is put upon the priest, not the Brother.

Within weeks the novitiate moved to Le Mans, but Andre was left behind in Ruillé to continue running the boarding school at the Grand Saint-Joseph. The school dwindled to half a dozen students so by August, 1836, the property was sold, and the last Brothers moved to Le Mans where Vincent assumed direction of a new boarding school to be opened in November 1836.

Near the end of November in 1835 Brother Leonard and the new priest-director (Moreau) went to visit Jean-Marie de Lamennais, founder of the Brothers of Christian Instruction. De Lamennais was staying at Chesnaie near Dinan in Brittany with his renegade brother Félicité-Robert. Moreau asked to meet the infamous brother, but de Lamennais discouraged him: "The sight of a priest would not go over well with my brother" (Charles Moreau 1.115). After three days, Moreau returned to Le Mans, but Leonard went up to Ploërmel in Brittany where he stayed three weeks with the Brothers of Christian Instruction. Brother Leonard himself got to live among the Ploërmel Brothers for weeks, but Moreau never met them and thus relied on Leonard's experience to help him craft daily life for the new Le Mans novitiate. Moreau got from de Lamennais and Leonard the information he needed to finalize the structure of the Brothers of St. Joseph and helped him in his attempts to get the novices at Le Mans exempt from military service, navigating political red tape in the La Sarthe Department.

Not only had Moreau taken Leonard (not Andre) along with him on the visit to La Chesnaie, but when Moreau opened his new boarding school at Sainte-Croix in November, 1836, it was Brother Vincent who was put in charge, not Andre. Catta suggests that Vincent was chosen because he had a teaching license (*Moreau* 1.353), but Andre's license actually predated Vincent's by one year. Of course, Andre may very well have been left behind in Ruillé to look after his aging mentor (Dujarié) and the boarding school there in its waning years. But when Moreau moved the novitiate to Sainte-Croix, there were only five or six students left in the Ruillé boarding school. It could be that Vincent, who spent years out teaching away from the motherhouse, was chosen to head the new Le Mans school over Andre because Andre's talent at Ruillé had been the formation of novices, not actual school teaching. But eventually Andre was not without an assignment at Le Mans: "Moreau in the chapel made Andre novice master and Leonard 'general director of the congregation'" (Jan. 1, 1836, in Klawitter, *Mottais* 128).

Why did Moreau demote Andre Mottais? Thomas Maddix has analyzed at length Moreau's understanding of a Brother's vocation and concluded that Moreau's understanding differed radically from Dujarié's understanding (Maddix 76). Under Dujarié, all Brothers were equal and shared one apostolate, the evangelization of children. When Moreau shifted some Brothers out of the classroom into manual labor, he created two tiers of membership in the Brothers. However, some of the men may have, in fact, welcomed the opportunity to leave a profession for which they had no taste or talent, an opportunity that allowed them to remain within the religious society doing some kind of work. But it was, nevertheless, a big shift in the basic dynamics of a brother's vocation and worked against the very sense of democracy that Dujarié and Andre had fostered. Under Moreau, some men who could not handle classroom duties were relegated to manual labor: hierarchy was thus born in the Brothers of St. Joseph. Heston notes the shift was made at the 1836 retreat when Moreau interviewed each Brother and decided if that Brother would continue teaching or be moved into manual labor (Heston 54). Did Andre confront Moreau on this shift in paradigm? Did Moreau react negatively to any questioning of his decisions and sideline Andre? We do not know. What we do know is that once Moreau assumed control of the Brothers, Andre began to fade from administration, in spite of his fifteen years' experience, in spite of his being a man of enormous talent and virtue in the prime of his life. Moreau was one year younger than Andre (they were born in the same month one year apart), yet in 1836 one's star continued to rise and the other's started to fall.

Could the Brothers have survived and thrived in Ruillé under the guidance of Brother Andre Mottais and his three capable assistants (Leonard, Henry, and Vincent)? It was not in the nature of the Ruillé organization, however, to look for a leader anywhere outside of a cleric. They had worked happily under their priest-founder, and his person remained dear to them as he aged and sickened. Naturally they would have looked to a similar churchman to take his place. Familiar already for years with the energetic assistant-rector of the Le Mans seminary, they would easily look to him as a replacement for their elderly founder, especially since the Le Mans priest had already proven himself a guide to religious by founding and guiding a community of Good Shepherd Sisters.

A curious assumption by some historians is that the Brothers of St. Joseph were incapable of governing themselves or did not want to govern themselves. Catta writes, "Like M. Dujarié, he [Moreau] was persuaded that the frail little tree had to be grafted on to a stronger trunk, which would be the Society of Priests which the Founder had thought of but which he had been unable to realize" (Catta, *Dujarié* 261-2). In other words, a "frail" organization of some fifty teaching Brothers had to be put under the control of a non-existent group of religious priests. The lack of logic is bewildering. At the end of the same summer that Moreau assumed direction of dozens of seasoned Brothers, he had attracted exactly two priests and two seminarians to his auxiliary band, which was apparently already superior to the established group of Brothers.

Is it to Andre's credit or discredit that he knuckled under? If he had engineered in Ruillé a break from a priest-director as Mother Marie Lecor had done from Dujarié, would the Brothers have survived? They had scores of hard working men, a little property, and the promise of a new set of rules. Would these assets have been enough to float them under Andre's leadership? They had, however, grown up tightly enmeshed with a priest at their head, a priest whom they revered, and when they had to rethink their organization, they quite naturally would think about revitalizing their community under a structure similar to the one that had brought them great growth in the years before 1830. They may have sensed, however, that Moreau would not be Dujarié, and Andre was one of their first sacrifices to the new order. It is important, of course, that organizations get new blood from time to time in administrative posts, but it was a good idea for Moreau to give Andre some type of supervisory work. Andre did keep his novice-master position for four years after the move north.

Moreau's original plan in 1831 for a male community was for an association of auxiliary priests alone. With the death of Bishop Carron in 1833 and the accession of Bouvier, Moreau had in his new prelate a man who had himself long recognized the value of such an auxiliary group of priests in the diocese. It was not, however, until June, 1835, a year after Brother Andre had himself written to the bishop about a mixed community, that Moreau formalized his plans to found an association of auxiliary priests.

Moreau brought to the Brothers a canonical regimentation that they had not had before. Himself familiar with semi-monastic life, he was able to forge a community that, like the Christian Brothers, blended monastic ideals of discipline with non-monastic apostolates, primarily teaching in French elementary schools. One of the first requests he made of the remnants of Dujarié's Brothers was that they profess religious vows, which Moreau felt were needed to give the group a stability and cohesiveness which they had lacked in Ruillé. The first man to profess in Le Mans was Brother Andre Mottais. His commitment was made on August 25, 1836, with vows of poverty, celibacy, obedience, and stability. The vows, which would show his unfaltering faith in Moreau's leadership, were the first perpetual vows pronounced in the community.

Brother Vincent made his profession of permanent vows one year later, on August 30, 1837. His final vow document (August 22, 1838) reads as follows:

> I, John Pieau, Brother Vincent, in the presence of Him who must judge the living and the dead, under the protection of Mary ever Virgin, of Saint Joseph and of my guardian angel, vow to God and promise to keep to death, poverty, obedience, and chastity, according to the rules of the Society of the Brothers of Saint Joseph and under the authority of our Reverend Father Rector [Moreau], requiring me, by vow, to persevere in my vocation and to fulfill all the tasks that it will please my legitimate superiors to assign me. (Klawitter, *Early* 109)

There is no vow of stability in this formula. Some men took longer to profess: Etienne Gauffre (the fourth man to answer Dujarié's call, did not profess any vows until 1842, some twenty-two years after he had joined the Brothers.

But retention would continue to be a problem. Of the fifteen men who entered the Brothers previous to Vincent, only five were still around when the group came to Le Mans. At this time in Le Mans none of Moreau's auxiliary priests had taken religious vows. They were, in effect, "ordained novices." Even by 1837 none of the ordained novices had taken religious vows.

Although acceptance into the Community became more formal (as far as entry dates are concerned) at Le Mans, exceptions were still made. For example, by 1836 it seems February 2 was one of two dates in the year when groups of men were given the religious habit and a new name, but Nicolas Pierre Drouin came to Le Mans twelve days after Jean François Hulot and was not given a habit or a new name until March 19, the feast of St. Joseph. Why the delay? Had the new administration put in place a minimum time of adjustment to religious life before a recruit would be given a habit and name? Or was it simply that Nicolas needed more time than Jean François needed, in the judgment of the novice-master, to settle into the religious routine? Or it could be that the novice-master had some concerns over Nicolas' health because he died at St-Aignan on June 28, 1837, just a little over a year after receiving the name "François d'Assise." He was 19 years old and probably teaching there at the time of his death, it not being uncommon that novices were sent out on assignment before completing a full year of canonical novitiate.

On March 1, 1837, the Brothers and priests accepted a document called the "Fundamental Act of Union," which prepared for their eventual union as two societies in one Community. Papal approval would come two years later—on March 12, 1838. Although the Brothers had been taking vows since 1836, none of Moreau's priests took religious vows until 1841. Thus the first four years of the new Community consisted of vowed religious Brothers and secular priests. Moreau himself took religious vows in 1840, but no other priest took religious vows until 1841.

What exactly was the "Fundamental Act of Union"? As the Brothers at Sainte-Croix saw Moreau's auxiliary priests beginning to assume a teaching apostolate, the Brothers grew concerned that their assets would be swallowed up. Moreau summoned all the men together (fifty-four Brothers, five priests, and three seminarians) to outline the Brothers' assets. Then he drew up the "Fundamental Act," which served as a stepping-stone to the eventual joining of the two societies, just as their two properties and schools adjoined in Sainte-Croix. Moreau really believed that if the Brothers were to survive, they would eventually need priests to be responsible for supervising them, as Article IX of the "Fundamental Act" clearly states:

> Article IX. Abbé Moreau will present later the principles by which he desires to establish the government of the members of the Congregation of the Brothers of Saint Joseph, which direction is to be confided to the Auxiliary Priests. (in Connolly 24, trans. Dufresne)

Here could be the source of Andre's fall from power: he was not a priest. Moreau, in fact, notes elsewhere: "The Institutes [of the Brothers] shall be governed by an ecclesiastic as long as the Auxiliary Priests exist in Society" (Heston 56). But did Moreau really believe Dujarié could have held the Brothers together for fifteen years without Andre's help? Probably not, but Moreau did believe that his priests should hold the positions of leadership over the Brothers: it was one of his requirements before he would merge the two "societies." It remains a sad testimony to clericalism.

Basil Moreau was bright and knew the right people. He was unfailingly honest and vitally interested in church work. Setting his headquarters in the Le Mans neighborhood known as Holy Cross (Sainte Croix), he thus created a religious organization that soon became known as the Brothers and priests from (of) Holy Cross. The Brothers continued to be styled "Josephites" and the priests "Salvatorists," but to the outside world they were the religious from Holy Cross. A letter from Bishop Angory dated July 19, 1856, refers to the "Frères de Ste. Croix." There were probably earlier uses of the phrase.

Moreau was a well-educated man who had connections to ecclesiastics and government officials, but as we look back at history, we know that in the same period of French history Mother Marie Lecor was not ordained and had succeeded very well in governing the Sisters of Providence. Why did Moreau believe that only priests could govern Brothers? Moreover, why did the Brothers let him proceed with his clerical imposition? Were they that demoralized by the loss in membership of recent years, the lack of a working set of rules, and the sad state of their academic preparation for teaching careers? Was Moreau the only answer to their crisis? He certainly came with excellent credentials: assistant superior of the local seminary, proven educator, and founder of the Good Shepherd Sisters in Le Mans. He was a man of immense talent and energy. But so was Andre Mottais who, apparently in the interests of saving his community, accepted Moreau's theory of clerical governance. If Andre had had some of Mother Marie

Lecor's vinegar and fighting spirit, the history of the Brothers of St. Joseph would be much different than it came to be.

Ages often tell us much. When Madame du Roscoät arrived in Ruillé, she was forty. She died four years later. Perrine Lecor, the future Mother Marie, arrived at age twenty-eight, a hardened peasant woman. Softened somewhat by association with Madame du Roscoät and the du Roscoät family, Perrine actually never lost her original toughness. Andre arrived at Ruillé at age twenty and lived alongside Dujarié for eighteen years, always deferential to the man who had nurtured him spiritually. Andre was only a year younger than Moreau, but no match for the priest's education, position, and tenacity. It is easy to see how Andre, accustomed for half his life to clerical rule, would naturally slide from under the authority of one priest to another. He knew no other pattern—except for the example of Mother Marie Lecor and the Sisters of Providence, but the separation of finances from the Sisters in 1831 surely left him with a distaste for the direction that the women so determinedly set out for themselves against his priest-mentor. Dujarié was a friend whom Andre possibly hoped to find replicated in Moreau, but one should never count on finding a spiritual clone, especially in a person one's own age. Andre might have been in a way a threat to Moreau's vision, and the Brother had to be controlled if Moreau's vision were to strengthen, a vision that would strengthen on the backs of the Brothers. Moreau was, after all, only bringing to realization the paradigm of a mixed community that both Dujarié and Andre had dreamed about.

Where did Moreau's clericalism, as reflected in Article IX of the "Fundamental Act," originate? Gallicanism, which stressed the hegemony of French bishops over Rome, died a slow death after the Revolution, but die it did, along with a sizable chunk of anti-clericalism. Within forty years of the Revolution, religious orders had established major beachheads, the Benedictines at Solesme under Abbé Guéranger and the Dominicans at various locales under Lacordaire. Jansenism breathed its last thanks to the mindset of saintly theologians like Alphonsus Liguori, and France's disparate forms of liturgical practice came to a kind of unity because of Guéranger's work and influence. Bishops, of course, were reluctant to cede power, but gradually under the extremely long pontificate of Pius IX (1846-1878) hierarchical rule solidified in Rome. By 1838 anti-clericalism had softened (Dansette 1.228), and the period between 1833 and 1840 was a remarkably peaceful time in French history. Political turbulence would surge again in 1848, but during the time of transition of the Brothers of St. Joseph from Ruillé to Le Mans (1835), religious orders were valued throughout France for their church work, especially in the area of education. The Brothers needed a cleric like Moreau, who was astute and more careful about teacher preparation than Dujarié or Andre had been or could have been. Red tape could be maddening.

For example, teaching credentials for Brothers were important. In May of 1837 the pastor of Ruillé-le-Gravelais (as of 2016 part of the commune Loiron-Ruillé) wrote to the Mayenne prefect for permission to let Brother Célestin (Louis Forton) be approved as a teacher for that little town. Two months later the prefect sent a short note to the pastor rejecting Célestin for the position and returning the Brother's dossier. No reasons were given for the rejection. These letters of application were not perfunctory because town councils were serious about their supervisory duties, concerned as they were that the town's children be afforded a solid education by well-trained teachers. Extracts from the May 7, 1837, deliberations of the town council at Ruillé-le-Gravelais show that the council did indeed have Brother Célestin's teaching license in hand—it was awarded him on September 2, 1835. The council extracts give no indication of their evaluation of the candidate's aptitudes.

Officials even higher up the ladder were solicitous of new teachers. In a three page form letter dated July 12, 1837, and intended for new teachers, the Angers Academy rector, Collet-Dubiguon, gives a hearty pep-talk about the obligations of good teaching—sowing virtue in one's students, treating them with respect and care. The new teacher is reminded that each teacher must be evaluated twice a year (January and July) by the local mayor and reported to Angers headquarters because, after all, Brother teachers were exempt from military service. Moreau and Leonard had to supervise over fifty Brothers or more, getting the men approved by authorities for school positions.

We know little about Andre's new life at Sainte-Croix. We do know that he was novice master up to 1840 and sat on the council with Brother Vincent, Brother Léopold, Father Marseul, and Father Chappé. One happy chore he was given was to travel back to Ruillé in October 1836 to help Dujarié move to Sainte-Croix. A little over a year later, Dujarié died (February 17, 1838), having been able to live his final year in the same home as Andre, who had been his stalwart religious helper for fifteen years in Ruillé. One sad duty that Andre was called upon to share was to watch at the bedside of Dujarié, who lay dying on February 17, 1838. Moreau kept only three Brothers in the room: Vincent, Andre, and Antonin. They whispered encouragement to the dying man and witnessed his final breaths a little past noon. For Andre the death would have meant the loss of his first superior, the man who saw in Andre promising virtue and the talents of a valuable educator.

The Ruillé priest-founder was buried four times, the first three times in Le Mans, the last in Ruillé. Having purchased on his deathbed a four meter square piece of property at Sainte-Croix for his own burial, he was laid to rest in it when he died in 1838. Moreau had thus far been unable to get permission from local authorities for a Community cemetery, but finally on July 17, 1841, the mayor allowed Moreau to open a Community cemetery. Augustin Nourry, a priest who had joined the auxiliary priests in 1835, had died on June 4, 1836, at the Le Mans seminary, where the auxiliary priests were still living. He had been buried in a city cemetery so it was fitting to have his remains finally returned to Community property. It seemed also fitting to take advantage of the new permission to transfer the Ruillé founder's remains into a more solid casket, one made of oak. Thus on August 21, 1841, Dujarié's remains were exhumed, the day before the closing of the Brothers' annual retreat.

Presiding at the exhumation were the Holy Cross priest Henri Philbert (who would leave Holy Cross five years later), Brother Eloi Leroy (a twenty-three-year-old novice who was a locksmith and had been a novice for a month), and thirty-nine- year-old Brother Marc Galinand, who persevered until his death in 1879. Auxiliary priests stood in front of the grave reciting the Divine Office, and Brothers stood reciting the rosary. Six Brothers lifted the old casket out of the ground. It had been made of poplar wood, except the ends, which had been made of oak. The ends were in good shape, oak being a hardier wood than poplar.

> Then they lifted up the boards which covered the cadaver, and it seemed in every respect as if the ravages of the tomb had really affected him. His head, which had been covered with an amice at the time of his exhumation, was nothing more than a shapeless ball, featureless; the linen was stuck to the skin and colorless; the rest of the body was covered with a soutane, which had kept its black color, and all the buttons were visible. The stocking and shoes were well preserved; the hands were placed on the sides of the body, the skin sticking to the fingers, the nails intact. Brother Mark, told by the Rector [Moreau] to open the clothes and display the body, saw that the skull was whole and every bone in its place, the flesh totally eaten away. Then he took up the rather well preserved scapula. They nested it

carefully with some of the hair, a tooth, the nail of the left thumb, and some pieces of the soutane that Brother Mark cut with a scissors; after these various actions, prompted by affection for, not horror at the cadaver, Brother Mark gave a final kiss to the father founder's forehead. (Vanier 130, trans. Klawitter)

Then Moreau had the entire Community participate in a final ceremony to honor the remains of the Ruillé curé: the priests approached first, two by two, followed by the Brothers, finally the Sisters. The new oak casket was nailed shut and replaced in the grave. Next to Dujarié's casket were placed the caskets of two other deceased: Brother Dosithée Leblanc, who had died on February 8, 1838, at age 21, and Father Augustin Nourry. Dujarié was on the left, Nourry in the middle, Dosithée on the right.

On August 22, 1849, Dujarié's casket was dug up for a second time for transfer to a new Community cemetery. Here he was buried outside the funeral chapel where he remained for twenty-four years until in 1873, at the request of the Sisters of Providence, his remains were transferred to their Ruillé motherhouse chapel. His old nemesis Mother Marie Lecor was still alive, having retired two years earlier (1871) after forty-three years heading the Sisters. The former Mother General, who had effected this translation of Dujarié, said, "Now I can die," (Catta *Dujarié* 281), remembering, no doubt, the grief she had caused their founder over many troubled years.

In addition to Dujarié's remains being disturbed on August 22, 1849, other remains were also moved. Brother Dosithée and Augustin Nourry were exhumed and buried in the new cemetery, as well as were Brother Philip Neri (died August 24, 1842), Brother Andre Mottais (died March 16, 1844), Brother Theodore (died April 12, 1848), Brother Mary-Basil (died June 17, 1848), and Basil Moreau's sister Cécile Moreau (died February 19, 1848). Only a few bones remained of Nourry. Theodore, Mary-Basil, and Cécile Moreau were reburied quickly because of their state of decomposition, but the remains of Andre, Philip Neri, and Dosithée were kept overnight in the cemetery guarded by a few of the Brothers. The next day the remains of Dujarié, Nourry, and Brother Louis (who drowned in Algiers September 16, 1841) were brought to the cemetery (Vanier 132).

The demotion of Brother Andre Mottais continues to bother me. Why did he end his religious life in an abject humility that he himself recognized and even embraced as an antidote to his scattered spirituality? Surely he was the product of success—a natural leader, a generous and kind formator of souls. Yet in his move north to Le Mans, he accepted a fate of psychological servitude, broken by a charismatic rector-priest of unbounded energy, a priest of evident zeal, a priest driven by vision and self-conviction. In 1835 Andre's day as leader was finished, and he only half-realized it as he supervised the packing and moving of the Brothers of St. Joseph from Ruillé to Le Mans.

With every step he took north, he must have sensed the erosion of his authority because he already knew quite well the drive of his new major superior. Yet he went. He bowed his head and accepted the usurpation of his primary role. Leonard Guittoger took over what Andre had held for thirteen years—the day-to-day decision-making that the fluctuating band of men had grown to expect and respect under Andre's hand.

Leonard was not Andre. Leonard was an aggressive thinker, a spontaneous decision-maker, a man who saw injustice and went after it. Could he have guided the Brothers of St. Joseph instead of Basil Moreau? Could he have been for the Brothers of St. Joseph what Mother Marie Lecor was for the Sisters of Providence? Andre was not the impulsive leader that Leonard was. Andre was deliberate, thoughtful, a man of prayerful quietude. Leonard was a bull in a china shop—he got things done, but his methods could be heavy-handed. Andre was never heavy-handed—he was a father-protector, circumspect, tractable. Leonard, like his new priest-director in 1835, was self-motivated, imbued with a high sense of his own righteousness. Such qualities build strong religious communities, but they can leave wreckage in their wake.

And where was gentle Vincent Pieau in this 1835 trauma-transition? Ever faithful Vincent, ever the consummate classroom teacher, remained rooted in a solid sense of community. But he remained in the background, a man to be consulted for his quiet wisdom, a man incapable of heading a community of men. Valued for his advice, Vincent was never very good at superiorship—except, of course, when he faced a classroom of children. He was much cherished by the men of Ruillé, Le Mans, and Indiana, but he was not a leader. Nor did he seek to be. Vincent was not one to shirk work, and he was obedient to a fault. Once at Notre Dame when he was well advanced into old age, the priest-president told him to drink a glass of wine. Vincent demurred because wine did not agree with him. The president insisted. Then as Vincent touched the glass to his lips, the president told him to stop, put the glass down, and leave the room. Brothers of St. Joseph took their vow of obedience at the words' intent: they subjected their will to that of a religious superior, no questions asked. The Brother Vincent of Ruillé did not morph into a new Brother Vincent at Le Mans or at Notre Dame: he remained the same integral person in all three places, his personality and his religious commitment of one melody.

And the other Brother-Director, Henry Taupin? Where was he in all this transition? Gone. Born before the other three directors, the elder Henry was the only Brother-Director not to persevere, dismissed in fact by Andre from the group under circumstances Andre shared in his August 18, 1834 letter to the bishop. Henry was apparently a bad influence on other Brothers and defied orders at least on one occasion specified to the bishop by Andre. We know little about Henry because we have none of his letters (if he wrote any). In a circular letter dated October 17, 1834, Brother Andre wrote: "Michael Taupin (Brother Henry) is no longer with us. If he had any correspondence with you, our superior would like to be informed of that." Henry had been master of novices 1824 to 1826 and a Brother-Director 1826 to 1834. He left the Community on October 2, 1834. Washed out of the community, he is an enigma, prized simply as one of the four directors at Ruillé, but tarnished for some rash acts that remain lost to history. According to Brother Rémi, Michael Taupin died soon after he was dismissed from the Brothers (Rémi to Champeau, February 27, 1878, qtd. Vanier 555).

At what point did Brother Leonard begin to rise in the ranks? He had been entrusted with the foundation of a second novitate at Esclimont, but the venture did not work out. By October of 1834, Leonard had returned from Esclimont to Ruillé to be on site as the little community devolved from Dujarié's hands to Basil Moreau's. One would think that as Moreau developed his ideas for rules and the direction of the Brothers of St. Joseph, he would have kept at his right hand Andre, the man most responsible for moving the community away from Dujarié's direction to Moreau's care. It was Andre, after all, who wrote behind Dujarié's back to Bishop Bouvier about the aged founder's failing health and inability to oversee the group. It was Andre who for all intents and purposes ran the community in Ruillé, not Leonard. But as of September 1, 1835, Leonard had been made Master of Novices in Le Mans, while Andre remained at Ruillé to direct the remnants of the community there and oversee the boarding school with its tiny enrollment.

As both the Brothers and the priests started to grow in Le Mans, Moreau saw the need for a more complex system of running operations. The system of four Brother Directors may have worked in little Ruillé, but a more representative system was needed at Le Mans. Moreau did away with the concept of the Four Brother-Directors in favor of a government run by a General Council and a Particular Council. In 1836 Leonard was third in rank on the Particular Council and held the title "Master of the House" at the new school in Le Mans. Early that year he was elected secretary of the General Council and named Director of the Brothers' Society. On August 19, 1838, he took religious vows in Moreau's Holy Cross Community, but then within a year he supposedly began his attempts to separate the Brothers from the auxiliary priests. It was a cause to which he would be linked, whether he liked it or not, for most of the rest of his life.

That Leonard enjoyed a good deal of respect from Moreau is obvious when one reads Leonard's letters to Moreau. In fact, Leonard had the same "frankness" (Klawitter, *Early* 84) that Moreau valued as a trait in himself. Writing confidentially to Moreau, Leonard could raise sensitive issues about his own removal from office as well as the assignments of various other Brothers. Moreau had a tranquillizing effect on Leonard's insistence, possibly because he sensed in Leonard gifts valuable to Holy Cross. Thus Leonard honestly submitted to Moreau's judgment: "In all these circumstances [just enumerated] and others I am grateful for, I have never acted against you for purely personal reasons, but only for reasons suitable for religion and the Congregation...I have the highest confidence in you" (Oct. 15, 1847, qtd. Klawitter, *Early* 81). This is not to say, however, that Leonard did not confide in other Brothers his concerns about the direction the Community was taking under Moreau's leadership.

In a letter to Brother Hilarion dated June 17, 1849, Leonard reveals his concerns about the novitiate: he wants it distanced from Le Mans for reasons unspecified other than for "incessant disturbances." Presumably he wanted novices kept away from community intrigue, or he may have wanted the Brothers' novitiate separated from the priests' novitiate. He asks Hilarion to communicate these views to Brother Louis Gonzaga but not to tell Louis that they originated with Leonard: "I don't want to be an instigator—I want everyone to have freedom of initiative for the community's needs—I frankly do not want to be behind the others as they write or speak, do not want either to harm nor constrict what may come" (June 17, 1849, Klawitter, *Early* 82). Although Leonard here again uses the word "frankly," he is being disingenuous for not being willing to show openly his behind-the-scenes efforts to move action on the relocation of the novitiate: we can learn much about the man from what he may not think he is doing.

Furthermore, Leonard is concerned that he is being watched because a long letter to Brother Pascal four months earlier has not elicited a reply from Pascal: "I suspect it has been intercepted," he tells Hilarion. Intercepted or not, a truly frank person would not let paranoia dissuade him from letting his own name be attached to his efforts and ideas. We do not know where Brother Pascal was living in the winter of 1849. If he were at Le Mans, the implication would be that Moreau was canvassing incoming mail, something totally out of character for Moreau. If Pascal were not in Le Mans, the implication is even more devastating—that Leonard's reputation for intrigue was such that others besides the Superior General were interested in preventing Leonard's correspondence from reaching its designated addressee. What we should not overlook, however, are two other eventualities: the letter may have been lost en route (a very slight possibility) or the letter may have been received by Pascal but not answered for whatever reason. The important point for Leonard, of course, is that he suspects it had been intercepted.

By the end of the summer in 1849, Leonard had become such a concern to Moreau that Moreau wrote to Bishop Bouvier:

> Since Brother Leonard has upset a dozen Brothers by saying you approved of their society's being governed by a Brother rather than by a priest, I beg you to please tell me if this is really your thinking, because it is important for the future of this institute, especially when I will no longer be around, that no one sow seeds of division which would overwhelm it one day. (August 19, 1849, qtd. Klawitter, *Early* 82)

It is significant in this letter that Moreau does not know if Leonard has actually communicated with the bishop. Moreau was not one to impede his subjects from having correspondence with higher authorities. Nor does Moreau ask Bouvier if Leonard has approached the bishop for an opinion. It would be foolish for Moreau to ask anything about a bishop's correspondence or involvement with religious matters. It was none of Moreau's business whom the bishop corresponded with or what the bishop said to correspondents. Moreau is very careful simply to ask Bouvier if he is indeed in favor of a Brother directing the Brothers' society. Moreau's letter to Bouvier proves how firmly Moreau believed in his system of governance for Holy Cross: after all, by this time he had spent fourteen years creating and refining the rules of governance, and even though his Constitutions were yet six years from papal approbation, they were solidly in place in a Community thriving on three continents.

One month after Moreau's letter to Bouvier, Leonard himself writes from St. Berthevin to the bishop requesting advice on letters that Leonard has received from various Brothers. He wants to know if he can simply summarize the contents of the letters for Moreau instead of turning over the letters themselves. He is most intent on preserving the anonymity of the Brothers who have written to him presumably in confidence on sensitive matters, possibly the matter of the novitiate location. There is no indication that the letters may have concerned the matter of a Brother director for the Brothers' society, but since the matter was probably hot at the time, we might presume that the Brother director matter was indeed touched upon in the letters in question. As harmless as a separate Brother director may seem to us today, it was probably perceived as the first step, a very important step, on the way to separation of the two societies. Moreau undoubtedly would have seen it in that light.

In May of 1853 Leonard writes again to Bouvier. It is getting close to Bouvier's death (1854) and the approbation of the Holy Cross Constitutions (1857), both events having significant impact on the firming up of governance within Holy Cross. Leonard, in fact, remarks in his first paragraph on the movement in Rome towards approbation. Eighteen Brothers and Father Chappé have met at Bouère to discuss confidentially what they might say to Bouvier. Leonard says he could have summarized the meeting to the Apostolic Nuncio but has not for two reasons: the nuncio has recently been changed, and secondly Leonard has great confidence in Bouvier. The telling paragraph follows:

> I told Father Moreau confidentially eighteen months ago when he thought about sending me to Rome that in this case, if I were admitted to an audience with the pope or with some Roman prelate, there would be some question about our society—I would speak in all frankness about our congregational weaknesses and thus the necessity to prolong the [Constitutional] experiments. Good grief! He was offended at my frankness and divulged my confidences—to my great surprise. (May 13, 1853, qtd. Klawitter, *Early* 84)

The significance of this paragraph cannot be understated. First of all, we learn that Leonard was still held in such high regard that Moreau actually considered using him in Rome as advocate for the approbation of the Constitutions—at least according to Leonard, and we have no reason to doubt his veracity since he is, after all, telling such to the bishop who could easily confirm the information with Moreau. Secondly, we are confronted with something we rarely see in Moreau—a show of pique, an abrupt loss of face, and most importantly a misreading of one of his closest and most talented Brothers. Moreau would never have suggested sending Leonard to Rome if he were not sure that Leonard was of his mind on the importance of getting the Constitutions approved as soon as possible. After all, such approbation would lend not only dignity to the Community but also a kind of permanence that would attract vocations and reassure prelates and pastors that Holy Cross was viable and worthy of trust. But the most significant insight we can take away from this letter is a softening of our century old evaluation of Bouvier in regard to the Holy Cross Constitutions. We have always believed that Bouvier withheld his approval of the document (a politic if not necessary step before they could be passed by Rome) because of some nastiness that existed between himself and Moreau, his former assistant at St. Vincent's Seminary, some nastiness that could never be resolved: Bouvier gave excuses for not forwarding the document (e.g., he had misplaced it, he needed another copy). But in reality his motive may very well have been a valid concern that the document was flawed because a number of Brothers were dissatisfied with the matter of the Brother director. Bouvier would have seen no point in approving a code of governance that might one day explode in Rome's face—as indeed it would a century later in 1945.

It is good to soften our appreciation of former nemeses, and just as Bouvier as a Gallican bishop has alternately endeared himself to or distanced himself from various historians, times change and attitudes toward Rome change. So too in Holy Cross our own appreciation of Bishop Bouvier has tilted to favorable where it might once have been negative. Bouvier may very well have had the welfare of the Brothers very much in mind as he failed to approve the Holy Cross Constitutions (right up to his death). After all, he must have had immense respect for men like Leonard and Andre Mottais. Even though Andre was more in the confidence of Bouvier's predecessor (Carron) as Andre helped engineer the transition of the Josephites from Dujarié to Moreau, Bouvier would have known, as rector of the seminary, all of the good work that Andre was doing in the diocese, at least second hand from Moreau, in the years 1830-1833 when the Ruillé community was falling apart. Then when the novitiate was transferred to Le Mans under Leonard's direction, in the second year of Bouvier's tenure as bishop, Bouvier would have knowledge of Leonard as well as of Vincent Pieau and others. Bouvier was, after all, bishop of all his people, not just his priests. So when one of his prime religious expressed doubt to him in letters about the need to reconsider the matter of a Brother director, Bouvier would have listened, not to block the heady success of his previous assistant Moreau, but simply out of a valid concern that Holy Cross Brothers be afforded justice as they saw it.

At the end of the September Ruillé retreat in 1835 there were sixty-two Brothers of St. Joseph. By the end of the year there would be sixty-four (Appendix II). In 1836 seventeen men would join the Brothers, two would die as Brothers, and sixteen would leave or be sent away. The total membership at year's end was sixty-three. In 1837 fifteen would join, one die, and eight leave or be sent away. The total at year's end was sixty-nine. On March 1 of that year when the "Fundamental Act of Union" was signed, there were sixty-three members, no one having entered in the first two months of the year. The Brothers of St. Joseph were slowly regaining members. 1838 was a boom year with forty-eight new men arriving at Le Mans—word must have gotten around about the new leadership for the newly "mixed" community of Brothers and priests. Twenty-one Brothers left that year so membership just counting the Brothers was ninety-six at year's end. Of course, after the 1837 "Fundamental Act of Union" we must add to the count thirteen Salvatorist novices (nine priests and four seminarians) for 1837 and three Salvatorist priest-novices for 1838. But the next year (1839) was not a good year—only three new Brothers of St. Joseph entered, sixteen left or were dismissed. Membership for the Brothers dropped to eighty-three. And 1840 was even worse for recruitment: only two entered, but six left or were dismissed, with a total membership of seventy-nine for year's end.

What exactly did "community" mean at Le Mans when Basil Moreau brought fifty-plus Brothers of St. Joseph up from Ruillé to Sainte-Croix in 1835? Did it mean that the Brothers lived with his four "auxillary" priests? Yes and no. First of all, he was attempting to blend two different kinds of organizations. The Brothers originally banded together based on their apostolate, teaching in little parish elementary schools, but they also embraced the ideals of semi-monasticism and wanted from their founders Jacques Dujarié and André Mottais a rule to guide them. That rule did not lay down prescriptions for good teaching—it was a guide to their spiritual development. By 1838 when Moreau added new apostolates for the Brothers, their basic glue was no longer teaching because some Brothers were carpenters, some farmers, some cooks. Their apostolates proliferated. Thus to define themselves ("What makes a Brother of St. Joseph a Brother?") they had to look to something other than apostolate.

Moreau's auxiliary priests never made that transition, or rather they did it slowly and awkwardly. Thoughts of "once a priest always a priest" began in seminary days when they looked forward to celebrating Mass. To their deaths they always thought of themselves primarily as priests and only secondarily as semi-monks. In other words, most of them came to Sainte-Croix already defined, and they accepted "community" as an accretion to their apostolic work. Any teachers who came to the Brothers could not do that because they found themselves in a "community" of men with divergent jobs so to be a "Brother" did not necessarily mean to be a teacher. Any apostolate comes with baggage, the priesthood especially, controlled as it is with ecclesiastical regulations and expectations. There is, of course, a pride that is engrained with ordination so that today with great joy Holy Cross priests celebrate jubilees of their priestly ordination. Brothers of St. Joseph, on the other hand, celebrate jubilees of their first vows.

It is difficult to accept the Holy Cross Community's birthing as an 1837 event when scores of men just like Andre and Vincent made the move from one priest-director to another priest-director with no change in their spiritual life or their work ethic. The evangelical counsels which they began taking publically in 1836 did not impose any more restrictions on their mental or spiritual lives than the restrictions they had been accepting since 1820, one restriction (the promise of obedience) formal and the other two restrictions (poverty and celibacy) implicit in their day-to-day lives. What I am therefore arguing for is that we no longer begin the history of "Holy Cross" at the 1837 "Fundamental Act." We should begin the history in 1820 with the arrival of Pierre Hureau at the Ruillé rectory. This means that two groups did not initially merge into one unit, but rather that one group (the auxiliary priests) were spliced into a viable and vibrant extant community of Brothers, the original fabric of Holy Cross.

CHAPTER FIVE

1840 and Beyond

Brother Andre Mottais himself would not stay long at Sainte-Croix after Dujarié's death. In the fall of 1839, Moreau was asked to send missionaries to Algeria, and in April 1840 he announced the names of the Brothers to be sent: Andre, Alphonsus, and the novice Ignatius. Andre was designated director of the houses in Africa, but in May an auxiliary priest was designated superior of the group so Andre would effectively not be in charge. In May another novice and another priest were added to the band. Andre, waiting at Lyons to embark, wrote a long letter to Brother Vincent Pieau, who had been chosen to go on the American mission. Andre tells Vincent to ask Moreau to write up the chronicles of the Brothers, using himself (Vincent) as chief witness to the events. Vincent is told to give Moreau everything Andre had already written on the history of the Brothers up to 1826. Then Andre adds a most interesting and important phrase: "take care to erase my name anywhere it is found, because I don't wish to be named anywhere" (May 18, 1840).

What prompted this supreme act of abnegation? Some who suffer humiliation in a cause to which they have devoted themselves generously experience a sudden twinge of anger and frustration so they wish to disassociate themselves from the project. It is a way of saying, "You do not appreciate me, and therefore I do not want to be remembered or associated with you." The sentiment is a mixture both of admirable self-abnegation and not so admirable resentment born of frustration, sometimes the only recourse after losing a battle. As Andre watched Moreau, he may have felt some resentment, no longer having the premier role he had enjoyed under Dujarié, especially the increment of power that gathered to him as Dujarié grew old and sick. Getting the chance to distance himself by going to Africa, he would have felt relieved of the daily reminders of his own loss of power.

Moreau, ever a wise judge of character, probably sensed in Andre a need for a change, and so the obedience to go to Algeria was a blessing for both men: it gave Andre a dignified way to use his talents in a new venue, albeit still under obedience to a priest.

What stands out in Andre's 1840 Lyons letter to Vincent are the careful instructions Andre gives to set his affairs in order. It is almost as if he were writing his last will and testament. He asks Vincent to preserve carefully the notes on the 1831 financial separation from the Sisters of Providence. He notes how this event hurt Dujarié deeply. He wants the narrative of Dujarié's final illness preserved. Everything is to be attended to with the utmost care. Andre cautions, "I'm holding to this in my final wishes. Let it [the Dujarié narrative] be read to the Brothers at the retreat and let them have the liberty to speak their feelings and make their observations with total honesty, prudence, civility, and submissiveness" (Klawitter, *Mottais* 24). It sounds like an order rather than a request. Underneath Andre's desire to preserve the memory of the father-founder was possibly a desire that the Brothers air honestly their feelings about the transfer of authority. He then turns his attention to his present state of mind and remarks that at long last, away from the milieu he has known for twenty years, he is at last able to have a kind of novitiate experience, become a new person. The former Andre Mottais is dead and the new Andre is emerging. He tells Vincent that he has learned that the house the Brothers were destined to live in half a league from Algiers has been besieged by the Arabs. The man who knew only the calm beauty of Ruillé and Sainte-Croix is heading into hell. His farewell to Vincent, whom he had worked beside for so long, is touching: "Good-by then my very dear Brother Vincent. Good-by for eternity undoubtedly, because you are for America, we for Africa. Good-by—I embrace you with all my heart" (Klawitter, *Mottais* 25). At last the man has time for himself, time to assess his own situation and feelings. Almost from the day he arrived at Ruillé, his concern had been for others. Now there is only Andre himself. Andre is free. But his purification was only beginning.

The three letters we have from Andre in Africa show us a person we had barely known up to this point. Finally at age forty, freed from the cares of running the day-to-day operations of a community, he was free to look inside himself and reveal a character we before had to reconstruct from events and duties. The Africa letters are the most important letters Andre wrote. His 1834 and 1835 letters to Bishop Bouvier were extremely important, of course, for the history of Holy Cross, but nothing is more valuable to the history of Andre Mottais the person than the letters from

Africa. Andre's demotion afforded him at last the opportunity to make an extended retreat—just himself and his God. The three letters are, in this way, amazing.

The first letter, written from Moustapha on July 11, 1840, is directed to his parents. He tells them he arrived on May 27 and lives with orphans in a building adjacent to the seminary that his superior directs. One can only imagine the emotions that Jean and Jeanne Mottais would have felt on receiving the letter and sharing it with their children Jeanne and Joseph. (Andre's older brother Jean was already dead.) The crossing had not been easy: his five companions were all seasick. Since they had only four beds among them, Andre had given up his share of a bed and slept on deck "wrapped in a cloak among the soldiers." They passed by Minorca and Majorca, stopped briefly at Mahon, before arriving at Algiers on a Tuesday evening.

On going into the city, they met two sons of King Louis Philippe: the young men were returning to France after military duty. The sounds of war were everywhere. Andre called the cannon shots that started the day at 4 AM and ended the day at 8 PM "the sound of the Angelus in Africa." On first arriving, the Brothers were placed by the bishop in a hospice where they had to help care for two hundred and fifty sick and mentally ill people, under the supervision of the religious of St. John of God. Andre comments on the various nationalities that have converged in Algiers, the language, patois, and jargon that dominate the streets. He comments on ceremonies that the bishop presides over and the prospects for evangelization in a war torn country. Andre has an eye for detail: native clothing (or lack thereof), sleeping habits, modes of transportation, local cuisine. He comments at great length on the crops and livestock, the Larchamp farmer coming back to life in him. Finally he mentions his own health: he is so weak he can hardly write. During a two-week period he has suffered terribly. Before the days of vaccinations and vitamins, one can only imagine the multiple germs and diseases that would meet a European coming to a dirty village where hygiene was primitive and food preparation less than sterile. Something from Africa would, in fact, eventually kill Andre Mottais.

The second letter from Africa is addressed to Father Moreau and dated August 1, 1840, several weeks after the letter to the Mottais family. We learn that after six weeks the Brothers were given charge of an orphanage. There were only fourteen orphans, eight of whom boarded. Where the "six external" orphans slept is anyone's guess. Since the Brothers cannot get authorization to open a school, Brother Louis is studying arithmetic, grammar, and history as he bides his time. The novice Ignatius is not a very good student, so the priest superior has put him in charge of the refectory and food purchases. Brother Alphonsus works as a joiner (carpenter). Andre takes care of the orphans from 10 to 11:45 each morning and from 4 PM until supper. Louis takes care of them at the other times. Andre sleeps in a dorm with the littlest ones, Louis in a dorm with the biggest. Andre's bed, we learn later, is a mattress on the floor. The orphans can stay until they reach the age of twenty.

In this letter Andre further elaborates on his health problems. He had earlier reported that bathing in the sea had made him ill, but now he attributes his sickness to hemorrhage, loss of appetite, and a weakness that has led to fainting. A local doctor prescribes "sitting baths," a procedure which suggests that Andre was suffering from anemia brought on by untreated hemorrhoids and loss of blood. Andre has a relapse every third day. He then turns to a particular account of the state of his soul and rejoices that the superior, Father Leboucher, has relieved him of supervising the other Brothers: "That makes me happy because I no longer have any responsibility on that matter, and anyway I already have too much to watch over myself." He has overcome a preoccupation with death, is resigned to God's will, and in spite of his health problems, is determined to stay in Algeria for three reasons: he tells Moreau all who come are customarily sick for three to six months, the doctor has not advised him to leave, and many people suffer as he has until the end of September. Then he descends into the depths of self-loathing:

> I really want to end my career in this land of Africa that I cherish. If it rejects me from its breast, it is because I am more unworthy than the least of its inhabitants. Then please, my very reverend Father, have the kindness to send me to America, if you have the least task (temporarily or not, it doesn't matter) that I can fill. Otherwise if you call me back to France, I beg you on my knees, get into God's plans, which are evidently to cure my folly and my pride, as well as to convince me of my lack of ability in everything and everywhere, because this God out of His goodness allows every job like every country to vomit me out as soon as it gets a taste of me. So I beg you, if you recall me to France, in the name of charity, give me the last and the lowest job in the Congregation. Dressed in a shirt if necessary, rather than the religious habit which I now

believe I am unworthy of, I will clean shoes, wash dishes,
etc. I have but little time to repair my unworthy life.

How could a grown man drop to such a poor self-image? He has been
convinced that nothingness means saintliness, and he craves oblivion. He
clearly does not want to return to France where God "allows every job like
every country to vomit me out as soon as it gets a taste of me." Where did
he get the idea that he is unworthy to wear a religious habit, he who was
one of the first two to receive the habit of the Brothers of St. Joseph, and is
good for nothing but to clean shoes and wash dishes? This is the dark night
of the soul when all the good he had effected in twenty years seems erased
by his being "vomited" first out of France and then out of Algeria.

Thankfully, the sentiments passed away: two weeks later he adds to
the letter two paragraphs that are joyous and upbeat. He looks forward
to spring (coming at the end of September) when the planting is to begin.
He will need vegetable seeds. Possibly a return to health brought him out
of gloom or possibly the fear that the despair he expressed earlier would
prompt Moreau to summon him back to France. The latter explanation is
probably not true because, after all, he did not destroy the dark paragraph
before mailing the letter to Moreau. Anything but return to the work that
had rejected him. Better to live and die meagerly in a foreign land. So he
changes his tone and ends the letter upbeat.

The third and final letter of Andre from Africa is dated December 1,
1841, fifteen months after the second letter. It is sent from Philippeville,
where Andre had been sent to open a school. He expresses shock to learn
(via Moreau, not anyone in Algeria) that Brother Louis, a fellow Algerian
missionary, had drowned in the Mediterranean a month and a half earlier
while swimming with the orphans. At Moreau's request, Andre here
assesses the suitability of each of the Brothers, something Andre does
reluctantly. He then remarks that his hemorrhoids are worse than ever,
and he is having difficulty with the parish priest who denies him classroom
furniture, clothing, or a salary. The water is putrid and teems with "little
critters." He teaches six hours a day to varying numbers of the thirty-six
students enrolled in various courses: computation, spelling, penmanship.
He receives no salary while the public school teacher, who has only ten
students, is paid by the government. The classroom ceiling leaks dust from
the pastor's bedroom above. There is no bathroom: Andre has to trek "into
the mountains" while the parish priest has a bedpan that the maid empties
at night. Andre takes Thursdays off, his only break because on Sunday he
has to clean the church, teach catechism, perform baptisms, and wind the

clock! For breakfast he has a piece of bread and some dried fruit or a lump of sugar. His afternoon meal is generally something cold or sometimes a cup of soup.

The bad situation in Algeria for Holy Cross did not improve. Moreau finally recalled all the men in June, 1842. Andre returned to Sainte-Croix in broken health. At age forty-three, he was a man near death. In a letter to Brother Vincent he tells Vincent that the Brothers are soon to go back to Algeria. As for Andre himself, Moreau has made him a member of all the councils at Sainte-Croix and given him the title "Assistant." At Sainte-Croix, Andre reports, there are forty-six Brothers and postulants, not counting another thirty men at the Solitude. Andre teaches bookkeeping, writing, and reading. He is convinced that the Brothers have turned a corner under Moreau's direction, and that the union of Brothers and priests is solid: "I cannot grow tired of thanking the Lord and praying that He will maintain forever the union of priests with the Brothers" (May 26, 1843). He ends with the hope that he and Vincent will rest together in heaven.

Andre died at Sainte-Croix at 8 PM on Saturday, March 16, 1844. The chapel was draped in black linen, and the boarding school students, four of them carrying torches, processed with the body up the hill to the community cemetery. We do not know where he is buried today because all the graves of the early Holy Cross Brothers and priests were later used for graves of Marianite Sisters. History should never again underestimate his importance at Ruillé or at Sainte-Croix. Philéas Vanier, CSC, who was the first to name Andre the "second founder" of Holy Cross, summarizes Andre's contributions to Holy Cross:

> Four directors had been established to head the Institute [at Ruillé]: but the last three are more assistants than equals. Brother Andre directs everything: he rules on everything and is the judge of last resort. He is responsible for formation of subjects; he is master of novices; he presides over all exercises including meals; he gives all permissions; he resolves all difficulties between religious; he harries the lukewarm; he encourages the zealous; he gives direction. (Vanier 136)

These were the day-to-day necessities of running a community, and Andre carried them out well for thirteen years. If Dujarié was the heart of the organization, Andre was the head: without him, Dujarié's group would not have lasted as long as it did. The Cattas too in their monumental biography of Basil Moreau accept the importantance of Andre Mottais:

> Modestly and in his humble role as intermediary, the "first director" of the Brothers of St. Joseph deserves honorable mention alongside M. Dujarié and M. Moreau in the history of the early origins of Holy Cross, as one who had a providential role in the evolution of these "three societies in one," whose outlines he saw taking shape from afar and whose realization he hoped for "with ardent desire." (1.331)

The Cattas do not exactly call Andre a "founder," but they do note that he was the one who encouraged Moreau to form an association of auxiliary priests and join them to the Brothers (Catta, *Moreau* 1.331).

It is no easy task to convince an established religious community that it has three founders instead of two or one. Part of the problem may be iconographic: we have no idea what Andre Mottais looked like. We have no photo, no oil painting, no statue. Therefore we have nothing to help anchor an image of the man in our imagination. Moreau, Dujarié, Mary of the Seven Dolors—these people are fixed in our brain from graphic images. But what do we have for Andre? The mind works on image, and for Andre Mottais we can only fabricate. We do not even know if he were short or tall, fair haired or dark, brown eyed or blue eyed.

In a circular letter dated four days after Andre's death, Moreau does not apologize for removing Andre from a position of power in 1835 nor for sending him ill-prepared to Algeria and indirectly causing his death by exposure to harsh living condition, poor food, and isolation in a land Moreau had never investigated nor visited. Moreau's circular letter to the Community is all about himself and his grief, and how this death should inspire the living to work harder to be proper religious.

Andre was a man of talent and generosity, a man who worked tirelessly to make the Brothers of St. Joseph a success. He was not only solid in practical matters, he could also give gentle spiritual counsel. To Brother Adrien he wrote: "I hope, my dear brother, you are following as much as possible the school rules, because those of our brothers who observe them best are those who succeed in teaching. Take care to train yourself in training others to become a good school teacher, a pious and fervent religious, having no greater desire than to sanctify yourself and those Divine Providence has entrusted to you" (June 22, 1826).

Who then are the giants holding together the history of the Brothers of St. Joseph? Who are the men worth knowing? Surely three of the four Brother-Directors: Andre the founder, Vincent the obedient religious, and Leonard the fighter. We can add to them Hilarion the missionary and Rémi the chronicler. Anyone who wishes to know and live the history of the Brothers of St. Joseph should study these five men, read their letters, live their sorrows and joys. After all, the history of an organization is simply the aggregate history of its various members: a historian looks at the pieces and puts together the whole, but a reader looks at the whole and thrills back to its pieces. Hopefully both historian and reader come to the same conclusion: the Brothers of St. Joseph are a group of men valuable to each other, valuable to the Church, valuable to France, worthy still to be loved.

And how did other early great Brothers of St. Joseph fare under Moreau's direction? Because of his excellence as a teacher and his long, faithful relationship with the Brothers, Vincent was chosen by Moreau in 1841 to be one of seven missionaries sent to America. Touched by a plea from Celestine de la Hailandière, bishop of the Indiana Territory, Moreau assembled a group in the summer of 1841 and sent them off in the fall by steamship to begin work in the New World. The oldest of the group, Vincent at forty-four, was the only one certified as a teacher, chosen because he could train the two novices sent with the group, and he could train new recruits in Indiana.

Although Brother Vincent was almost a generation older than Edward Sorin, Vincent was not entrusted by Moreau with the primary leadership position for the group. That job was given to the chaplain. The young priest was talented, but his preeminence in the missionary group of seven can today only be understood in the light of Moreau's concept of authority for the new Holy Cross Community. The 1837 "Fundamental Act of Union" stipulated that the new group of auxiliary priests would be given the major superior roles. Thus Brother Vincent, with twenty years of religious communal living behind him, was entrusted to the care of a man with some three years experience living in religious life. That Vincent accepted such an arrangement is testament to his supreme sense of humility and his appreciation of Moreau's faith in Sorin's leadership qualities. Throughout his life Vincent never sought promotion or positions of authority, content to serve where he was needed, in whatever capacity he was asked to work. A master teacher, he was not above menial kitchen tasks. At St. Peter's in Indiana he did laundry and baked bread, which he pronounced "not bad" with his customary understatement in matters relating to his own talents. In the notes for the Notre Dame Council of Administration, an entry for

1844 shows that Brother Vincent is to "attend to sugar making." What he used as a base for sugar is not indicated. At Notre Dame Brother Vincent settled into an active routine and died, much revered, in 1890 at Notre Dame in Indiana.

On Sorin's orders in late spring of 1861 a double burial vault had been dug in the chapel of the novitiate at Notre Dame. Sorin intended it to be the final resting place for himself and Brother Vincent with, as lugubrious as it may sound, Moreau's right hand in a reliquary positioned above the two graves. Brother Vincent was never buried in the novitiate chapel, nor was Sorin. They both rest today in the quiet Community cemetery on St. Mary's Lake at Notre Dame, Vincent with the Brothers, Sorin with the Indiana provincials. Death came to the patriarch Vincent on July 23, 1890, at the age of 93. His most striking portrait is now displayed at the retirement facility named after him: the Brother Vincent Pieau Residence in Austin, Texas. Brother Vincent in the painting matches what we know of him through letters and tradition: he appears calm, wise, and kind, an old man with a full gray beard, the gentlest of smiles completing his face. He remains, along with Andre Mottais, one of the most significant of the early Brothers of St. Joseph.

Vincent saw little turbulence in his elder years, but Brother Leonard Guittoger, another great early Brother-Director of the Brothers of St. Joseph, had a very troubled life as he aged. Unlike Andre's sufferings, which were extraneous, Leonard's were self-induced. While Andre and Vincent grew in wisdom and happiness, much to our edification today, we cannot forget the lion Leonard, who used his prime years for a cause neither Andre nor Vincent endorsed.

Edward Sorin was elected Superior General of the Congregation on July 15, 1868, in a chapter which mercifully included Basil Moreau, who had been refused attendance at the 1866 General Chapter where he was denounced (without benefit of formal hearing) for the financial woes of Holy Cross. While the Congregation wrestled with its problems in the spring of 1868, Brother Leonard worked to separate the Brothers from the priests. By May of 1868 the General Council became aware of machinations Leonard had begun at Easter time. The minutes of the May 8, 1868, General Council meeting indicate that the matter of Brother Leonard needed serious and quick attention:

> In spite of Brother Leonard's promise, he has not stopped following his plan as is plain from the following passage in his April 29 letter: "Would you let me add, Reverend

Father, that our request has twenty-four signatures and
would have sixty more if we were permitted to present it
to Propaganda as we asked." Despite long years and many
retreats, this Brother followed up by sowing among his
Brothers the deadly idea to separate the Brothers from
the priests, and in 1855 had proposed the break between
the two societies to such a point that the General Council,
after being made aware of it, found themselves obliged to
threaten expulsion from the Congregation if he did not
desist. (*Minutes*, Gen. Council May 8, 1868, qtd. Klawitter,
Early 91).

Although the Council does not indicate what exactly it would do to punish
Leonard, they are unanimous in their will that he stop his campaign as
they perceived it. Father Moreau's vision for Holy Cross remained for the
majority of its members the desired structure of their religious institute, and
since at the time there were over five hundred priests, Brothers, and Sisters
serving in ninety-three houses in three different countries (Catta, *Moreau*
2.772), one can assume that the separatists were a minority: only eighteen
signatures appeared on Leonard's circulating document.

But rather than think of Brother Leonard as a separatist, that is, someone
who wanted to fracture Holy Cross, one should think of him as someone
who wanted to save the Josephites should the Congregation crumble. The
documents of 1868 make this point clear. We cannot read Leonard's heart,
but the documents come as close to his heart as anything we can get. But
once Edward Sorin was established as leader of Holy Cross, Leonard was
up against a more formidable superior than any he had met to date. He
knew Sorin well, but since the priest had been in America for twenty-seven
years, Leonard's recollection of the young Edward Sorin would have had to
have been radically altered after the priest's heady success first in Indiana
and then at the Rome General Chapter of 1868. At the end of the year 1868
Leonard wrote kindly to Sorin, but the issue of the Brothers' grievances
was not dead.

Leonard himself, in fact, was quite reconciled to the state of the
Congregation in the years following the 1868 Chapter as he asserts to
Sorin in that letter dated August 20, 1870: "I can affirm in good conscience
that I have said to no one since our chapter in Rome that I desire and ask
for the separation of the Brothers from the priests" (qtd. Klawitter, *Early*
95). He goes on to say that it was the desertion of Holy Cross priests in
1867 and 1868 as well as Pierre Dufal's resignation as Superior General

that prompted him to petition Cardinal Barnabo to save the Brothers in case Holy Cross were to fold. We have no reason to doubt the sincerity of Leonard's remarks. That he would be working secretly behind the scenes while telling his Superior General the contrary would be unthinkable for a religious of Leonard's age and prestige.

Leonard, however, may have overplayed his hand, and unfortunately the ax was soon to fall. In the minutes of the August 15, 1871, General Council meeting, drastic action was taken on this grand old man of Holy Cross:

> For many years Brother Leonard, scorning infractions of his vows, his oaths, his promises to repent, his repeated promises constantly broken, has worked to sow discord among his Brothers and has become the instrument of the devil, regarding the Constitutions, in order to trap them in a kind of coalition having for its purpose the separation of what God has united by the authority of his Vicar on earth. Nothing would correct him, neither multiple public humiliations nor threats from superiors, nor his protests to Rome during the Chapter, especially to Cardinal Barnabo; his vows today and his new protests not assuring the administration nor sufficiently repairing the scandal given, the General Council, after reading the last deliberation of the Provincial Chapter, decides:
>
> 1) that Brother Leonard, so often relapsed from amending, no longer merits the Congregation's confidence
> 2) that he will be deprived of all honor and any voice in the chapter
> 3) that he will be publicly stripped of his professed insignia, that is the statue of St. Joseph and the blessed cord
> 4) that he will always be placed after the last professed person
> 5) that he can correspond with no member of the Congregation, except his superiors, until he has given sufficient proof of conversion
> 6) that he will accept the obedience to be given to him, or better yet, if he wishes, he will receive permission to leave the Congregation. (*Minutes* Gen. Council, August 15, 1871, qtd. Klawitter, *Early* 97)

These are unbelievably harsh pronouncements on the head of one of the oldest members of Holy Cross. Leonard, after all, entered the Brothers of St. Joseph in 1825, just five years after its foundation, and he had risen to the highest positions possible for a Brother in Moreau's Community. But this was no longer Moreau's Community. It was Sorin's, and the harsh hand of Sorin is evident in Leonard's public fall from grace. Leonard was no doubt as shocked by the Council's decrees as we are today. Moreau himself commiserated in January 1872 that Leonard had not been afforded due process (Catta, *Moreau* 2.1013).

There is no evidence that Leonard attempted to defend himself after the 1871 summer retreat where he was demoted and disgraced. Unlike Moreau, who fought vigorously after the 1864 and 1866 chapters to salvage his good name, Leonard did nothing but accept his punishments. Does this indicate he was guilty? Not necessarily. Having seen the slanders leveled at Moreau year after year not only by Edward Sorin, Louis Champeau, and Victor Drouelle, but also by the rank and file men of Holy Cross who deserted Moreau, Leonard may have been traumatized enough simply to give up and try to live with whatever simple dignity he could muster for the remaining years of his life. He would still have sixteen years in Holy Cross before his death. Sorin, of course, was not content to leave Leonard anywhere near the center of the French community where the Brother could refresh his stained reputation. Sorin not only took away Leonard's religious insignia, he also took away his career. After decades of teaching, Leonard was sent as a cook to a small town where he was to prepare meals for a single Brother (a young one at that) under, let us remember, the injunction to correspond with no one besides his superiors.

Was Sorin so threatened by a Brother that he had to have the man isolated? Apparently so, and yet there is no evidence that Leonard ever intended to work to separate the Brothers from the priests—his goal was to make sure only that the Brothers would endure as a unit if the Congregation folded. His fault, if any, was a lack of concern for the fate of those priests who had joined Holy Cross in good faith and zeal. We have precious little from Brother Leonard after his downfall: four letters in sixteen years. He lived a quiet life until his death on June 9, 1877.

A happier Brother of St. Joseph is a man who was much younger than Brother Leonard, but one who died long before Leonard. Brother Hilarion Ferton is the fourth of our indispensible early heroes among the Brothers of St. Joseph. His life and letters have been examined elsewhere (Klawitter, *Algeria* xx-xxii and *Early Men* 47-76). He was a true pioneer to Africa and gave his life in a land foreign to France. Hardworking and edifying, he should be remembered forever for his missionary zeal and his joy.

We must look more intently, however, at a Brother who lived a long life as a Brother of St. Joseph and in his old age chronicled the Brothers, praising their amalgamation with Basil Moreau's auxiliary priests. The joining of two organizations is rarely accomplished without wrinkles and heartache, especially if one of the two organizations is fifteen years old and the other is fledgling. Add to this mixture a hierarchy of education, and the result can be less than conflict free. So it was with the amalgamation of the Brothers of St. Joseph and Basil Moreau's auxiliary priests in 1837, the Brothers some fifty strong and teaching in thirty schools, the priests five in number with three seminarians. The joining of two such religious organizations was, however, accomplished with minimum chaos thanks to the gentle sanctity of Dujarié, the consummate efficiency of Andre Mottais, and the charismatic energy of Moreau. At stake was a revolutionary idea of joining as equals (more or less equals) clerics and non-clerics. Originally the apostolates of the two groups were to be separate but complementary, the Brothers as teachers, the priests as pastoral substitutes in parishes, but rather rapidly the priests moved into school management and teaching, thus preventing some of the Brothers trained under Dujarié from managing their own schools. It did not help, of course, that the priests generally enjoyed a lengthy and deep education-preparation for apostolic work while the Brothers cobbled together a few months or at most one or two years of study before being shuttled out to the primary schools.

The majority of Holy Cross men, of course, both Brothers and priests, never agitated in Moreau's lifetime to separate the two groups. Moreau sent Brothers and priests together as units to found settlements in Africa, Indiana, Canada, and Bengal, and these missionaries valued each other, respected each other, and worked deliberately together to extend Holy Cross abroad from France. In Indiana, for example, Brother Vincent Pieau and Father Edward Sorin had a smooth working relationship based on mutual trust for half a century as they labored side by side to mold Notre Dame from a boys' boarding school into a university. In France, one of the most respected voices for a united Holy Cross over the same length of time was Brother Rémi Mérianne, who labored for sixty-three years in education, supported his priest-supervisors, and on occasion counseled provincial superiors. We can appreciate him today as a man who entered Dujarié's group when it was moving toward Moreau's stewardship and who recognized that groups evolve like any other organic being. Rémi accepted that evolutionary movement in Holy Cross as inspired by the Holy Spirit for the betterment of Church work. He did not fight to preserve the old ways, the old order, the old system of community used under Dujarié. Rather, he saw that change for the Brothers, and at the same time for the priests, was dynamic, envisioned and nurtured by Moreau, who based his vision on earlier visions for a mixed community, visions by both Dujarié and Brother Andre Mottais. We would do well, therefore, to study Brother Rémi Mérianne's correspondence to understand how beautifully the dynamic of Holy Cross worked in its first half-century.

Brother Rémi was born Etienne Mérianne in La Quinte (Sarthe) February 10, 1809, the son of Etienne Mérianne and Marie Ivon. He became a novice on September 21, 1825, nine months after entering, but did not profess final vows until August 19, 1838, ten years after he had received his teaching credentials on October 7, 1828. By the age of nineteen he was considered by the government to be prepared to teach French children, and throughout his years as a religious Brother, he apparently excelled in the teaching profession.

From his correspondence we can tell that Rémi was an active and respected member of the Brothers' Society. In 1847 in a letter thanking Moreau for the rules and constitutions, he states that the superior of the Brothers' Society should be elected before the superior for the priests' Society. He does not elaborate on his reasoning, but he adds this very telling sentence: "The Rector [Moreau] will always have more rapport with the priests than with the Brothers because he lives with them" (Oct. 19, 1847, qtd. Klawitter, *Early* 241-2). If we have ever wondered about the living arrangements at Sainte-Croix, this letter should not only illuminate for us the physical separation between the two societies by way of living conditions, but it should also hint at the psychological separation between the two societies as well. In its earliest days Moreau's two societies did not live together in one group as we may have thought, and the founder chose to live with his fellow priests rather than with the Brothers. I do not think that Rémi is simply referring to the fact that the majority of the Brothers were away from Le Mans living singly or in small groups in various parish schools around Sarthe. There actually were Brothers living at Sainte-Croix—teaching in the school there and supervising the Brothers' novitiate—but Moreau did not physically live with them. He lived with his priests. Such an arrangement may have fed the fires of separatists like Brother Leonard Guittoger.

In a letter to Edward Sorin on February 14, 1878, a good ten years into Sorin's tenure as Superior General, Brother Rémi himself addressed the matter of separating the two societies and comes down firmly on the unity of the two societies in one community:

> From its foundation right up to the present day I see Providence at work. In our Congregation nothing has changed, yes, given direction from above, spiritual direction conferred not on regular ecclesiastics. Enemies of the status quo, more numerous than your Reverence could imagine, are working to separate religious priests from lay religious, as per the Christian Brothers, the Marists, the Delaménais Brothers, the St. Gabriel Brothers before their rule was approved by the Holy See. For us the matter is over, and thanks be to God really over, and curses on him who wants to put his hand on the holy ark. (Feb. 14, 1878, qtd. Klawitter, *Early* 242)

For Rémi, the subject has obviously been settled once and for all—he is happy with the structure of Holy Cross uniting priests with Brothers.

We should note, however, that the illogical yoking of two groups based on different identifications had not crossed Rémi's mind. The religious vows taken by priests at Sainte-Croix were identical to those taken by Brothers, and thus the priests were basically religious Brothers. To discriminate them further on the basis of their ministry (priesthood) or sacred character makes as little sense as discriminating another group (e.g., the teachers) on the basis of their ministry (education). When Basil Moreau amalgamated his band of auxiliary priests with Dujarié's Brothers of St. Joseph, he was not amalgamating religious with religious because no auxiliary priest at Sainte-Croix took religious vows until 1841, six years after Moreau had brought to Sainte-Croix Dujarié's Brothers, who had taken a single promise (of religious obedience). By 1838 most of these Brothers had taken perpetual vows, with Brother Andre Mottais in the first position, three years before any of the auxiliary priests took any religious vows. The priests, of course, followed the practice of celibacy and sacerdotal obedience, but they had professed no vows in a religious community. One could argue, I suppose, that they were living at Sainte-Croix in a kind of extended novitiate from 1835 to 1841, but novices are never categorized as religious per se and enjoy none of the protection that professed religious enjoy.

Such reasoning apparently never crossed the minds of most Holy Cross men in 1878 when the Congregation had already enjoyed Vatican approval of the Constitutions for a generation. Brother Rémi was quite satisfied with Holy Cross as constituted, and if he ever thought about the separatists (e.g., Brother Leonard Guittoger), he condemned their thinking and their tactics as evidenced in his 1878 letter to Edward Sorin. What was not to like in Holy Cross? The Congregation was working and thriving on three continents (not four since Louis Champeau, the French provincial, had pulled all Brothers out of Africa in 1873), so Holy Cross was obviously blessed in its organization, i.e., Brothers and priests united in one religious unit.

The relationship of Holy Cross Brothers and priests was very much on Rémi's mind when he wrote to his French provincial Champeau in February 1878. He outlined six points on the matter. First of all, he notes that the Congregation was inspired by the Holy Spirit and birthed by Bishop Claude-Madeleine de la Myre-Mory at the annual clergy retreat in 1818. Its apostolate was to give religious instruction to boys in the Le Mans diocese and surrounding dioceses. It was first to be composed of Brothers and later joined by priests who would teach in secondary schools. We should notice two things in this first point: Rémi does not date the "beginning" of the Congregation to Moreau's assuming its direction in 1835 so in his mind the Congregation started with Dujarié and merely continued under Moreau. Rémi's second point to Champeau says as much: "the addition of priests joined to the Brothers was not a second beginning but simply the complement to Dujarié's original plan, which Dujarié tried to start" (Feb. 17, 1878, Vanier 542). Dujarié actually did try to attract priests to his projected community of auxiliary priests (one of whom was Basil Moreau). We know also that Brother Andre Mottais tried to move on this vision (Klawitter, *Early* 319, n. 13), as we have seen in an earlier chapter.

Thirdly, the plan for the Brothers of St. Joseph was not the same as that for the Christian Brothers, Delamenais Brothers, or the Marists of St. Gabriel. Curious in the wording of Rémi's fourth point is the following: the Holy Cross priests' society and the Brothers' society are "two sisters who must walk together, animated by the same spirit although their functions are different" (Klawitter, *Early* 244). That choice of the word "sisters" is telling because it enables Rémi to skirt the issue of priests as "Brothers"— i.e., call them all "sisters" and you do not have to stumble over the awkward idea that priests and Brothers walk together as "brothers," using the same word for two different meanings. What this suggests is that early in the Congregation, members struggled to mix a ministry (priesthood) with a lifestyle (brotherhood) in the same Congregation by isolating one ministry for separate treatment over other ministries. Surely in his subconscious Rémi and others must have wrestled with this odd organizational principle.

Fifthly, Rémi says that the two societies need each other to fulfill the destiny that Divine Providence wanted in creating this one unified Congregation. He warns that neither society could break off without ruining the plan sanctioned by God through the approbation of the rules and constitutions under Pius IX. Rémi represents the majority opinion on this matter of unity, i.e., a unity that persisted in spite of the majority of the members being defined negatively as "non-clergy" instead of all members being defined as "Brothers" in various ministries.

Rémi apparently enjoyed a close and cordial relationship with the French provincial Louis Champeau. After a circular letter by Edward Sorin in 1878 had made its rounds, Rémi wrote to Champeau (March 23, 1878) to express surprise at its contents. Waxing poetic, Rémi notes that the Sorin letter was like a lead ball dropped on an anthill (Rémi's image): "it broke through the roof and went as deeply as it could into the living quarters" (Klawitter, *Early* 245). The Brothers, Rémi adds, have been similarly affected by the circular letter, and, although some calm has returned, the anthill "of separatist ideas" has been destroyed, undermined at its base before it could ruin the Congregation. Rémi was particularly concerned about novices who had been infected by separatist ideas.

By 1877 Rémi was a trusted source for the history of the Brothers. In September of that year the General Administration (through Brother Gregory LeRoy) wrote to Rémi asking him about his memories of the old days under Father Dujarié. Rémi replies that he no longer has copies of the circular letters that summoned the men to the annual end-of-summer retreat year by year under Dujarié, but as he recalls, those convocation letters were not well written, as he put it, "not a masterpiece of enscribed eloquence" ("n'était point un chef d'oeuvre d'éloquence écrit"). The memoirs, covering his own entrance into the Brothers of St. Joseph up to Dujarié's death, are completed, but he has to make a copy of them before he can forward them. His hope, he confides to Gregory, is that the memories can be looked at by other elder members of the Community, who can correct or add to his recollections.

An important letter dated September 1, 1879 by Rémi to Champeau is the last letter we have by him, written nine years before his death in 1888. In it he gives details on the early days of the Brothers whom he asserts were founded as "The Brothers of St. Joseph," not "The Josephites." Why he insists on this point is not made clear in the letter. According to Rémi, around 1825 Dujarié gave direction of the Brothers over to three men: Andre Mottais, Henry Taupin, and Leonard Guittoger. (He does not include Vincent.) Thereafter, Dujarié tried to interest three priests to take over the Brothers: one named Duclos, the second a Norman priest (no name given in Rémi's letter), and a Breton (also unnamed). This third priest was, with Brother Leonard, trying to start a novitiate on the property of the Duchess of Montmorency in the Chartres diocese sometime in 1834, an enterprise that did not succeed. Finally at the annual retreat in 1835 at the end of the summer, Bishop Bouvier turned the Brothers over to Basil Moreau. Rémi states definitely that there was no talk at the time of having a Brother direct the group—the Brothers always thought in terms of a priest as director. Curiously Rémi attributes the actual founding of the Brothers to Bishop Myle-Mory, who initially told Dujarié to start a group of Brothers. Rémi may only raise this point in the letter to Champeau to show that the bishop's successor (Bouvier) could therefore be the only one to decide the fate of the Brothers. It is hard for us to imagine a successful group of male religious not wanting to direct themselves, but Rémi insists that no one, not even any of the four Brother-Directors (he here includes Vincent) wanted a Brother as a replacement for Dujarié.

A certain frustration comes with the reading of Rémi's letters because just as he is about to give us some wonderful details about the history of the Brothers, he launches into exultation over the unity of the Congregation or the excellence of priesthood. He must have been a philosopher of sorts, armchair variety, who thought through fact to idea. If he had stuck more to fact, how wonderful it would be to have from him a physical description of Andre Mottais or some insight into the personality of Henry Taupin. As a scion of the early Community, he can be treasured for his endurance, but we wish he had been more particular in his details. Of course, who knows what has been lost in his correspondence, his dozens of letters to fellow Brothers, men in the field who never kept their correspondence for the sake of history because, unlike provincial superiors, they never felt the need to preserve a paper trail of their apostolate. For Rémi then we must be content with what we have—a handful of letters and a legacy of respectability.

Brother Rémi died at Angers on February 12, 1888. He had given all but the first fifteen years of his life to the Brothers first known as the Brothers of St. Joseph and later known as the Brothers from Holy Cross. He was a champion of Brothers and priests united in one religious community, never wavering in this heartfelt vision.

How does Holy Cross enjoy unity today and avoid the peril of clericalism? Recently in Holy Cross it was suggested that clericalism and anti-clericalism are two extreme positions that threaten the harmony within mixed provinces. Such a suggestion implies that both positions are evil. But such a suggestion would imply that slavery and anti-slavery, for example, are attitudes worthy of reconciliation, or that homophobia and anti-homophobia are of equal moral disdain. Such thinking, of course, is illogical. If, therefore, we have to jettison one attitude, it would seem logical that clericalism must go, and with it, of course, anti-clericalism, which would no longer have a *raison d'être*. "Clerical" in its best sense should simply mean "acting like a priest," but the term has acquired a pejorative sense that will not go away easily. It has come to mean acting as if deference and privilege are due to one by reason of ordination. Clericalism is not simply the flip side of anti-clericalism. Clericalism is an evil. Privileging a small segment of the Church poisons the entire Church. Clerical privilege is unfair to the men who enjoy it most because by setting them apart as special, it places upon them the onus of living a kind of supernatural life of perfection that is beyond human. The failure to achieve clerical perfection can lead to frustration, an accelerated drive for power, and spiritual suicide.

As readers continue to meditate on the Brothers of St. Joseph, I will not rehearse here the transformation of the Brothers' "root metaphor," as that term has already been explored by Thomas Maddix, CSC, in *Naming the Options*:

> For the original brothers rooted in the Christian Brother tradition of brother as evangelizer, a distinctive religious habit, and a "motherhouse, the Grand St. Joseph" in Ruillé, the changes demanded by Basil Moreau meant not only a loss of symbolic meaning and rootedness but also a possible loss of religious and ministerial identity. (Maddix 57, qtd. Klawitter, *Mottais* 78)

Maddix blames not only Moreau for the change in the Brothers' symbolic presence, but also all members of Holy Cross who have followed Moreau in a mist of "historical amnesia" (Maddix 34, qtd. Klawitter, *Mottais* 67). Resistant to change from an "originating vision," Maddix has fought to return the Brothers of St. Joseph to their founding charism, but we should not forget that the shift from Ruillé to Le Mans, from Dujarié to Moreau, was more than physical—it was incrementally dynamic. If a religious community does not respond to immediate social needs, how can it survive? The Brothers carved out a niche for themselves in responding to a primary-school crisis in post-revolutionary France. Under the guidance of a later superior general (Gilbert Français), they moved into high school teaching. It is up to the young Brothers of St. Joseph today to effect change, salvaging what is good from the past, and jettisoning what is no longer useful for the evangelizing mission: "si le grain ne meurt..."

Readers may disagree with the basic argument of this book, this insistence on the pre-eminence of brotherhood over ministry in Holy Cross. An important voice in Holy Cross has written the following on the matter:

> What is clear historically is that Fr. Dujarié is considered as the founder of the Brothers of St. Joseph, a congregation *which doesn't exist anymore as such.* [Italics mine.] On the other hand, Fr. Moreau is the founder of the Association of Holy Cross, of which the Brothers of Holy Cross are a part. (Dionne, "Review" 88)

Gérard Dionne, CSC, in a way, wants to freeze Holy Cross and deny it evolution as much as the person he attacks (Maddix) attempted to freeze history at an earlier date. Dionne accuses Maddix of romanticizing" history:

> Is the reclaiming of the "founding vision of James Dujarié as brother-as-evangelizer" for example more a possible fantasizing about the founding vision, a romanticizing about our origins than a courageous and critical reading of all our history and originating vision? (Dionne, "Review" 100)

But if Maddix "romanticizes" and freezes history, does not Dionne also freeze it, albeit at a later date, and thus indulge in his own "romanticizing"? Is the "originating vision" of 1837 any more sacrosanct than the "originating vision" of 1820?

Holy Cross is a living, evolving, social institution: what it becomes in the future, as new Holy Cross members shape it, will be a wonder. That I wish to call us all (priests included) "Brothers of St. Joseph" should not be taken as an endgame. The future of Holy Cross belongs to the young in Africa, Bangladesh, India, Peru, and Haiti. Let us look with hope to their visions. Brother Rémi wrote in 1878: "What is a community or religious Congregation? It's a society or family created by the breath of God to help in the Lord's warfare, by prayer or religious instruction in the Church Militant" (qtd. Vanier 546). Let us live out Brother Rémi's vision. The Brothers of St. Joseph today are alive and healthy, their ministries not divisive but complementary.

Top: Mottais house in Larchamp and baptismal font in
Larchamp church. Bottom: La Charbonnière novitiate
building and Monsimer home (Brother Gatian).

APPENDIX I

Register of the Brothers of Saint Joseph

This register has been arranged from the *Matricule Générale* assembled by Brother Bernard Gervais, CSC, when he was on the General Council. This new arrangement of the material has been done to effect quick analysis of total membership, year by year, for the Brothers of St. Joseph from their inception at Ruillé-sur-Loir up to 1840. The legal name for each Brother is given in parentheses. The number in parentheses is the Brother's rank in the *Matricule Générale*. Also given in each item is the age of the Brother, when known. The total number of Brothers remaining at each year's end is found in the far right column. The items in this chronicle beyond 1838 include material only for Brothers who entered before 1839. The cumulative numbers = previous year's total plus the number entering new, minus number leaving (or dismissed). Italics are used to indicate leaving or death.

1820

July 15	Ignace (Pierre Hureau) 24, enters (2)	
Aug 20	Louis (Louis Duchêne) 19, enters (3)	
Oct 22	André (André Pierre Mottais) 20, enters (4)	
Nov 16	Etienne (Etienne Gauffre) 28, enters (5)	4

1821

June 25	Michel (Michel Jouseau) 17, enters (6)
June []	*Ignace (Pierre Hureau) 25, leaves (2)*
Nov 18	Jean (Jean Vayer) 26, enters (7)
Dec 7	Baptiste (Baptiste Verger) 24, enters (8)
Dec 7	Charles (Charles Faribault) 21, enters (9)

Dec 11   Victor (Victor Loupil) 19, enters (10)

Dec 15   François (Pierre François Blanchet) 29, enters (11)   **4 + 6 - 1 = 9**

1822

Apr 19   Joseph (Pierre Bourdon) 17, enters (12)

Apr 24   Augustin (Jean-Baptiste Riet) 22, enters (13)

Apr 24   Pierre (Pierre Oger) 17, enters (14)

May 10   Basile (René Derouet) 25, enters (15)

May 29   Julien (Jean Neveu) 32, enters (16)

July 17   Dominique (Pierre Gautier) 16, enters (17)

Sept 28   Benjamin (Benjamin Poirier) 22, enters (25)

Oct 9   Vincent (Jean Pieau) 26, enters (18)

Oct 31   Bernard (_____ Bonneau) 33, enters (19)

Nov 9   Martin (Jean Verger) 24, enters (20)

Nov 21   Pascal (François Gareau) 20, enters (21)

Nov 23   Léon (Jean Marsollier) [age unknown] enters (22)

Nov 23   Arsène (Arsène Echard) [age unknown] enters (23)

Nov 23   Félix (Jean Taupin) 28, enters (24)

Dec 11   Daniel (Pierre Launay) 14, enters (26)   **9 + 1 5 = 24**

1823

Jan 3   Stanislas (Jean Blaise) [age unknown] enters (27)

Mar 11   Paul (Paul Petit) 22, enters (28)

Apr 2   *Stanislas (Jean Blaise) [age unknown], sent away (27)*

Apr 13   Athanase (Charles Richard) [age unknown] enters (29)

Apr 26   Marin (Michel Bulanger) 27, enters (30)

Apr 30   Dorothée (Armand-Adolphe Aumas) 16, enters (31)

Apr []   *Léon (Jean Marsollier) [age unknown], leaves (22)*

May 12   Antoine (Joseph Jousse) 30, enters (32)

May 27   Clément (Louis-François Pottier) [age unknown] enters (33)

May []   *Pascal (François Gareau) 21, sent away (21)*

June 3   Alexis (Alexis-Alexandre Poule-Dupré) 27, enters (34)

July 2   Maurice (Pierre Chéan) 17, enters (35)

July 20   Henri (Michel Taupin) 31, enters (36)

Aug 19   Isidore (Isidore Bouvier) 20, enters (37)

Sept 4   Philippe de Néri (Jean-Baptiste Bougault) 21, enters (38)

Sept 4	Eléonore (Eléonore Hulot) 20, enters (39)
Oct 10	René (René Fromentin) [age unknown] enters (40)
Oct 14	Thadée (Pierre Papin) 24, enters (41)
Nov []	*Arsène (Arsène Echard) [age unknown], sent away (23)*
Nov 7	Romain (François Bouvier) 23, enters (42)
Nov 23	Elie (Jean Letessier) 23, enters (43)
Nov 29	Germain (Pierre-Antoine Blin) 32, enters (44)
Dec 4	Eusèbe (Jean-Pierre Coudriou) 26, enters (45)
[ ]	*Athanase (Charles Richard) [age unknown], sent away (29)*

24 +19 -5 = 38

1824

Jan 4	Léon-Louis de Gonzague (Louis Pottier) 14, enters (46)
Jan 17	Grégoire (Julien Lépinay) 13, enters (47)
Jan 21	Alexandre (Pierre Neveu) [age unknown] enters (48)
Jan []	*Isidore (Isidore Bouvier) 21, leaves (37)*
Mar 4	Siméon (Charles Bouvier) 17, enters (49)
Mar 6	Marie-Joseph (Pierre-Joseph Duval) 19, enters (50)
Mar 11	Jean-Baptiste (Jean-Baptiste Lardeau) 25, enters (51)
Mar 16	Jérôme (René Porcheré) 24, enters (52)
Mar 30	Pascal (Pierre Bignon) 28, enters (53)
Apr 1	Simon (Simon Guy) 21, enters (54)
Apr 15	Ignace (Pierre Hureau) 28, re-enters (2)
May 14	Zozime (Pierre Desmares-Vicaire) [age unknown] enters (55)
May 23	Jacques (Jacques Hamon) 18, enters (56)
May []	Isidore (René-Isidore Janvier) 24, enters (57)
June 5	Jean-Marie (Jean-Marie Gauchet) 25, enters (58)
July 1	Laurent (Joseph Chartier) 16, enters (59)
July 3	Gabriel (Pierre Marsollier) 24, enters (60)
July 6	Arsène (Louis-Pierre Bouvet) 19, enters (61)
Aug []	*Clément (Louis-François Pottier) [age unknown], leaves (33)*
Aug 23	Denis (René-Auguste Touti) 20, enters (62)
Oct 1	*Dorothée (Armand-Adolphe Aumas) 18, sent away (31)*
Oct 15	Didier (Jean-Didier Mousseau) 29, enters (63)
Oct 22	Alexis (Jean-Pierre Chabrun) 15, enters (64)
Oct 24	*Alexis (Alexis-Alexandre Poule-Dupré) 29, leaves (34)*
Nov 1	Saturnin (François Oger) 16, enters (65)

Nov 4   Maxime (François Boisramé) 19, enters (66)

Nov 12   Hilarion (Jean Lagarde) 29, enters (67)

Nov 13   Pacôme (Louis Laffay) 13, enters (68)

Nov 20   Thomas (Jacques-Thomas Peloille) 34, enters (69)

Dec 13   Césaire (Alexis Poirier) 18, enters (70)

Dec 14   Sévère (Jean-Louis Bellouard) 25, enters (71)

Dec 16   Cyprien (Jean Chambon) 26, enters (72)

Dec 23   Fulgence (René Ridereau) 28, enters (73)

Dec 29   Jean de la Croix (Jean Cabot) 19, enters (74)

[   ]   *Eléonore (Eléonore Hulot) 21, sent away (39)*

[   ]   *René (René Fromentin) [age unknown], sent away (40)*

[   ]   *Zozime (Pierre Desmares-Vicaire) [age unknown], leaves (55)*   **38 +30-7 = 61**

1825

[   ]   Hermas (_____ _____) [age unknown] enters (75)

Jan []   *Maurice (Pierre Chéan) 25, leaves (35)*

Jan 1   Adrien (Louis Legeai) 21, enters (76)

Jan 4   Abraham (Etienne Cormier) 24, enters (77)

Jan 7   Jean de Dieu (Louis Duportail) 29, enters (78)

Jan 8   Rémi (Etienne Mérianne) 15, enters (79)

Feb 3   Ambroise (Pierre Dupont) 31, enters (80)

Feb 5   Hippolyte (François Dureau) 25, enters (81)

Feb 18   Vincent-de-Paul (Jean-Baptiste Vincent Plat) 18, enters (82)

Feb 23   Hilaire (Augustin Jubault) 15, enters (83)

Feb 24   Bertrand (Pierre Paineau) 15, enters (84)

Mar []   *Abraham (Etienne Cormier) 24, leaves (77)*

Apr 6   Vital (Auguste-Casimir Breton) 16, enters (85)

Apr 18   Edmond (François Edon) 17, enters (86)

Apr 18   René (René-Michel Lépineau) 33, enters (87)

Apr 19   Stanislas (Louis-Joseph-Grégoire Derve) 21, enters (88)

Apr 19   Urbain (Louis Jubault) 19, enters (89)

Apr 21   Armand (Armand Maisonnier) 14, enters (90)

Apr 23   Prosper (Guillaume Herbelle) 24, enters (91)

Apr 28   Athanase (Michel-Etienne Tarault) 24, enters (92)

Apr []   *Elie (Jean Letessier) 24, leaves (43)*

May 4   Théophile (Alexandre-Jean Cosson) 24, enters (93)

May 10	Justin (Michel Ragot) 20, enters (94)
May 19	Théodore (René Gouadon) 16, enters (95)
May 27	Symphorien (Denis Bourgneuf) 21, enters (96)
May 29	Bruno (Paul-Jean Bouilly) 20, enters (97)
May []	*Didier (Jean-Didier Mousseau) 30, leaves (63)*
June 10	Dorothée (Joseph Bigot) 22, enters (98)
June 16	Epiphane (Jean-Simon Billard) 13, enters (99)
June []	*Jean de Dieu (Louis Duportail) sent away (78)*
July 10	Benoît (François Bazile) 13, enters (100)
July 24	Jean-Climaque (Jean-Baptiste Contamin) 27, enters (101)
Aug 4	*Daniel (Pierre Launay) 20, leaves (26)*
Aug 25	Alphonse (Julien Landemaine) 21, enters (102)
Aug []	*Eusèbe (Jean-Pierre Coudriou) 28, leaves (45)*
Aug []	*Alexandre (Pierre Neveu) [age unknown], leaves (48)*
Aug []	*Jean-Baptiste (Jean-Baptiste Lardeau) 25, leaves (51)*
Sept 3	Almire (Charles-François Lelièvre) 23, enters (103)
Sept 8	Marc (François-Charles-Marthe Galinand) 23, enters (104)
Sept 8	Abraham (Joseph-Louis Veaufleury) 18, enters (105)
Sept 10	*Louis (Louis Duchêne) 24, leaves (3)*
Sept 15	Léonard (Pierre-François Guittoger) 23, enters (106)
Sept 22	Ambroise (Victor-Gabriel-Charles Corbière) 24, enters (107)
Sept []	*Bernard (_____ Bonneau) 25, sent away (19)*
Oct 8	Elie (Joseph Rétif) 16, enters (108)
Oct 11	Hyacinthe (Hyacinthe Hutin) 14, enters (109)
Oct []	Léandre (Léandre Debray) 23, enters (110)
Oct 12	Maurice (Pierre Chéan) re-enters (35)
Oct 24	*Sévère (Jean-Louis Bellouard) 25, sent away (71)*
Nov 3	Irénée (Joseph-Almire Trassard-Deslandes) 18, enters (111)
Dec 3	Matthieu (Pierre Plumard) 16, enters (112)
Dec 8	Constantin (Jean Vivens) 22, enters (113)
Dec 13	*Jacques (Jacques Hamon) 19, sent away (56)*
Dec 22	Clément (Pierre-Jacques Richard) 22, enters (114)
Dec 27	Eugène (Louis-Gustave Fossé) 20, enters (115)
Dec []	Gervais (Pierre Esnault) [age unknown] enters (116)
[ ]	*Ambroise (Pierre Dupont) 32, sent away (80)*
[ ]	*Fulgence (René Ridereau) 29, sent away (73)*

[   ]   *Hermas (_____) [age unknown], leaves (75)*

[   ]   *Urbain (Louis Jubault) 31, sent away (89)*

[   ]   *Théophile (Alexandre-Jean Cosson) 25, leaves (93)*

[   ]   *Théodore (René Gouadon) 16, sent away (95)*   **61 + 43 − 19 = 85**

1826

[   ]   Paulin (Cannet) [age unknown] enters (117)

Feb 20   Alexandre (Paul Gautier) 16, enters (118)

Feb 20   Anselme (René Mercier) 28, enters (119)

Feb 20   Magloire (Pierre-Charles Sage) 13, enters (120)

Mar 12   *Jean-Marie (Jean-Marie Gauchet) 27, dies (58)*

Mar 30   Jean-Baptiste (Jean-François Guilmet) 14, enters (121)

Mar []   *Thomas (Jacques-Thomas Peloille) 37, leaves (69)*

Apr 9   Edouard (François-Jean Delalande) 19, enters (122)

Apr 11   Marie (François-Jean-Marie Delorière) 20, enters (123)

May 25   *Jérôme (René Porcheré) 26, dies (52)*

June 10 *Gervais (Pierre Esnault) [age unknown], leaves (116)*

June 17 Gatien (Jean Fouquet) 16, enters (124)

June 18 Eugène (Pierre James) 19, enters (125)

June 18 Eustache (François Marchand) 18, enters (126)

June 23 Sylvain (Louis Veaufleury) 19, enters (127)

June 29 Jérôme (François Emond) 23, enters (128)

June [] *Almire (Charles-François Lelièvre) 24, sent away (103)*

June [] *Ambroise (Victor-Gabriel-Charles Corbière) 25, sent away (107)*

July 1   Placide (François-Jaqcques Beauté) 18, enters (129)

July 1   Damien (Jean-François Pivard) 13, enters (130)

July 25 Jerome (François Fourmont) 23, enters (131)

July [] *Félix (Jean Taupin) 23, sent away (24)*

July [] *Hilaire (Augustin Jubault) 17, sent away (83)*

Aug 5   Médard (Jean-Michel-Médard Proust) 19, enters (132)

Aug 23   Honoré (Auguste-François Brunet) 14, enters (133)

Aug 23   Casimir (Julien Bardou) 14, enters (134)

Aug 23   Théophile (Jean Fréard) 13, enters (135)

Aug []   *Charles (Charles Faribault) 26, leaves (9)*

Aug []   *Edmond (François Edon) 18, sent away (86)*

Aug []   *Hilarion (Jean Lagarde) 30, leaves (67)*

Sept 1	Hilaire (Matthieu-Charles Bourgeteau) [age unknown] enters (136)	
Sept 15	*Symphorien (Denis Bourgneuf) 22, sent away (96)*	
Sept 18	Georges (Victor Guisbé) [age unknown] enters (137)	
Sept 21	Barthélémy (Julien-Mathieu-Louis Guinegaut) 15, enters (138)	
Oct 3	Thomas (François Cochon) 17, enters (139)	
Oct 4	Jude (Henri-Baptiste Bougault) [age unknown] enters (140)	
Oct 10	*Jean-Baptiste (Jean-François Guilmet) 14, sent away (121)*	
Oct 12	Maurice (Pierre Chéan) 20, re-enters (35)	
Oct 18	Eloi (Louis-Jean Cosnier) 19, enters (141)	
Oct 26	Frumence (Pierre Saulnier) [age unknown] enters (142)	
Oct []	*Simon (Simon Guy) 23, leaves (54)*	
Nov 2	Quentin (Augustin Chesnel) 17, enters (143)	
Nov 3	Ambroise (Louis-Ambroise-Marie Desloriers) 22, enters (144)	
Nov 6	*Damien (Jean-François Pivard) 13, leaves (130)*	
Nov 15	Sébastien (Pierre Poirier) 22, enters (145)	
Nov []	Cyrille (René Renard) 16, enters (146)	
Nov []	Marcel (Jean Brard) 16, enters (147)	
Nov []	Daniel (Pierre Launay) 18, re-enters (26)	
Nov []	*Clément (Pierre-Jacques Richard) 26, sent away (114)*	
Dec 5	*Hilaire (Matthieu-Charles Bourgeteau) [age unknown], sent away (136)*	
Dec 7	Gervais (Pierre-Jacques-Gervais Langlois) 16, enters (148)	
Dec 7	Charles (Charles Rousseau) [age unknown] enters (149)	
Dec 13	Louis (Auguste Ménage) 22, enters (150)	
Dec 15	Eusèbe (Armand Béranger) 14, enters (151)	
Dec 15	Liboire (Marie-François Meunier) 16, enters (152)	
Dec 29	Mathurin (Pierre Leroyer) 18, enters (153)	
Dec []	Nicolas (Jules-Nicolas Guesnot) 18, enters (154)	
[ ]	*Léon-Louis de Gonzague (Louis Pottier) 17, leaves (46)*	
[ ]	*Laurent (Joseph Chartier) 19, sent away (59)*	
[ ]	*Eugène (Louis-Gustave Fossé) 21, leaves (115)*	
[ ]	*Magloire (Pierre-Charles Sage) 14, leaves (120)*	
[ ]	*Jérôme (François Emond) 23, sent away (128)*	**85 + 40 - 22 = 101**

1827

Jan 7	Victorin (Jean Brunet) 16, enters (155)
Jan 11	*Victorin (Jean Brunet) 16, leaves (155)*

[ ]	*Liboire (Marie-François Meunier) 17, sent away (152)*
Jan 18	Liboire (Elie Launay) 15, enters (156)
Jan 18	Victorin (Henri Lion) 17, enters (157)
Jan 28	Laurent (Antoine Rouchy) 29, enters (158)
Feb 24	Christophe (Christophe Murat) 25, enters (159)
Feb 25	Silvestre (Ambroise Corni) 22, enters (160)
Mar 1	*Georges (Victor Guisbé) [age unknown], sent away (137)*
Mar1	*Gervais (Pierre-Jacques-Gervais Langlois) 16, sent away (148)*
Mar 1	*Nicolas (Jules-Nicolas Guesnot) 15, sent away (154)*
Mar 4	Agathange (Nicolas Berson) 25, enters (161)
Mar 26	Zozime (Ferdinand Prout) 15, enters (162)
Apr 22	Norbert (Louis Bailleul) 28, enters (163)
Apr 23	*Barthélémy (Julien-Mathieu-Louis Guinegaut) 16, sent away (138)*
May 5	Onésime (Mathurin-Pierre-François Pillard) 30, enters (164)
May 5	Bonaventure (Pierre Tulou) 30, enters (165)
May 5	François d'Assise (François-Marie Tulou) 29, enters (166)
May 18	Mathias (Mathias Chapelière) 29, enters (167)
June 17	Florent (Jean-Rodolphe Jouandy) 23, enters (168)
July 11	Ulphace (Louis Oger) 14, enters (169)
July 29	Célestin (Louis Forton) 12, enters (170)
July []	*Florent (Jean-Rodolphe Jouandy) 24, sent away (168)*
Sept 4	Théodoret (Grégoire Gilette) 15, enters (171)
Sept 7	Isaac (François-Clément Coutard) 15, enters (172)
Sept 7	Gérasime (Florent Duval) 14, enters (173)
Sept 7	François-Xavier (François Fleurinet) [age unknown] enters (174)
Sept 7	Principe (Principe Manoury) [age unknown] enters (175)
Sept 7	Flavien (Louis-Victor Manceau) 18, enters (176)
Oct 8	*Hippolyte (François Bureau) 27, sent away (81)*
[Oct] 24	Jean-Chrysostôme (Jean Martin) 20, enters (177)
Oct []	*Principe (Principe Manoury) [age unknown], leaves (175)*
Nov 4	Bernard (Gilles Lecavorsin) 32, enters (178)
Nov 30	Damase (Jean Poilpré) 21, enters (179)
Nov []	*Hyacinthe (Hyacinthe Hutin) 16, leaves (109)*
Dec 22	Raphael (Arsène Forton) 10, enters (180)
[ ]	Philippe (_____ _____) [age unknown] enters (181)
[ ]	*Léandre (Léandre Debray) 25, leaves (110)*

[ ]	*Marie (François-Jean-Marie Delorière) 22, leaves (123)*	
[ ]	*Honoré (Auguste-François Brunet) 16, leaves (133)*	
[ ]	*Thomas (François Cochon) 18, sent away (139)*	
[ ]	*Jude (Henri-Baptiste Bougault) [age unknown], leaves (140)*	
[ ]	*Frumence (Pierre Saulnier)[age unknown], leaves (142)*	
[ ]	*Quentin (Augustin Chesnel) 18, sent away (143)*	
[ ]	*Ambroise (Louis-Ambroise-Marie Desloriers) 23, sent away (144)*	
[ ]	*Charles (Charles Rousseau) [age unknown], leaves (149)*	
[ ]	*Louis (Auguste Ménage) 24, leaves (150)*	
[ ]	*Silvestre (Ambroise Corni) 23, leaves (160)*	
[ ]	*Zozime (Ferdinand Prout) 16, leaves (162)*	
[ ]	*Norbert (Louis Bailleul) 28, leaves (163)*	**101 + 27 - 23 = 105**

1828

Jan 5	Théotime (Jean-Pierre Coquand) 27, enters (182)
Jan 18	Philibert (Louis Launay) 17, enters (183)
Jan 18	Théodore (Vital Chaumezière) 19, enters (184)
Feb 14	Clément (Clément Cheron) 24, enters (185)
Feb 23	*Marcel (Jean Brard) 17, leaves (147)*
Feb 27	*Clément (Clément Chéron) 24, sent away (185)*
Mar 1	Barnabé (Louis Balleux) 28, enters (186)
Mar 4	*Flavien (Louis-Victor Manceau) 19, leaves (176)*
Mar 6	François de Paule (Victor Défoumeaux) 24, enters (187)
Mar 6	*Isidore (René-Isidore Janvier) 28, leaves (57)*
Mar 13	*François de Paule (Victor Defoumeaux) 24, leaves (187)*
Mar 15	Dosithée (Jean-Marie Tulou) 14, enters (188)
Mar []	*Constantin (Jean Vivens) 25, leaves (113)*
Apr 8	*Eusèbe (Armand Beranger) 15, leaves (151)*
Apr 11	*René (René Fromentin) [age unknown], leaves*
Apr 11	*Thadée (Pierre Papin (29, leaves (41)*
Apr []	*Sébastien (Pierre Poirier) 25, sent away (145)*
Apr []	*Agathange (Nicolas Berson) 21, leaves (161)*
May 17	Antonin (Pierre Lefèbvre) 23, enters (189)
May 22	Flavien (Louis-Victor Manceau) 19, re-enters (176)
May 29	Jean-François (François-Jean Royer) 39, enters (190)
June 9	Samuel (Louis Frêne) 17, enters (191)

June 10	*Jean-François (François-Jean Royer) 39, leaves (190)*
June 13	Avit (Sébastien Bunel) 24, enters (192)
June 23	Elisée (Félix-Hippolyte Réau) 15, enters (193)
June 28	Marie (Julien-Marie Paquet) 41, enters (194)
July 13	*Barnabé (Louis Balleux) 29, leaves (186)*
July 19	Lucien (Alphonse-François Dagoreau) 16, enters (195)
July 19	*Bertrand (Pierre Paineau) 19, leaves (84)*
July 31	*Eugène (Pierre James) 22, leaves (125)*
July []	*Prosper (Guillaume Herbelle) 27, sent away (91)*
July []	*Mathias (Mathias Chapelière) 30, sent away (167)*
Aug 7	Honoré (Pierre Bouhour) 14, enters (196)
Aug 7	Emeri (Louis Guerin) 13, enters (197)
Aug 17	Louis (Etienne-Joseph Rouillon) 14, enters (198)
Aug 18	Charles (Ferdinand Raimond) 13, enters (199)
Aug 19	Firmin (Alexis Gorget) 46, enters (200)
Aug 19	Léon (Louis Mottais) 13, enters (201)
Aug []	*Honoré (Pierre Bouhour) 14, leaves (196)*
Aug []	*Pascal (Pierre Bignon) 32, leaves (53)*
Sept 15	Marcel (Jean Brard) 18, re-enters (147)
Sept [?]	Corentin (Corentin Chevalier) 14, enters (202)
Sept 23	Anaclet (Joseph Hallier) 22, enters (203)
Sept 25	Chrysostôme (Pierre David) 22, enters (204)
Sept []	*Victor (Victor Loupil) 26, leaves (10)*
Sept []	*Paul (Paul Petit) 27, leaves (28)*
Sept []	*Anselme (René Mercier) 31, sent away (119)*
Sept []	*Gérasime (Florent Duval) 15, leaves (173)*
Oct 9	Thomas d'Aquin (Alexandre Meleux-Laperrière) 13, enters (205)
Oct 15	Georges (Georges Lorain-Laval) 24, enters (206)
Oct 23	Hilaire (Silvin Vernon) 28, enters (207)
Nov 5	Gervais (François Houlbert) 17, enters (208)
Nov 6	Simon (Michel Péard) 32, enters (209)
Nov 15	*Chrysostôme (Pierre David) 22, leaves (204)*
Dec 3	*Simon (Michel Péard) 32, leaves (209)*
Dec 10	*Gervais (François Houlbert) 17, sent away (208)*
Dec 15	*Corentin (Corentin Chevalier) 14, sent away (202)*
[ ]	Rodriguez (Besnard) [age unknown] enters (210)

[ ]	Zozime (Cossom) [age unknown] enters (211)	
[ ]	Eugène (_____ Dubriel) [age unknown] enters (212)	
[ ]	*Daniel (Pierre Launay) 20, leaves again (26)*	
[ ]	*Gabriel (Pierre Marsollier) 29, leaves (60)*	
[ ]	*Alphonse (Julien Landemaine) 24, leaves (102)*	
[ ]	Jean-Baptiste (Jean-François Guilmet) 16, re-enters (121)	
[ ]	*Jean-Baptiste (Jean-François Guilmet) 16, leaves again (121)*	
[ ]	*Liboire (Elie Launay) 17, leaves (156)*	
[ ]	*Théodoret (Grégoire Gilette) 16, leaves (171)*	
[ ]	*Jean-Chrysostôme (Jean Martin) 21, leaves (177)*	
[ ]	*Philippe (_____ _____) [age unknown], leaves (181)*	
[ ]	*Dosithée (Jean-Marie Tulou) 15, leaves (188)*	**105 + 34 - 36 = 103**

1829

Jan 2	*Georges (Georges Lorain-Laval) 24, sent away (206)*
Jan 12	Alphonse (Julien Landemaine) 24, re-enters (102)
Feb 3	Jules (Jean Chancerel) 17, enters (213)
Feb 20	*Anaclet (Joseph Hallier) 22, leaves (203)*
Feb 23	Gervais (Augustin Bemier) 22, enters (214)
Feb 23	*Firmin (Alexis Gorget) 46, sent away (200)*
Feb 27	Donatien (André-Louis-Paul Nail) 23, enters (215)
Mar 5	*Gervais (Augustin Bemier) 22, sent away (214)*
Mar 15	*Jules (Jean Chancerel) 17, sent away (213)*
Mar 19	*Michel (Michel Jouseau) 25, leaves (6)*
Mar 28	Jude (René Maçon) 25, enters (216)
Apr 3	Barthélémy (Joseph Monvoisin) 30, enters (217)
Apr 4	Philéas (Henri Gonet) 17, enters (218)
Apr 24	Abel (Abel Guyon) 34, enters (219)
Apr []	*Epiphane (Jean-Simon Billard) 17, leaves (99)*
June 26	*Samuel (Louis Frêne) 18, sent away (191)*
June []	*Charles (Ferdinand Raimond) 13, leaves (199)*
July 2	*Jude (René Maçon) 25, leaves (216)*
Aug 19	Gervais (Jean Guibon) 20, enters (220)
[ ]	*Vincent-de-Paul (Jean-Baptiste Vincent Plat) 23, leaves (82)*
Aug 21	Vincent-de-Paul (Jean-Baptiste Vincent Plat) 23, re-enters (82)
Aug 26	Louis de Gonzague (Louis-Michel Gondard) 15, enters (221)

Aug 28   Bertin (Jean Bouthmis) 25, enters (222)

Aug 29   Théodule (Jean-Marie Hillion) 28, enters (223)

Aug []   *Mathurin (Pierre Leroyer) 21, leaves (153)*

Aug []   *Nicolas (Jules-Nicolas Guesnot) 15, leaves (154)*

Aug []   *Marie (Julien-Marie Paquet) 44, sent away (194)*

Sept 2   Adolphe (Pierre-Philippe Barbot) 16, enters (224)

Sept 2   Moise (Joseph Marin Boureau) [age unknown] enters (225)

Sept 16   Anaclet (Joseph Hallier) 23, re-enters (203)

Sept []   *Elie (Joseph Rétif) 20, leaves (108)*

Oct 6   Macaire (Guillaume-Michel Chauvin) 19, enters (227)

Oct 14   *Moise (Joseph Marin Boureau) [age unknown], leaves (225)*

Oct 25   Théodore (Alain-Marie Mevel) 18, enters (226)

Oct []   *Philippe de Néri (Jean-Baptiste Bougault) 27, leaves (38)*

Oct []   Barnabé (Louis Balleux) 30, re-enters (186)

Nov 6   Théodose (Louis-Michel Prieul) 17, enters (228)

Nov []   *Laurent (Antoine Rouchy) 32, sent away (158)*

Dec 3   *Théodore (Alain-Marie Mevel) 18, leaves (226)*

Dec 16   Florentin (Jean-Amand Mottay) 25, enters (229)

[   ]   *Alphonse (Julien Landemaine) 25, leaves again (102)*

[   ]   Sébastien (Pierre Poirier) 26, re-enters (145)

[   ]   *Christophe (Christophe Murat) 28, leaves (159)*

[   ]   *Théodore (Vital Chaumezière) 21, leaves (184)*

[   ]   *Rodriguez (Besnard) [age unknown], leaves (210)*

[   ]   *Zozime (Cossom) [age unknown], leaves (211)*

[   ]   *Eugène (Dubriel) [age unknown], leaves (212)*   103 + 22 - 25 = 100

1830

Jan 17   Jean Chrysostôme (Joseph Lecavorzin) 29, enters (235)

Feb 16   Jules (Guillaume-Victor Glaume) 17, enters (236)

Feb 16   *Flavien (Louis-Victor Manceau) 21, dies (176)*

Feb 18   Prudence (Joseph Loiseau) 26, enters (237)

Feb 27   Basilde (Justin Renault) 18, enters (238)

Mar 17   Joseph de Jésus (Gentien-Julien Faucheux) 21, enters (239)

Apr []   *Philibert (Louis Launay) 19, leaves (183)*

May 15   Félix (Adolphe Guenes) 30, enters (240)

June []   *Paulin (_____ Cannet) [age unknown], sent away (117)*

July 1	Jérôme (François Fourmont) 32, leaves (131)

July 1   *Jérôme (François Fourmont) 32, leaves (131)*
July 12   Léopold (Pierre-Nicholas Putiot) 25, enters (241)
July []   *Jérôme (François Fourmont) 27, leaves (131)*
Aug 5   *Armand (Armand Maisonnier) 19, sent away (90)*
Aug []   *Antoine (Joseph Jousse) 37, leaves (32)*
Aug []   *Barnabé (Louis Balleux) 31, leaves again (186)*
Aug []   *Avit (Sébastien Bunel) 27, sent away (192)*
Aug []   *Louis (Etienne-Joseph Rouillon) 16, sent away (198)*
Aug []   *Philéas (Henri Gonet) 19, leaves (218)*
Aug []   *Marie (Julien-Marie Paquet) 44, sent away (194)*
Sept 8   *Emeri (Louis Guerin) 16, leaves (197)*
Sept []   *Alexandre (Paul Gautier) 21, sent away (118)*
Sept []   *Isaac (François-Clément Coutard) 18, leaves (172)*
Sept []   *Hilaire (Silvin Vernon) 30, leaves (207)*
Oct 1   *Ignace (Pierre Hureau) 34, leaves again (2)*
Oct?   *Germain (Pierre-Antoine Blin) 38, leaves (44)*
Oct []   *René (René-Michel Lépineau) 39, sent away (87)*
Nov 17   *Saturnin (François Oger) 22, leaves (65)*
Nov 21   *Siméon (Charles Bouvier) 23, dies (49)*
Nov []   *François-Xavier (François Fleurinet) [age unknown], leaves (174)*
Nov []   *Barthélémy (Joseph Monvoisin) 31, leaves (217)*
Dec 27   *Benoît (François Bazile) 18, sent away (100)*
[   ]   Théodoret (_____ Essellard) [age unknown] enters (230)
[   ]   François de Paule (_____ Hureau) [age unknown] enters (231)
[   ]   Silvestre (_____ Hubert) [age unknown] enters (232)
[   ]   Victor (_____ Huet) [age unknown] enters (233)
[   ]   Anastase (_____ Messager) [age unknown] enters (234)
[   ]   *Bertin (Jean Bouthmis) 26, leaves (222)*
[   ]   *Florentin (Jean-Amand Mottay) 26, leaves (229)*
[   ]   *Théodoret (_____ Essellard) [age unknown], leaves (230)*
[   ]   *François de Paule (_____ Hureau) [age unknown], leaves (231)*
[   ]   *Silvestre (_____ Hubert) [age unknown], leaves (232)*
[   ]   *Victor (_____ Huet) [age unknown], leaves (233)*
[   ]   *Anastase (_____ Messager) [age unknown], leaves (234)*
[   ]   *Jules (Guillaume-Victor Glaume) 18, leaves (236)*
[   ]   *Basilde (Justin Renault) 19, leaves (238)*   **100 + 12 – 33 = 79**

1831

Jan 14	*Joseph de Jésus (Gentien-Julien Faucheux) 22, leaves (239)*
Feb []	*Ulphace (Louis Oger) 18, leaves (169)*
Mar 21	Salomon (Augustin Mordret) 23, enters (242)
June 1	*Médard (Jean-Michel-Medard Proust) 23, sent away (132)*
June 16	*Marcel (Jean Brard) 20, sent away (147)*
June 18	*Cyprien (Jean Chambon) 32, leaves (72)*
July 7	*Placide (François-Jaqcques Beauté) 23, sent away (129)*
Aug 17	*Théotime (Jean-Pierre Coquand) 31, leaves (182)*
Aug []	*Jean (Jean Vayer) 35, leaves (7)*
Sept []	*Maurice (Pierre Chéan) 25, leaves again (35)*
Sept []	*Jean de la Croix (Jean Cabot) 25, leaves (74)*
Sept 29	*Julien (Jean Neveu) 41, leaves (16)*
Nov 23	Paul (Joseph-Etienne Collet) 25, enters (243)
Nov []	*Joseph (Pierre Bourdon) 25, leaves (12)*
Dec 30	Jean-Baptiste (Jean-Baptiste Beunèche) 20, enters (244)
[ ]	*Denis (René-Auguste Touti) 27, leaves (62)* 79 + 3 - 13 = 69

1832

Feb 8	*Maxime (François Boisramé) 26, dies (66)*
Feb 19	*Théophile (Jean Fréard) 19, dies (135)*
Apr 25	*Sylvain (Louis Veaufleury) 25, leaves (127)*
May []	*Edouard (François-Jean Delalande) 25, leaves (122)*
July 8	Dosithée (François Leblanc) 16, enters (245)
July 24	*François (Pierre François Blanchet) 39, sent away (11)*
Aug 24	*Salomon (Augustin Mordret) 25, leaves (242)*
Aug []	*Gatien (Jean Fouquet) 22, leaves (124)*
Aug []	*Damase (Jean Poilpré) 26, leaves (179)*
Aug []	*Adolphe (Pierre-Philippe Barbot) 19, leaves (224)*
[ ]	*Léon (Louis Mottais) 18, leaves (201)*
[ ]	*Prudence (Joseph Loiseau) 28, leaves (237)* 69 + 1 - 11 = 59

1833

Jan 1	*Eloi (Louis-Jean Cosnier) 36, leaves (141)*
Feb 23	Gatien (Gatien Dutertre) 17, enters (246)
Feb 27	Julien (Julien Henry) 19, enters (247)

Mar 4	*Anaclet (Joseph Hallier) 26, dies (203)*
Mar 30	Laurent (Jean-Joseph Moreau) 21, enters (248)
Apr 25	Patrice (Thomas Brière) 23, enters (249)
May 23	*Théodule (Jean-Marie Hillion) 32, sent away (223)*
Aug 27	Jacques (Jacques Nourry) 33, enters (250)
Aug 28	Barnabé (Louis Grangé) 18, enters (251)
Sept 11	Alphonse (Jacques-Félix Perrin) 19, enters (252)
Oct 9	*Barnabé (Louis Grangé) 18, sent away (251)*
Oct 24	Léon (Vincent-Léon Ringuenoir) 22, enters (253)
Nov 6	Ignace (Louis Boissé) 15, enters (254)
Nov 19	Céleste (François Boissé) 19, enters (255)
Nov 30	Benoît (François Galbin) 26, enters (256)
Dec 2	Eugène (Joseph Desneux) 15, enters (257)
Dec 12	*Laurent (Jean-Joseph Moreau) 22, sent away (248)*
Dec 17	Charles (Jacques-Charles Felquin) 14, enters (258)
Dec 17	Isidore (Pierre Verdier) 14, enters (259)
[ ]	*Grégoire (Julien Lépinay) 23, leaves (47)*
[ ]	Jérôme (François Fourmont) 30, re-enters (131)
[ ]	*Paul (Joseph-Etienne Collet) 28, leaves (243)* **59 + 15 - 7 = 67**

1834

Jan 4	Paul (Jérôme Tessier) 21, enters (260)
Jan 29	Rodolphe (Jean Chollet) 19, enters (261)
Feb 20	Laurent (Joseph Pieau) [age unknown], enters (262)
Mar 20	Daniel (Léon-Etienne Boidier) 23, enters (263)
Apr 3	Pascal (Pascal Thorin) 24, enters (264)
Apr 3	*Laurent (Joseph Pieau) [age unknown], sent away (262)*
June 1	*Pacôme (Louis Laffay) 23, leaves (68)*
June 25	*Rodolphe (Jean Chollet) 19, sent away (261)*
June 27	Victor (Pierre Enjourbault) 18, enters (265)
Aug 9	Ephrem (Pierre-Laurent Guérin) 14, enters (266)
Aug 9	Siméon (Jean-Marin Pieau) 26, enters (267)
Aug 13	Théophile (Thomas-Marie Chainais) 22, enters (268)
Aug 21	Jérémie (Edmond Empetit) 14, enters (269)
Aug 26	Mathurin (Mathurin Rué) 26, enters (270)
Aug 20	*Victorin (Henri Lion) 25, leaves (157)*

Aug 20   *Jean-Baptiste (Jean-Baptiste Beunèche) 23, sent away (244)*

Aug 26   *Eugène (Joseph Desneux) 16, sent away (257)*

Aug []   *Justin (Michel Ragot) 30, leaves (94)*

Aug []   *Cyrille (René Renard) 24, leaves (146)*

Sept 6   *Ignace (Louis Boissé) 16, dies (254)*

Sept 13 *Pascal (Pascal Thorin) 25, leaves (264)*

Sept 19 Gerault (Julien-Vincent Chauvois) 28, enters (271)

Sept 21 *Céleste (François Boissé) 21, dies (255)*

Oct 2   *Henri (Michel Taupin) 42, leaves (36)*

Oct 4   *Abraham (Joseph-Louis Veaufleury) 27, dies (105)*

[   ]   *Théophile (Thomas-Marie Chainais) 22, leaves (268)*   **67 + 12 - 14 = 65**

1835

Feb 2   *Charles (Jacques-Charles Felquin) 15, leaves (258)*

Feb 4   *Benoît (François Galbin) 27, sent away (256)*

May 29   *Ephrem (Pierre-Laurent Guerin) 14, leaves (266)*

May []   *Benjamin (Benjamin Poirier) 34, sent away (25)*

Sept 6   *Ignace (Louis Boissé) 17, dies (254)*

Sept 21 *Céleste (François Boissé) 21, dies (255)*

Sept [] *Jean Chrysostôme (Joseph Lecavorzin) 34, leaves (235)*

Oct 30   Hilaire (Pierre Beaury) 18, enters (282)

Nov 16   Sosthènes (François Radiguet) 16, enters (283)

Dec 11   Charles (Jacques-Charles Felquin) 16, re-enters (258)

Dec 14   Narcisse (Jean-François Hulot) 18, enters (280)

Dec []   *Louis de Gonzague (Louis-Michel Gondard) 22, sent away (221)*

[   ]   Philippe de Néri (Jean-Baptiste Bougault) 33, re-enters (38)

[   ]   Auguste (François-Joseph Bodinier) 19, enters (281)

[   ]   Jean-Marie (Toussaint-Julien Gigon) 49, enters (284)   **65 + 7 - 8 = 64**

1836

Jan 1   *Jérôme (François Fourmont) 32, sent away (131)*

Jan 8   *Thomas d'Aquin (Alexandre Meleux-Laperriere) 20, dies (205)*

Jan []   *Basile (René Derouet) 38, sent away (15)*

Feb 2   Thomas d'Aquin (Jean-Baptiste Garnier) 15, enters (279)

Feb 20   Clément (François Deschamps) 26, enters (287)

Feb 29   *Sébastien (Pierre Poirier) 33, sent away (145)*

Feb []	*Léon (Vincent-Léon Ringuenoir) 25, leaves (253)*
Mar 4	*Julien (Julien Henry) 22, dies (247)*
Mar 8	Hyacinthe (Louis-Stanislas-Xavier Côme) 20, enters (286)
Mar 22	*Isidore (Pierre Verdier) 16, sent away (259)*
Apr 9	Grégoire de Nazianze (Henri Leroy) 13, enters (289)
July 19	*Bernard (Gilles Lecavorsin) 41, leaves (178)*
July 26	*Alphonse (Jacques-Félix Perrin) 22, sent away (252)*
July 26	*Emile (Joseph-Zacharie Barat) 27, sent away (293)*
July 27	*Daniel (Léon-Etienne Boidier) 25, sent away (263)*
Aug []	*Jérémie (Edmond Empetit) 15, leaves (269)*
Aug []	*Antoine (Jules Joubert) 14, leaves (294)*
Oct 15	*Benoît (Jean Plantay) 40, leaves (290)*
Nov []	*Isidore (François Leroy) 40, sent away (291)*
Dec 1	Louis de Gonzague (Pierre Galmard) 19, enters (308)
[ ]	*Charles (Jacques-Charles Felquin) 17, leaves again (258)*
[ ]	*Eustache (François Marchand) 33, leaves (126)*
[ ]	*Victor (Pierre Enjourbault) 20, leaves (265)*
[ ]	François d'Assise (Nicolas-Pierre Drouin) 18, enters (285)
[ ]	Louis (François-Julien-Michel Letessier) 39, enters (288)
[ ]	Benoît (Jean Plantay) 40, enters (290)
[ ]	Isidore (François Leroy) 40, enters (291)
[ ]	Alexandre (François-Pierre Bédouet) 29, enters (292)
[ ]	Emile (Joseph-Zacharie Barat) 27, enters (293)
[ ]	Antoine (Jules Joubert) 14, enters (294)
[ ]	Adolphe (Pierre-André Moriceau) 15, enters (295)
[ ]	Agathange (Victor-Pierre Dagonneau) 16, enters (296)
[ ]	Camille (Louis Gastineau) 25, enters (297)
[ ]	Roch (Pierre-François Cabaré) 19, enters (298)
[ ]	Jérôme (François Régnier) 23, enters (299) **64 + 17 − 18 = 63**

1837

Jan 18	Basile (Michel Gary) 24, enters (311)
Feb 26	*Roch (Pierre-François Cabaré) 20, leaves (298)*
Mar 30	Roch (Pierre-François Cabaré) 20, re-enters (298)
Apr 7	Théodore (François Feau) 12, enters (313)
May 3	Zacharie (Jean-Baptiste Cognet) 19, enters (314)

May 20	Hilarion (Louis Ferton) 20, enters (315)
June 28	*François d'Assise (Nicolas-Pierre Drouin) 19, dies (285)*
July 1	*Roch (Pierre-François Cabaré) 20, sent away (298)*
July []	*Félix (Adolphe Guenes) 37, sent away (240)*
July []	*Gatien (Gatien Dutertre) 22, leaves (246)*
Sept 1	*Alexandre (François-Pierre Bédouet) 29, leaves (292)*
Sept 1	*Camille (Louis Gastineau) 25, leaves (297)*
Sept 15	*Thomas d'Aquin (Jean-Baptiste Garnier) 16, leaves (279)*
Nov 16	Valéry (Jean Bruneau) 18, enters (307)
Dec 10	Alexandre (François-Pierre Bédouet) 30, re-enters (292)
[ ]	Aldric (Etienne Anglade) 17, enters (304)
[ ]	Hildebert (Alexandre Jarry) 17, enters (305)
[ ]	Gonzales (Romain Angot) 19, enters (306)
[ ]	Sylvain (Joseph-François Lesné) 22, enters (309)
[ ]	*Sylvain (Joseph-François Lesné) 23, sent away (309)*
[ ]	Roch (René Loisnard) 15, enters (310)
[ ]	Gabriel (Victor Chédebois) 22, enters (312)
[ ]	Théophile (_____ Hervé) 18, enters (316)
[ ]	Henri (René Compain) 19, enters (317)

63 + 15 − 9 = 69

1838

Jan 4	Elie (Auguste-Nicholas-Patrice Pérony) 22, enters (338)
Jan 19	Julien (François Corbin), 22, enters (350)
Jan 30	*Siméon (Jean-Marin Pieau) 29, leaves (267)*
Jan 31	*Jacques (Jacques Nourry) 37, leaves (250)*
Feb 8	*Dosithée (François Leblanc) 21, dies (245)*
Feb 15	Eugène (Constant-Julien Leroux) 14, enters (339)
Feb 23	*François Régis (François Prioux) 25, leaves (320)*
Feb []	*Gerault (Julien-Vincent Chauvois) 32, leaves (271)*
Mar 1	Edmond (René Marteau)19, enters (340)
Mar 5	Emmanuel (Léon-Pierre-Marie Guyon) 14, enters (341)
Mar 10	*Louis (François-Julien-Michel Letessier) 40, leaves (288)*
Apr 20	*Mathurin (Mathurin Rué) 30, leaves (270)*
Apr 21	*Gabriel (Victor Chédebois) 22, leaves (312)*
Apr 28	*Victor (Jacques Delmas) 17, leaves (327)*
May 8	*Almire (Nicolas Eustache) 27, leaves (321)*

May 8	Héliodore (Joseph-Clément Leblanc)17, enters (344)
May 21	*Henri (René Compain) 20, leaves (317)*
June 4	Placide (Urbain Alard) 26, enters (351)
June 6	*Liboire (André Gelin) 19, leaves (329)*
June 10	Hippolyte (Léonard-Louis-François Pieau) 13, enters (346)
June 12	*Hippolyte (René Roboam) 19, leaves (324)*
June 17	Justin (Louis Gautier) 37, enters (373)
July 2	Théodule (François Barbé) 20, enters (347)
July 9	Léon (Norbert-Auguste Cotin) 19, enters (345)
July 25	*Auguste (François-Joseph Bodinier) 22, leaves (281)*
Aug 11	Saturnin (François Oger) 29, re-enters (65)
Aug 11	Bernard (Adolphe-Jean Legras) 14, enters (352)
Aug 11	Dosithée (René Pierre Foret) 16, enters (353)
Aug 19	*Saturnin (François Oger) 29, leaves again (65)*
Aug []	*Hildebert (Alexandre Jarry) 19, leaves (305)*
Sept 16	Isidore (Michel-Céleste Garnier) 15, enters (323)
Sept 18	Liguori (Louis Guyard) 18, enters (355)
Oct 1	Maxime (François Berger) 13, enters (356)
Oct 16	*Ferdinand (André Lérourneau) 30, leaves (330)*
Oct []	*Bruno (Paul-Jean Bouilly) 33, sent away (97)*
Nov 8	*Blaise (Louis Vermeil) 23, leaves (349)*
Nov 18	*Roch (René Loisnard) 16, leaves (310)*
Nov 29	Sylvain (Victor-Ephrem-Marie Gareau) 15, enters (367)
Dec 1	*Anatole (Louis Veau) 13, leaves (342)*
Dec 14	François-Xavier (Joseph Ménand) 16, enters (368)
[ ]	François Régis (François Prioux) 25, enters (320)
[ ]	Almire (Nicolas Eustache) 26, enters (321)
[ ]	Edouard (Louis Moutain) 13, enters (322)
[ ]	Hippolyte (René Roboam) 19, enters (324)
[ ]	Gustave (Eugène Rose) 14, enters (325)
[ ]	Antoine (Jean Bersange) 15, enters (326)
[ ]	Victor (Jacques Delmas) 17, enters (327)
[ ]	Marie (Louis Gizard) 16, enters (328)
[ ]	Liboire (André Gelin) 18, enters (329)
[ ]	Ferdinand (André Lérourneau) 30, enters (330)
[ ]	Jules (Pierre Heurtebize) 16, enters (331)

[   ] Alfred (Eugène-Dominique Gônet) 27, enters (332)

[   ] Joachim (Auguste Reimbert) 31, enters (333)

[   ] Louis (_____ Garreau) age unknown, enters (336)

[   ] Ernest (Joseph Nicolas Fournier) 13, enters (337)

[   ] Anatole (Louis Veau) 13, enters (342)

[   ] Joseph (Emmanuel Gandais) 14, enters (343)

[   ] Blaise (Louis Vermeil) 23, enters (349)

[   ] Joseph (Jean-Baptiste Pottier) 17, enters (354)

[   ] François d'Assise (Jean Biron) 17, enters (357)

[   ] Benoît (François Guiller) 19, enters (358)

[   ] Moïse (Pierre Plédran) 37, enters (359)

[   ] Bruno (Bernard Audoux) 19, enters (360)

[   ] Frédéric (Louis Boinay) 16, enters (361)

[   ] Alexandre (Prosper Lehoux) 14, enters (362)

[   ] Gabriel (Hippolyte Marcheaux) 19, enters (363)

[   ] Ambroise (Georges Parel) 35, enters (364)

[   ] Ferdinand (Pierre Pivière) 16, enters (365)

[   ] Valentin (Louis Masseron) 15, enters (366) $69 + 48 - 21 = 96$

1839

Jan 15   *Anatole (Louis Veau) 13, leaves (342)*

Jan 17   *Aldric (Etienne Anglade) 18, leaves (304)*

Feb 21   *Alexandre (François-Pierre Bédouet) 31, leaves again (292)*

June 22   *Moïse (Pierre Plédran) 38, enters (359)*

Aug 1   *Théophile (_____ Hervé) 20, leaves (316)*

Aug 5   *Gonzales (Romain Angot) 21, leaves (306)*

Aug 20   *Ernest (Joseph Nicolas Fournier) 14, leaves (337)*

Aug []   *Gabriel (Victor Chédebois) 24, re-enters (312)*

Sept 6   *Jules (Pierre Heurtebize) 18, leaves (331)*

Sept 6   *Alfred (Eugène-Dominique Gônet) 27, leaves (332)*

Sept 8   *Antoine (Jean Bersange) 17, leaves (326)*

Sept 8   *Marie (Louis Gizard) 17, leaves (328)*

Sept 8   *François d'Assise (Jean Biron) 17, leaves (357)*

Sept 10   *Louis (_____ Garreau) age unknown, leaves (336)*

Oct 9   *Césaire (Alexis Poirier) 32, leaves (70)*

Oct 15   *Jérôme (François Régnier) 25, leaves (299)*

Oct 18	*Bruno (Bernard Audoux) 20, leaves (360)*	
Oct 19	Jules (Pierre Heurtebize) 18, re-enters (331)	
Dec 28	*Joachim (Auguste Reimbert) 33, leaves (333)*	96 + 3 -16 = 83

1840

Mar 16	*Ambroise (Georges Parel) 37, leaves (364)*	
Aug 1	*Benoît (François Guiller) 20, leaves (358)*	
Aug 3	*Adolphe (Pierre-André Moriceau) 18, leaves (295)*	
Aug 3	*Alexandre (Prosper Lehoux) 16, leaves (362)*	
Aug 3	*Valentin (Louis Masseron) 17, leaves (366)*	
Aug 23	Ferdinand (Pierre Pivière) 18, enters (365)	
Sept 25	Mathias (Mathias Chapelière) 42, re-enters (167)	
Oct []	*Mathias (Mathias Chapelière) 42, leaves again (167)*	83 + 2 -6 = 79

1841

Jan 10	*Casimir (Julien Bardou) 29, dies (134)*	
Apr 14	*Gervais (Jean Guibon) 32, leaves (220)*	
July 8	*Gabriel (Hippolyte Marcheaux) 21, dismissed (363)*	
Aug 7	Gervais (Jean Guibon) 32, re-enters (220)	
Aug 20	*Dominique (Pierre Gautier) 35, sent away (17)*	
Aug 24	*Philippe de Néri (Jean-Baptiste Bougault) 40, dies (38)*	
Aug []	*Abel (Abel Guyon) 47, leaves (219)*	
Aug []	*Joseph (Jean-Baptiste Pottier) 20, leaves (354)*	
Sept 13	*Célestin (Louis Forton) 27, dies (170)*	
Nov 13	*Gervais (Jean Guibon) 33, leaves again (220)*	
[ ]	*Edouard (Louis Moutain) 17, leaves (322)*	

1842

| Aug 5 | *Gabriel (Victor Chédebois) 27, leaves again (312)* | |
| [   ] | *Frédéric (Louis Boinay) 20, leaves (361)* | |

1843

| Nov 4 | Mathias (Mathias Chapelière) 45, re-enters (3rd time) (167) | |
| Dec 12 | Gonzales (Romain Angot) 26, re-enters (306) | |

1844

Mar 16   André (André Pierre Mottais) 44, dies (4)

Mar 16   Gonzales (Romain Angot) 26, leaves again (306)

Mar 27   Mathias (Mathias Chapelière) 45, leaves again (3rd time) (167)

Apr 20   Paul (Jérôme Tessier) 31, sent away (260)

Aug []   Théodose (Louis-Michel Prieul) 32, leaves (228)

Aug []   Agathange (Victor-Pierre Dagonneau) 24, leaves (296)

1845

Aug 8   Gustave (Eugène Rose) 22, leaves (325)

Aug 17   Jules (Pierre Heurtebize) 24, leaves again (331)

1846

May 31   Liguori (Louis Guyard) 27, leaves (355)

1847

Dec 26   Théodore (François Feau) 23, leaves (313)

1848

Aug 25   Héliodore (Joseph-Clément Leblanc)28, leaves (344)

Sept 16   Donatien (André-Louis-Paul Nail) 42, leaves (215)

1849

Aug 2   Maxime (François Berger) 25, leaves (356)

Oct 15   Hilarion (Louis Ferton) 32, dies (315)

1850

Apr 22   Dorothée (Joseph Bigot) 47, leaves (98)

June 7   Dorothée (Joseph Bigot) 47, re-enters (98)

Oct 20   Raphael (Arsène Forton) 33, leaves (180)

Nov 6   Placide (Urbain Alard) 38, dies (351)

1851

Jan 29   Marie-Joseph (Pierre-Joseph Duval) 46, sent away (50)

Apr 1 [?]   Dorothée (Joseph Bigot) 70 dies (98)

Sept 2   Clément (François Deschamps) 42, dies (287)

Sept 6   *Etienne (Etienne Gauffre) 58, dies (5)*

July 5   *Jean-Marie (Toussaint-Julien Gigon) 65, dies (284)*

1852

Mar 25   *Irénée (Joseph-Almire Trassard-Deslandes) 44, dies (111)*

July 15   *Hippolyte (Léonard-Louis-François Pieau) 27, leaves (346)*

1853

Mar 24   *François d'Assise (François-Marie Tulou) 55, dies (166)*

June 25   *Théodule (François Barbé) 45, dies (347)*

1856

May 10   *Bonaventure (Pierre Tulou) 59, dies (165)*

1857

May 8   *Donatien (André-Louis-Paul Nail) 51, re-enters (215)*

1859

Aug 6   *Isidore (Michel-Céleste Garnier) 37, leaves (323)*

Aug 25   *Baptiste (Baptiste Verger) 61, dies (8)*

1860

June 1   *Marin (Michel Bulanger) 64, dies (30)*

Dec 3   *Augustin (Jean-Baptiste Riet) 60, dies (13)*

1864

Jan []   *Dosithée (René Pierre Foret) 41, leaves (353)*

Oct []   *Emmanuel (Léon-Pierre-Marie Guyon) 40, leaves (341)*

Nov 13   *Léopold (Pierre-Nicholas Putiot) 59, dies (241)*

1865

May 24   *Martin (Jean Verger) 66, dies (20)*

1866

Apr 28   *Jean-Climaque (Jean-Baptiste Contamin) 68, dies (101)*

1867

June 21   *Ernest (Joseph Nicolas Fournier) 53, dies (337)*

1869

Aug 15   *Edmond (René Marteau) 50, leaves (340)*

Sept 15   *Pierre (Pierre Oger) 64, dies (14)*

1870

Jan 10   *Romain (François Bouvier) 69, dies (42)*

Dec 20   *Justin (Louis Gautier) 69, dies (373)*

1871

Jan 7   *Alexis (Jean-Pierre Chabrun) 61, dies (64)*

1873

Feb 24   *Athanase (Michel-Etienne Tarault) 72, dies (92)*

Apr 1   *Dorothée (Joseph Bigot) 70, dies (98)*

Apr 14   *Adrien (Louis Legeai) 70, dies (76)*

Aug 22   *Vincent-de-Paul (Jean-Baptiste Vincent Plat) 67, dies (82)*

1875

Aug 4   *Patrice (Thomas Brière) 65, dies (249)*

1876

Aug 12   *Onésime (Mathurin-Pierre-François Pillard) 79, dies (164)*

1879

July 8   *Marc (François-Charles-Marthe Galinand) 77, dies (104)*

1880

June 5   *Macaire (Guillaume-Michel Chauvin) 70 dies (227)*

1881

Aug 30   *Bernard (Adolphe-Jean Legras) 57, dies (352)*

1882

116

Dec 2   *Antonin (Pierre Lefèbvre) 77, dies (189)*

1883

Oct 31   *Arsène (Louis-Pierre Bouvet) 78, dies (61)*

Dec 18   *Valéry (Jean Bruneau) 65, dies (307)*

1886

Feb 27   *Donatien (André-Louis-Paul Nail) 80, dies (215)*

June 30   *Vital (Auguste-Casimir Breton) 77, dies (85)*

1887

June 9   *Léonard (Pierre-François Guittoger) 84, dies (106)*

Dec 29   *Narcisse (Jean-François Hulot) 70, dies (280)*

1888

Feb 12   *Rémi (Etienne Mérianne) 79, dies (79)*

May 9   *Stanislas (Louis-Joseph-Grégoire Derve) 84, dies (88)*

May 12   *Matthieu (Pierre Plumard) 79, dies (112)*

Dec 13   *Basile (Michel Gary) 76, dies (311)*

Dec 23   *François-Xavier (Joseph Ménand) 64, dies (368)*

1889

June 4   *Lucien (Alphonse-François Dagoreau) 77, dies (195)*

1890

July 23   *Vincent (Jean Pieau) 93, dies (18)*

Nov 21   *Hilaire (Pierre Beaury 81, dies (282)*

1892

Nov 24   *Julien (François Corbin), 76, dies (350)*

1893

Feb 12   *Louis de Gonzague (Pierre Galmard) 76, dies (308)*

1894

Jan 21   *Léon (Norbert-Auguste Cotin) 74, dies (345)*

Feb 8   *Elisée (Félix-Hippolyte Réau) 81, dies (193)*

1897

May 7   *Zacharie (Jean-Baptiste Cognet) 79, dies (314)*

1900

Aug 31   *Grégoire de Nazianze (Henri Leroy) 77, dies (289)*

1904

May 29   *Sylvain (Victor-Ephrem-Marie Gareau) 81, dies (367)*

1913

April 17   *Eugène (Constant-Julien Leroux) 79, dies (339)*

APPENDIX II

Brothers of St. Joseph Arranged by Date of Entry

1820

2. Ignace	Pierre Hureau	left 1821, left 1830
3. Louis	Louis Duchêne	dismissed 1825
4. André	André Mottais	died 1844
5. Etienne	Etienne Gauffre	died 1851

1821

6. Michel	Michel Jouseau	left 1829
7. Jean	Jean Vayer	left 1831
8. Baptiste	[Baptiste] Verger	died 1859
9. Charles	Charles Faribault	left 1826
10. Victor	Victor Loupil	left 1828
11. François	Pierre François Blanchet	dismissed 1832

1822

12. Joseph	Pierre Bourdon	left 1831
13. Augustin	Jean-Baptiste Riet	died 1860
14. Pierre	Pierre Oger	died 1869
15. Basile	René Derouet	dismissed 1836
16. Julien	Jean Neveu	left 1831
17. Dominique	Pierre Gautier	dismissed 1841
18. Vincent	Jean Pieau	died 1890

19. Bernard	_____ Bonneau	dismissed 1825
20. Martin	Jean Verger	died 1865
21. Pascal	François Gareau	dismissed 1823
22. Léon	Jean Marsollier	left 1823
23. Arsène	Arsène Echard	dismissed 1823
24. Felix	Jean Taupin	dismissed 1826
25. Benjamin	Benjamin Poirier	dismissed 1835
26. Daniel	Pierre Launay	left 1825, left 1828

1823

27. Stanislaus	Jean Blaise	dismissed 1823
28. Paul	Paul Petit	left 1828
29. Athanase	Charles Richard	dismissed 1823
30. Marin	Michel Bulanger	died 1860
31. Dorothée	Armand-Adolphe Aumas	dismissed 1824
32. Antoine	Joseph Jousse	left 1830
33. Clément	Louis-François Pottier	left 1824
34. Alexis	Alexis-Alexandre Poule-Dupré	left 1824
35. Maurice	Pierre Chéan	left 1825, left 1831
36. Henri	Michel Taupin	left 1834
37. Isidore	Isidore Bouvier	left 1824
38. Philippe de Néri	Jean-Baptiste Bougault	left 1829, died 1842
39. Eléonore	Eléonore Hulot	dismissed 1824
40. René	René Fromentin	dismissed 1824
41. Thadée	Pierre Papin	left 1828
42. Romain	François Bouvier	died 1870
43. Elie	Jean Letessier	left 1825
44. Germain	Pierre-Antoine Blin	left 1830
45. Eusèbe	Jean-Pierre Coudriou	left 1825

1824

46. Léon-Louis de Gonzague	Louis Pottier	left 1826
47. Grégoire	Julien Lépinay	left 1833
48. Alexandre	Pierre Neveu	left 1825
49. Siméon	Charles Bouvier	died 1830
50. Marie-Joseph	Pierre-Joseph Duval	dismissed 1851

51. Jean-Baptiste	Jean-Baptiste Lardeau	left 1825
52. Jérôme	René Porcheré	died 1826
53. Pascal	Pierre Bignon	left 1828
54. Simon	Simon Guy	left 1826
55. Zozime	Pierre Desmares-Vicaire	left 1824
56. Jacques	Jacques Hamon	dismissed 1825
57. Isidore	René-Isidore Janvier	left 1828
58. Jean-Marie	Jean-Marie Gauchet	died 1826
59. Laurent	Joseph Chartier	dismissed 1826
60. Gabriel	Pierre Marsollier	left 1828
61. Arsène	Louis-Pierre Bouvet	died 1883
62. Denis	René-Auguste Touti	left 1831
63. Didier	Jean-Didier Mousseau	left 1825
64. Alexis	Jean-Pierre Chabrun	died 1871
65. Saturnin	François Oger	left 1830, left 1838
66. Maxime	François Boisramé	died 1832
67. Hilarion	Jean Lagarde	left 1826
68. Pacôme	Louis Laffay	left 1834
69. Thomas	Jacques-Thomas Peloille	left 1826
70. Césaire	Alexis Poirier	left 1839
71. Sévère	Jean-Louis Bellouard	dismissed 1825
72. Cyprien	Jean Chambon	left 1831
73. Fulgence	René Ridereau	dismissed 1825
74. Jean de la Croix	Jean Cabot	left 1831

1825

75. Hermas	_____ _____	left 1825
76. Adrien	Louis Legeai	died 1873
77. Abraham	Etienne Cormier	left 1825
78. Jean de Dieu	Louis Duportail	dismissed 1825
79. Rémi	Etienne Mérianne	died 1888
80. Ambroise	Pierre Dupont	dismissed 1825
81. Hippolyte	François Dureau	dismissed 1827
82. Vincent-de-Paul	Jean-Baptiste Vincent Plat	left 1829, died 1873
83. Hilaire	Augustin Jubault	dismissed 1826
84. Bertrand	Pierre Paineau	left 1828

85. Vital	Auguste-Casimir Breton	died 1886
86. Edmond	François Edon	dismissed 1826
87. René	René-Michel Lépineau	dismissed 1830
88. Stanislas	Louis-Joseph-Grégoire Derve	died 1888
89. Urbain	Louis Jubault	dismissed 1825
90. Armand	Armand Maisonnier	dismissed 1830
91. Prosper	Guillaume Herbelle	dismissed 1828
92. Athanase	Michel-Etienne Tarault	died 1873
93. Théophile	Alexandre-Jean Cosson	left 1825
94. Justin	Michel Ragot	left 1834
95. Théodore	René Gouadon	dismissed 1825
96. Symphorien	Denis Bourgneuf	dismissed 1826
97. Bruno	Paul-Jean Bouilly	dismissed 1838
98. Dorothée	Joseph Bigot	left 1850, died 1873
99. Epiphane	Jean-Simon Billard	left 1829
100. Benoît	François Bazile	dismissed 1830
101. Jean-Climaque	Jean-Baptiste Contamin	died 1866
102. Alphonse	Julien Landemaine	left 1828, left 1829
103. Almire	Charles-François Lelièvre	dismissed 1826
104. Marc	François-Charles-Marthe Galinand	died 1879
105. Abraham	Joseph-Louis Veaufleury	died 1834
106. Léonard	Pierre-François Guittoger	died 1887
107. Ambroise	Victor-Gabriel-Charles Corbière	dismissed 1826
108. Elie	Joseph Rétif	left 1829
109. Hyacinthe	Hyacinthe Hutin	left 1827
110. Léandre	Léandre Debray	left 1827
111. Iréné	Joseph-Almire Trassard-Deslandes	died 1852
112. Matthieu	Pierre Plumard	died 1888
113. Constantin	Jean Vivens	left 1828
114. Clément	Pierre-Jacques Richard	dismissed 1826
115. Eugène	Louis-Gustave Fossé	left 1826
116. Gervais	Pierre Esnault	left (?) 1826

1826

| 117. Paulin | _____ Cannet | dismissed 1830 |
| 118. Alexandre | Paul Gautier | dismissed 1830 |

119. Anselme	René Mercier	left 1828
120. Magloire	Pierre-Charles Sage	left 1826
121. Jean-Baptiste	Jean-François Guilmet	dis. 1826, left 1828
122. Edouard	François-Jean Delalande	left 1832
123. Marie	François-Jean-Marie Delorière	left 1827
124. Gatien	Jean Fouquet	left 1832
125. Eugène	Pierre James	left 1828
126. Eustache	François Marchand	left 1836
127. Sylvain	Louis Veaufleury	left 1832
128. Jérôme	François Emond	dismissed 1826
129. Placide	François-Jacques Beauté	dismissed 1831
130. Damien	Jean-François Pivard	left 1826
131. Jérôme	François Fourmont	left 1830, dis. 1836
132. Médard	Jean-Michel-Médard Proust	dismissed 1831
133. Honoré	Auguste-François Brunet	left 1827
134. Casimir	Julien Bardou	died 1841
135. Théophile	Jean Fréard	died 1832
136. Hilaire	Matthieu-Charles Bourgeteau	dismissed 1826
137. Georges	Victor Guisbé	dismissed 1827
138. Barthélémy	Julien-Mathieu-Louis Guinegaut	dismissed 1827
139. Thomas	François Cochon	dismissed 1827
140. Jude	Henri-Baptiste Bougault	left 1827
141. Eloi	Louis-Jean Cosnier	left 1833
142. Frumence	Pierre Saulnier	left 1827
143. Quentin	Augustin Chesnel	dismissed 1827
144. Ambroise	Louis-Ambroise-Marie Desloriers	dismissed 1827
145. Sébastien	Pierre Poirier	dis. 1828, dis. 1836
146. Cyrille	René Renard	left 1834
147. Marcel	Jean Brard	left 1828, dis. 1831
148. Gervais	Pierre-Jacques-Gervais Langlois	dismissed 1827
149. Charles	Charles Rousseau	left 1827
150. Louis	Auguste Ménage	left 1827
151. Eusèbe	Armand Béranger	left 1828
152. Liboire	Marie-François Meunier	dismissed 1828
153. Mathurin	Pierre Leroyer	left 1829
154. Nicolas	Jules-Nicolas Guesnot	dismissed 1827

1827

155. Victorin	Jean Brunet	left 1827
156. Liboire	Elie Launay	left 1828
157. Victorin	Henri Lion	left 1834
158. Laurent	Antoine Rouchy	dismissed 1829
159. Christophe	Christophe Murat	left 1829
160. Silvestre	Ambroise Corni	left 1827
161. Agathange	Nicolas Berson	left 1828
162. Zozime	Ferdinand Prout	left 1827
163. Norbert	Louis Bailleul	left 1827
164. Onézime	Mathurin-Pierre-François Pillard	died 1876
165. Bonaventure	Pierre Tulou	died 1856
166. François d'Assise	François-Marie Tulou	died 1853
167. Mathias	Mathias Chapelière	dis. 1828, left 1840, left 1844
168. Florent	Jean-Rodolphe Jouandy	dismissed 1827
169. Ulphace	Louis Oger	left 1831
170. Célestin	Louis Forton	died 1842
171. Théodoret	Grégoire Gilette	left 1828
172. Isaac	François-Clément Coutard	left 1830
173. Gérasime	Florent Duval	left 1828
174. François-Xavier	François Fleurinet	left 1830
175. Principe	Principe Manoury	left 1827
176. Flavien	Louis-Victor Manceau	left 1828, died 1830
177. Jean-Chrysostôme	Jean Martin	left 1828
178. Bernard	Gilles Lecavorsin	left 1836
179. Damase	Jean Poilpré	left 1832
180. Raphael	Arsène Forton	left 1850
181. Philippe	————— —————	left 1828

1828

182. Théotime	Jean-Pierre Coquand	left 1831
183. Philibert	Louis Launay	left 1830
184. Théodore	Vital Chaumezière	left 1829
185. Clément	Clément Chéron	dismissed 1828
186. Barnabé	Louis Balleux	left 1828, left 1830

124

187. François de Paule	Victor Défourneaux	left 1828
188. Dosithée	Jean-Marie Tulou	left 1828
189. Antonin	Pierre Lefèbvre	died 1882
190. Jean-François	François-Jean Royer	left 1828
191. Samuel	Louis Frêne	dismissed 1829
192. Avit	Sébastien Bunel	dismissed 1830
193. Elisée	Félix-Hippolyte Réau	died 1894
194. Marie	Julien-Marie Paquet	dismissed 1830
195. Lucien	Alphonse-François Dagoreau	died 1889
196. Honoré	Pierre Bouhour	left 1828
197. Emeri	Louis Guérin	left 1830
198. Louis	Etienne-Joseph Rouillon	dismissed 1820
199. Charles	Ferdinand Raimond	left 1829
200. Firmin	Alexis Gorget	dismissed 1829
201. Léon	Louis Mottais	left 1832
202. Corentin	Corentin Chevalier	dismissed 1828
203. Anaclet	Joseph Hallier	left 1829, died 1833
204. Chrysostôme	Pierre David	left 1828
205. Thomas d'Aquin	Alexandre Meleux-Laperrière	died 1836
206. Georges	Georges Lorain-Laval	dismissed 1829
207. Hilaire	Silvin Vernon	left 1830
208. Gervais	François Houlbert	dismissed 1828
209. Simon	Michel Péard	left 1828
210. Rodriguez	_____ Besnard	left 1829
211. Zozime	_____ Cossom	left 1829
212. Eugène	_____ Dubriel	left 1829

1829

213. Jules	Jean Chancerel	dismissed 1829
214. Gervais	Augustin Bernier	dismissed 1829
215. Donatien	André-Louis-Paul Nail	left 1848, died 1886
216. Jude	René Maçon	left 1829
217. Barthélémy	Joseph Monvoisin	left 1830
218. Philéas	Henri Gonet	left 1830
219. Abel	Abel Guyon	left 1842
220. Gervais	Jean Guibon	left 1837, left 1842

221. Louis de Gonzague	Louis-Michel Gondard	dismissed 1835
222. Bertin	Jean Bouthmis	left 1830
223. Théodule	Jean-Marie Hillion	dismissed 1833
224. Adolphe	Pierre-Philippe Barbot	left 1832
225. Moise	Joseph Marin Boureau	left 1829
226. Théodore	Alain-Marie Mevel	left 1829
227. Macaire	Guillaume-Michel Chauvin	died 1880
228. Théodore	Louis-Michel Prieul	left 1844
229. Florentin	Jean-Amand Mottay	left 1830
230. Théodoret	_____ Essellard	left 1830
231. François de Paule	_____ Hureau	left 1830
232. Silvestre	_____ Hubert	left 1830
233. Victor	_____ Huet	left 1830
234. Anastase	_____ Messager	left 1830

1830

235. Jean-Chrysostôme	Joseph Lacavorzin	left 1835
236. Jules	Guillaume-Victor Glaume	left 1830
237. Prudence	Joseph Loiseau	left 1832
238. Basilde	Justin Renault	left 1830
239. Joseph de Jésus	Gentien-Julien Faucheux	left 1831
240. Félix	Adolphe Guenes	dismissed 1837
241. Léopold	Pierre-Nicholas Putiot	died 1864

1831

242. Salomon	Augustin Mordret	left 1832
243. Paul	Joseph-Etienne Collet	left 1833
244. Jean-Baptiste	Jean-Baptiste Beunèche	dismissed 1834

1832

| 245. Dosithée | François Leblanc | died 1838 |

1833

246. Gatien	Gatien Dutertre	left 1837
247. Julien	Julien Henry	died 1836
248. Laurent	Jean-Joseph Moreau	dismissed 1833

249. Patrice	Thomas Brière	died 1875
250. Jacques	Jacques Nourry	left 1838
251. Barnabé	Louis Grangé	dismissed 1833
252. Alphonse	Jacques-Félix Perrin	dismissed 1836
253. Léon	Vincent-Léon Ringuenoir	left 1836
254. Ignace	Louis Boissé	died 1835
255. Céleste	François Boissé	died 1835
256. Benoît	François Galbin	dismissed 1835
257. Eugène	Joseph Desneux	dismissed 1834
258. Charles	Jacques-Charles Felquin	left 1835, dis. 1836
259. Isidore	Pierre Verdier	dismissed 1836

1834

260. Paul	Jérôme Tessier	dismissed 1844
261. Rodolphe	Jean Chollet	dismissed 1834
262. Laurent	Joseph Pieau	dismissed 1834
263. Daniel	Léon-Etienne Boidier	dismissed 1836
264. Pascal	Pascal Thorin	left 1834
265. Victor	Pierre Enjourbault	left 1836
266. Ephrem	Pierre-Laurent Guérin	left 1835
267. Siméon	Jean-Marin Pieau	left 1838
268. Théophile	Thomas-Marie Chainais	left 1834
269. Jérémie	Edmond Empetit	left 1836
270. Mathurin	Mathurin Rué	left 1838
271. Gerault (later Julien)	Julien-Vincent Chauvois	left 1838

1835

1836

279. Thomas d'Aquin	Jean-Baptiste Garnier	left 1837
280. Narcisse	Jean-François Hulot	died 1887
281. Auguste	François-Joseph Bodinier	left 1838
282. Hilaire	Pierre Beaury	died 1890
283. Sosthènes	François Radiguet	left 1846
284. Jean-Marie	Toussaint-Julien Gigon	died 1851
285. François d'Assise	Nicolas-Pierre Drouin	died 1837

286. Hyacinthe	Louis-Stanislas-Xavier Côme	left 1862
287. Clément	François Deschamps	died 1851
288. Louis	François-Julien-Michel Letessier	left 1838
289. Grégoire de Nazianze	Henri Leroy	died 1900
290. Benoît	Jean Plantay	left 1836
291. Isidore	François Leroy	dismissed 1836
292. Alexandre	François-Pierre Bédouet	left 1837, left 1839
293. Emile	Joseph-Zacharie Barat	dismissed 1836
294. Antoine	Jules Joubert	left 1836
295. Adolphe	Pierre-André Moriceau	left 1840
296. Agathange	Victor-Pierre Dagonneau	left 1844
297. Camille	Louis Gastineau	left 1837
298. Roch	Pierre-François Cabaré	dismissed 1837
299. Jérôme	François Régnier	left 1839
304. Aldric	Etienne Anglade	left 1839
305. Hildebert	Alexandre Jarry	left 1838
306. Gonzales	Romain Angot	left 1839, left 1844
307. Valéry	Jean Bruneau	died 1883
308. Louis de Gonzague	Pierre Galmard	died 1893
309. Sylvain	Joseph-François Lesné	dismissed 1837
310. Roch	René Loisnard	left 1838

1837

311. Basile	Michel Gary	died 1888
312. Gabriel	Victor Chédebois	left 1838, left 1842
313. Théodore	François Feau	left 1847
314. Zacharie	Jean-Baptiste Cognet	died 1897
315. Hilarion	Louis Ferton	died 1849
316. Théophile	_____ Hervé	left 1839
317. Henri	René Compain	left 1838

APPENDIX III

Brothers of St. Joseph Arranged by Religious Name

Abel	Abel Guyon	219	left 1842
Abraham	Etienne Cormier	77	left 1825
Abraham	Joseph-Louis Veaufleury	105	died 1834
Adolphe	Pierre-Philippe Barbot	224	left 1832
Adolphe	Pierre-André Moriceau)	295	left 1840
Adrien	Louis Legeai	76	died 1873
Agathange	Nicolas Berson	161	left 1828
Agathange	Victor-Pierre Dagonneau	296	left 1844
Aldric	Etienne Anglade	304	left 1839
Alexandre	Pierre Neveu	48	left 1825
Alexandre	Paul Gautier	118	dismissed 1830
Alexandre	François-Pierre Bédouet	292	left 1837, left 1839
Alexis	Alexis-Alexandre Poule-Dupré	34	left 1824
Alexis	Jean-Pierre Chabrun	64	died 1871
Almire	Charles-François Lelièvre	103	dismissed 1826
Alphonse	Julien Landemaine	102	left 1828, left 1829
Alphonse	Jacques-Félix Perrin	252	dismissed 1836
Ambroise	Pierre Dupont	80	dismissed 1825
Ambroise	Victor-Gabriel-Charles Corbière	107	dismissed 1826
Ambroise	Louis-Ambroise-Marie Desloriers	144	dismissed 1827
Anaclet	Joseph Hallier	203	left 1829, died 1833
Anastase	_____ Messager	234	left 1830

André	André Mottais	4	died 1844
Anselme	René Mercier	119	left 1828
Antoine	Joseph Jousse	32	left 1830
Antoine	Jules Joubert	294	left 1836
Antonin	Pierre Lefèbvre	189	died 1882
Armand	Armand Maisonnier	90	dismissed 1830
Arsène	Arsène Echard	23	dismissed 1823
Arsène	Louis-Pierre Bouvet	61	died 1883
Athanase	Charles Richard	29	dismissed 1823
Athanase	Michel-Etienne Tarault	92	died 1873
Auguste	François-Joseph Bodinier	281	left 1838
Augustin	Jean-Baptiste Riet	13	died 1860
Avit	Sébastien Bunel	192	dismissed 1830
Baptiste	[Baptiste] Verger	8	died 1859
Barnabé	Louis Balleux	186	left 1828, left 1830
Barnabé	Louis Grangé	251	dismissed 1833
Barthélémy	Julien-Mathieu-Louis Guinegaut	138	dismissed 1827
Barthélémy	Joseph Monvoisin	217	left 1830
Basilde	Justin Renault	238	left 1830
Basile	René Derouet	15	dismissed 1835
Basile	Michel Gary	311	died 1888
Benjamin	Benjamin Poirier	25	dismissed 1835
Benoît	François Bazile	100	dismissed 1830
Benoît	François Galbin	256	dismissed 1835
Benoît	Jean Plantay	290	left 1836
Bernard	? Bonneau	19	dismissed 1825
Bernard	Gilles Lecavorsin	178	left 1836
Bertin	Jean Bouthmis	222	left 1830
Bertrand	Pierre Paineau	84	left 1828
Bonaventure	Pierre Tulou	165	died 1856
Bruno	Paul-Jean Bouilly	97	dismissed 1838
Camille	Louis Gastineau	297	left 1837
Casimir	Julien Bardou	134	died 1841
Céleste	François Boissé	255	died 1835

Célestin	Louis Forton	170	died 1842
Césaire	Alexis Poirier	70	left 1839
Charles	Charles Faribault	9	left 1826
Charles	Charles Rousseau	149	left 1827
Charles	Ferdinand Raimond	199	left 1829
Charles	Jacques-Charles Felquin	258	left 1835, dis. 1836
Christophe	Christophe Murat	159	left 1829
Chrysostôme	Pierre David	204	left 1828
Clément	Louis-François Pottier	33	left 1824
Clément	Pierre-Jacques Richard	114	dismissed 1826
Clément	Clément Chéron	185	dismissed 1828
Clément	François Deschamps	287	died 1851
Constantin	Jean Vivens	113	left 1828
Corentin	Corentin Chevalier	202	dismissed 1828
Cyprien	Jean Chambon	72	left 1831
Cyrille	René Renard	146	left 1834
Damase	Jean Poilpré	179	left 1832
Damien	Jean-François Pivard	130	left 1826
Daniel	Pierre Launay	26	left 1825, left 1828
Daniel	Léon-Etienne Boidier	263	dismissed 1836
Denis	René-Auguste Touti	62	left 1831
Didier	Jean-Didier Mousseau	63	left 1825
Dominique	Pierre Gautier	17	dismissed 1841
Donatien	André-Louis-Paul Nail	215	left 1848, died 1886
Dorothée	Armand-Adolphe Aumas	31	dismissed 1824
Dorothée	Joseph Bigot	98	left 1850, died 1873
Dosithée	Jean-Marie Tulou	188	left 1828
Dosithée	François Leblanc	245	died 1838
Edmond	François Edon	86	dismissed 1826
Edouard	François-Jean Delalande	122	left 1832
Elénore	Elénore Hulot	39	dismissed 1824
Elie	Jean Letessier	43	left 1825
Elie	Joseph Rétif	108	left 1829
Elisée	Félix-Hippolyte Réau	193	died 1894

Eloi	Louis-Jean Cosnier	141	left 1833
Emeri	Louis Guérin	197	left 1830
Emile	Joseph-Zacharie Barat	293	dismissed 1836
Ephrem	Pierre-Laurent Guérin	266	left 1835
Epiphane	Jean-Simon Billard	99	left 1829
Etienne	Etienne Gauffre	5	died 1851
Eugène	Louis-Gustave Fossé	115	left 1826
Eugène	Pierre James	125	left 1828
Eugène	? Dubriel	212	left 1829
Eugène	Joseph Desneux	257	dismissed 1834
Eusèbe	Jean-Pierre Coudriou	45	left 1825
Eusèbe	Armand Béranger	151	left 1828
Eustache	François Marchand	126	left 1836
Felix	Jean Taupin	24	dismissed 1826
Félix	Adolphe Guenes	240	dismissed 1837
Firmin	Alexis Gorget	200	dismissed 1829
Flavien	Louis-Victor Manceau	176	left 1828, died 1830
Florent	Jean-Rodolphe Jouandy	168	dismissed 1827
Florentin	Jean-Amand Mottay	229	left 1830
François	Pierre François Blanchet	11	dismissed 1832
François d'Assise	François-Marie Tulou	166	died 1853
François d'Assise	Nicolas-Pierre Drouin	285	died 1837
François de Paule	Victor Défourneaux	187	left 1828
François de Paule	? Hureau	231	left 1830
François-Xavier	François Fleurinet	174	left 1830
Frumence	Pierre Saulnier	142	left 1827
Fulgence	René Ridereau	73	dismissed 1825
Gabriel	Pierre Marsollier	60	left 1828
Gabriel	Victor Chédebois	312	left 1838, left 1842
Gatien	Jean Fouquet	124	left 1832
Gatien	Gatien Dutertre	246	left 1837
Georges	Victor Guisbé	137	dismissed 1827
Georges	Georges Lorain-Laval	206	dismissed 1829
Gérasime	Florent Duval	173	left 1828

Gerault (later Julien)	Julien-Vincent Chauvois	271	left 1838
Germain	Pierre-Antoine Blin	44	left 1830
Gervais	Pierre Esnault	116	left (?) 1826
Gervais	Pierre-Jacques-Gervais Langlois	148	dismissed 1827
Gervais	François Houlbert	208	dismissed 1828
Gervais	Augustin Bernier	214	dismissed 1829
Gervais	Jean Guibon	220	left 1837, left 1842
Gonzales	Romain Angot	306	left 1839, left 1844
Grégoire	Julien Lépinay	47	left 1833
Grégoire de Nazianze	Henri Leroy	289	died 1900
Henri	Michel Taupin	36	left 1834
Henri	René Compain	317	left 1838
Hermas	———— ————	75	left 1825
Hilaire	Augustin Jubault	83	dismissed 1826
Hilaire	Matthieu-Charles Bourgeteau	136	dismissed 1826
Hilaire	Silvin Vernon	207	left 1830
Hilaire	Pierre Beaury	282	died 1890
Hilarion	Jean Lagarde	67	left 1826
Hilarion	Louis Ferton	315	died 1849
Hildebert	Alexandre Jarry	305	left 1838
Hippolyte	François Dureau	81	dismissed 1827
Honoré	Auguste-François Brunet	133	left 1827
Honoré	Pierre Bouhour	196	left 1828
Hyacinthe	Hyacinthe Hutin	109	left 1827
Hyacinthe	Louis-Stanislas-Xavier Côme	286	left 1862
Ignace	Pierre Hureau	2	left 1821, left 1830
Ignace	Louis Boissé	254	died 1835
Iréné	Joseph-Almire Trassard-Deslandes	111	died 1852
Isaac	François-Clément Coutard	172	left 1830
Isidore	Isidore Bouvier	37	left 1824
Isidore	René-Isidore Janvier	57	left 1828
Isidore	Pierre Verdier	259	dismissed 1836
Isidore	François Leroy	291	dismissed 1836

Jacques	Jacques Hamon	56	dismissed 1825
Jacques	Jacques Nourry	250	left 1838
Jean	Jean Vayer	7	left 1831
Jean-Baptiste	Jean-Baptiste Lardeau	51	left 1825
Jean-Baptiste	Jean-François Guilmet	121	dis. 1826, left 1828
Jean-Baptiste	Jean-Baptiste Beunèche	244	dismissed 1834
Jean-Chrysostôme	Jean Martin	177	left 1828
Jean-Chrysostôme	Joseph Lacavorzin	235	left 1835
Jean-Climaque	Jean-Baptiste Contamin	101	died 1866
Jean de Dieu	Louis Duportail	78	dismissed 1825
Jean de la Croix	Jean Cabot	74	left 1831
Jean-François	François-Jean Royer	190	left 1828
Jean-Marie	Jean-Marie Gauchet	58	died 1826
Jean-Marie	Toussaint-Julien Gigon	284	died 1851
Jérémie	Edmond Empetit	269	left 1836
Jérôme	René Porcheré	52	died 1826
Jérôme	François Emond	128	dismissed 1826
Jérôme	François Fourmont	131	left 1830, dis. 1836
Jérôme	François Régnier	299	left 1839
Joseph	Pierre Bourdon	12	left 1831
Joseph de Jésus	Gentien-Julien Faucheux	239	left 1831
Jude	Henri-Baptiste Bougault	140	left 1827
Jude	René Maçon	216	left 1829
Jules	Jean Chancerel	213	dismissed 1829
Jules	Guillaume-Victor Glaume	236	left 1830
Julien	Jean Neveu	16	left 1831
Julien	Julien Henry	247	died 1836
Justin	Michel Ragot	94	left 1834
Laurent	Joseph Chartier	59	dismissed 1826
Laurent	Antoine Rouchy	158	dismissed 1829
Laurent	Jean-Joseph Moreau	248	dismissed 1833
Laurent	Joseph Pieau	262	dismissed 1834
Léandre	Léandre Debray	110	left 1827
Leon	Jean Marsollier	22	left 1823
Léon	Louis Mottais	201	left 1832

Léon	Vincent-Léon Ringuenoir	253	left 1836
Léopold	Pierre-Nicholas Putiot	241	died 1864
Léon-Louis de Gonzague	Louis Pottier	46	left 1826
Léonard	Pierre-François Guittoger	106	died 1887
Liboire	Marie-François Meunier	152	dismissed 1828
Liboire	Elie Launay	156	left 1828
Louis	Louis Duchêne	3	dismissed 1825
Louis	Auguste Ménage	150	left 1827
Louis	Etienne-Joseph Rouillon	198	dismissed 1820
Louis	François-Julien-Michel Letessier	288	left 1838
Louis de Gonzague	Louis-Michel Gondard	221	dismissed 1835
Louis de Gonzague	Pierre Galmard	308	died 1893
Lucien	Alphonse-François Dagoreau	195	died 1889
Macaire	Guillaume-Michel Chauvin	227	died 1880
Magloire	Pierre-Charles Sage	120	left 1826
Marc	François-Charles-Marthe Galinand	104	died 1879
Marcel	Jean Brard	147	left 1828, dis. 1831
Marie	François-Jean-Marie Delorière	123	left 1827
Marie	Julien-Marie Paquet	194	dismissed 1830
Marin	Michel Bulanger	30	died 1860
Marie-Joseph	Pierre-Joseph Duval	50	dismissed 1851
Martin	Jean Verger	20	died 1865
Mathias	Mathias Chapelière	167	dis. 1828, left 1840, left 1844
Mathurin	Pierre Leroyer	153	left 1829
Mathurin	Mathurin Rué	270	left 1838
Matthieu	Pierre Plumard	112	died 1888
Maurice	Pierre Chéan	35	left 1825, left 1831
Maxime	François Boisramé	66	died 1832
Médard	Jean-Michel-Médard Proust	132	dismissed 1831
Michel	Michel Jouseau	6	left 1829
Moise	Joseph Marin Boureau	225	left 1829
Narcisse	Jean-François Hulot	280	died 1887

Nicolas	Jules-Nicolas Guesnot	154	dismissed 1827
Norbert	Louis Bailleul	163	left 1827
Onézime	Mathurin-Pierre-François Pillard	164	died 1876
Pacôme	Louis Laffay	68	left 1834
Pascal	François Gareau	21	dismissed 1823
Pascal	Pierre Bignon	53	left 1828
Pascal	Pascal Thorin	264	left 1834
Patrice	Thomas Brière	249	died 1875
Paul	Paul Petit	28	left 1828
Paul	Joseph-Etienne Collet	243	left 1833
Paul	Jérôme Tessier	260	dismissed 1844
Paulin	_____ Cannet	117	dismissed 1830
Philéas	Henri Gonet	218	left 1830
Philibert	Louis Launay	183	left 1830
Philippe	_____ _____	181	left 1828
Philippe de Néri	Jean-Baptiste Bougault	38	left 1829, died 1842
Pierre	Pierre Oger	14	died 1869
Placide	François-Jacques Beauté	129	dismissed 1831
Principe	Principe Manoury	175	left 1827
Prosper	Guillaume Herbelle	91	dismissed 1828
Prudence	Joseph Loiseau	237	left 1832
Quentin	Augustin Chesnel	143	dismissed 1827
Raphael	Arsène Forton	180	left 1850
Rémi	Etienne Mérianne	79	died 1888
René	René Fromentin	40	dismissed 1824
René	René-Michel Lépineau	87	dismissed 1830
Roch	Pierre-François Cabaré	298	dismissed 1837
Roch	René Loisnard	310	left 1838
Rodolphe	Jean Chollet	261	dismissed 1834
Rodriguez	_____ Besnard	210	left 1829
Romain	François Bouvier	42	died 1870

Salomon	Augustin Mordret	242	left 1832
Samuel	Louis Frêne	191	dismissed 1829
Saturnin	François Oger	65	left 1830, left 1838
Sébastien	Pierre Poirier	145	dis. 1828, dis. 1836
Sévère	Jean-Louis Bellouard	71	dismissed 1825
Silvestre	Ambroise Corni	160	left 1827
Silvestre	_____ Hubert	232	left 1830
Siméon	Charles Bouvier	49	died 1830
Siméon	Jean-Marin Pieau	267	left 1838
Simon	Simon Guy	54	left 1826
Simon	Michel Péard	209	left 1828
Sosthènes	François Radiguet	283	left 1846
Stanislaus	Jean Blaise	27	dismissed 1823
Stanislas	Louis-Joseph-Grégoire Derve	88	died 1888
Sylvain	Louis Veaufleury	127	left 1832
Sylvain	Joseph-François Lesné	309	dismissed 1837
Symphorien	Denis Bourgneuf	96	dismissed 1826
Thadée	Pierre Papin	41	left 1828
Théodore	René Gouadon	95	dismissed 1825
Théodore	Vital Chaumezière	184	left 1829
Théodore	Alain-Marie Mevel	226	left 1829
Théodore	Louis-Michel Prieul	228	left 1844
Théodore	François Feau	313	left 1847
Théodoret	Grégoire Gilette	171	left 1828
Théodoret	? Essellard	230	left 1830
Théodule	Jean-Marie Hillion	223	dismissed 1833
Théophile	Alexandre-Jean Cosson	93	left 1825
Théophile	Jean Fréard	135	died 1832
Théophile	Thomas-Marie Chainais	268	left 1834
Théophile	_____ Hervé	316	left 1839
Théotime	Jean-Pierre Coquand	182	left 1831
Thomas	Jacques-Thomas Peloille	69	left 1826
Thomas	François Cochon	139	dismissed 1827
Thomas d'Aquin	Alexandre Meleux-Laperrière	205	died 1836
Thomas d'Aquin	Jean-Baptiste Garnier	279	left 1837

Ulphace	Louis Oger	169	left 1831
Urbain	Louis Jubault	89	dismissed 1825
Valéry	Jean Bruneau	307	died 1883
Victor	Victor Loupil	10	left 1828
Victor	_____ Huet	233	left 1830
Victor	Pierre Enjourbault	265	left 1836
Victorin	Jean Brunet	155	left 1827
Victorin	Henri Lion	157	left 1834
Vincent	Jean Pieau	18	died 1890
Vincent-de-Paul	Jean-Baptiste Vincent Plat	82	left 1829, died 1873
Vital	Auguste-Casimir Breton	85	died 1886
Zacharie	Jean-Baptiste Cognet	314	died 1897
Zozime	Pierre Desmares-Vicaire	55	left 1824
Zozime	Ferdinand Prout	162	left 1827
Zozime	_____ Cossom	211	left 1829

APPENDIX IV

Brothers of St. Joseph Arranged by Family Name

Ranking Numbers from the *Matricule Générale*

Anglade, Etienne	304
Angot, Romain	306
Aumas, Armand-Adolphe	31
Bailleul, Louis	163
Balleux, Louis	186
Barat, Joseph-Zacharie	293
Barbot, Pierre-Philippe	224
Bardou, Julien	134
Bazile, François	100
Beaury, Pierre	282
Beauté, François-Jacques	129
Bédouet, François-Pierre	292
Bellouard, Jean-Louis	71
Béranger, Armand	151
Bernier, Augustin	214
Berson, Nicolas	161
Besnard, _____	210
Beunèche, Jean-Baptiste	244
Bignon, Pierre	53

APPENDIX V

Early schools of the Brothers of St. Joseph operational in a given year

Year represents start of academic year in September.
(Adapted from *Sainte-Croix en France*.)

1821

Larchamp	1821 to 1829 (8 years)
Saint-Denis d'Orques	1821 to 1833 (12 years)
Ruillé	1821 to 1870 (49 years)

1822

Larchamp	1821 to 1829 (8 years)
Les Autels-Saint-Eloi	1822 to 1826 (4 years)
Marçon	1822 to 1836 (14 years)
Ménil	1822 to 1824 (2 years)
Montourtier	1822 to 1835 (13 years)
Saint-Denis d'Orques	1821 to 1833 (12 years)
Saint-Germain-le-Guillaume	1822 to 1831 (9 years)
Saint-Pierre de Chevillé	1822 to 1823 (1 year)
Yvré-l'Evêque	1822 to 1831 (9 years)
Ruillé	1821 to 1870 (49 years)

1823

Aigné	1823 to 1850 (27 years)

Ardenay	1823 to 1828 (5 years)
Beaulieu	1825 to 1828 (3 years)
Bierné	1823 to 1830 (7 years)
Ecommoy	1823 to 1836 (13 years)
Ernée	1823 to 1824 (1 year)
Larchamp	1821 to 1829 (8 years)
Laval	1823 to 1827 (4 years)
Les Autels-Saint-Eloi	1822 to 1826 (4 years)
Marcillé-la-Ville	1823 to 1841 (18 years)
Marçon	1822 to 1836 (14 years)
Ménil	1822 to 1824 (2 years)
Meslay	1823 to 1870 (47 years)
Montourtier	1822 to 1835 (13 years)
Saint-Denis d'Orques	1821 to 1833 (12 years)
Saint-Germain-le-Guillaume	1822 to 1831 (9 years)
Saint-Mars-la-Brière	1823 to 1827 (4 years)
Yvré-l'Evêque	1822 to 1831 (9 years)
Ruillé	1821 to 1870 (49 years)

1824

Aigné	1823 to 1850 (27 years)
Ardenay	1823 to 1828 (5 years)
Beaulieu	1824 to 1828 (4 years)
Bierné	1823 to 1830 (7 years)
Daon	1824 to 1852 (28 years)
Désertines	1824 to 1828 (4 years)
Ecommoy	1823 to 1836 (13 years)
Larchamp	1821 to 1829 (8 years)
Laval	1823 to 1827 (4 years)
Le Breil	1824 to 1826 (2 years)
Les Autels-Saint-Eloi	1822 to 1826 (4 years)
Marcillé-la-Ville	1823 to 1841 (18 years)
Mamers	1824 to 1833 (9 years)
Marçon	1822 to 1836 (14 years)
Meung-sur-Loire	1824 to 1827 (3 years)
Montourtier	1822 to 1835 (13 years)

Nogent-le-Bernard	1824 to 1831 (7 years)
Romorantin	1824 to 1827 (3 years)
Ruillé	1821 to 1870 (49 years)
Ruillé (boarding school)	1824 to 1836 (12 years)
Saint-Denis d'Orques	1821 to 1833 (12 years)
Saint-Germain-le-Guillaume	1822 to 1831 (9 years)
Saint-Mars-la-Brière	1823 to 1827 (4 years)
Saint-Martin-du-Eois	1824 to 1827 (3 years)
Yvré-l'Evêque	1822 to 1831 (9 years)

1825

Aigné	1823 to 1850 (27 years)
Ardenay	1823 to 1828 (5 years)
Aubigné	1825 to 1830 (5 years)
Beaulieu	1824 to 1828 (4 years)
Bierné	1823 to 1830 (7 years)
Channay	1825 to 1828 (3 years)
Contres	1825 to 1830 (5 years)
Cré-sur-Loir	1825 to 1827 (2 years)
Daon	1824 to 1852 (28 years)
Désertines	1824 to 1828 (4 years)
Ecommoy	1823 to 1836 (13 years)
Genneteil	1825 to 1828 (3 years)
Hardanges	1825 to 1860 (5 years)
Larchamp	1821 to 1829 (8 years)
Laval	1823 to 1827 (4 years)
Le Breil	1824 to 1826 (2 years)
Les Autels-Saint-Eloi	1822 to 1826 (4 years)
Lignières-la-Doucelle	1825 to 1826 (1 year)
Loches	1825 to 1831 (6 years)
Mamers	1824 to 1833 (9 years)
Marcillé-la-Ville	1823 to 1841 (18 years)
Marçon	1822 to 1836 (14 years)
Mayenne	1825 to 1842 (17 years)
Meung-sur-Loire	1824 to 1827 (3 years)
Montourtier	1822 to 1835 (13 years)

Mortagne	1825 to 1830 (5 years)
Nogent-le-Bernard	1824 to 1831 (7 years)
Preuilly	1825 to 1826 (1 year)
Rochecorbon	1825 to 1830 (5 years)
Romorantin	1824 to 1827 (3 years)
Ruillé	1821 to 1870 (49 years)
Ruillé (boarding school)	1824 to 1836 (12 years)
Saint-Cyr-en-Pail	1825 to 1833 (8 years)
Saint-Denis d'Orques	1821 to 1833 (12 years)
Saint-Germain-le-Guillaume	1822 to 1831 (9 years)
Saint-Mars-la-Brière	1823 to 1827 (4 years)
Saint-Martin-du-Eois	1824 to 1827 (3 years)
Souday	1825 to 1827 (2 years)
Vouvray	1825 to 1831 (6 years)
Yvré-l'Evêque	1822 to 1831 (9 years)

1826

Abondant	1826 to 1870 (44 years)
Aigné	1823 to 1850 (27 years)
Ardenay	1823 to 1828 (5 years)
Aubigné	1825 to 1830 (5 years)
Authon	1826 to 1828 (2 years)
Beaulieu	1824 to 1828 (4 years)
Bierné	1823 to 1830 (7 years)
Bouère	1826 to 1888 (62 years)
Brou	1826 to 1833 (7 years)
Channay	1825 to 1828 (3 years)
Contres	1825 to 1830 (5 years)
Cré-sur-Loir	1825 to 1827 (2 years)
Daon	1824 to 1852 (28 years)
Désertines	1824 to 1828 (4 years)
Ecommoy	1823 to 1836 (13 years)
Genneteil	1825 to 1828 (3 years)
Grez-en-Bouère	1826 to 1832 (6 years)
Hardanges	1825 to 1860 (5 years)
La Loupe	1826 to 1828 (2 years)

Larchamp	1821 to 1829 (8 years)
Laval	1823 to 1827 (4 years)
Loches	1825 to 1831 (6 years)
Mamers	1824 to 1833 (9 years)
Marcillé-la-Ville	1823 to 1841 (18 years)
Marçon	1822 to 1836 (14 years)
Mayenne	1825 to 1842 (17 years)
Meung-sur-Loire	1824 to 1827 (3 years)
Montmirail	1826 to 1846 (20 years)
Montourtier	1822 to 1835 (13 years)
Mortagne	1825 to 1830 (5 years)
Nogent-le-Bernard	1824 to 1831 (7 years)
Rochecorbon	1825 to 1830 (5 years)
Romorantin	1824 to 1827 (3 years)
Ruillé	1821 to 1870 (49 years)
Ruillé (boarding school)	1824 to 1836 (12 years)
Saint-Cyr-en-Pail	1825 to 1833 (8 years)
Saint-Denis d'Orques	1821 to 1833 (12 years)
Saint-Germain-le-Guillaume	1822 to 1831 (9 years)
Saint-James	1826 to 1847 (21 years)
Saint-Mars-la-Brière	1823 to 1827 (4 years)
Saint-Martin-du-Eois	1824 to 1827 (3 years)
Souday	1825 to 1827 (2 years)
Vouvray	1825 to 1831 (6 years)
Yvré-l'Evêque	1822 to 1831 (9 years)

1827

Abondant	1826 to 1870 (44 years)
Aigné	1823 to 1850 (27 years)
Ardenay	1823 to 1828 (5 years)
Aubigné	1825 to 1830 (5 years)
Authon	1826 to 1828 (2 years)
Beaulieu	1824 to 1828 (4 years)
Beaune-la-Rolande	1827 to 1835 (8 years)
Bonnétable	1827 to 1832 (5 years)
Bierné	1823 to 1830 (7 years)

Bouère	1826 to 1888 (62 years)
Brou	1826 to 1833 (7 years)
Champgénéteux	1826 to 1833 (7 years)
Channay	1825 to 1828 (3 years)
Cheverny	1826 to 1831 (5 years)
Contres	1825 to 1830 (5 years)
Craon	1827 to 1903 (76 years)
Dampierre	1827 to 1878 (51 years)
Daon	1824 to 1852 (28 years)
Désertines	1824 to 1828 (4 years)
Ecommoy	1823 to 1836 (13 years)
Evron	1827 to 1831 (4 years)
Genneteil	1825 to 1828 (3 years)
Grez-en-Bouère	1826 to 1832 (6 years)
Hardanges	1825 to 1860 (35 years)
La Loupe	1826 to 1828 (2 years)
La Pooté	1827 to 1844 (17 years)
Larchamp	1821 to 1829 (8 years)
Loches	1825 to 1831 (6 years)
Mamers	1824 to 1833 (9 years)
Marcillé-la-Ville	1823 to 1841 (18 years)
Marçon	1822 to 1836 (14 years)
Mayenne	1825 to 1842 (17 years)
Montmirail	1826 to 1846 (20 years)
Montourtier	1822 to 1835 (13 years)
Mortagne	1825 to 1830 (5 years)
Nogent-le-Bernard	1824 to 1831 (7 years)
Parcay-sous-Rillé	1827 to 1829 (2 years)
Rochecorbon	1825 to 1830 (5 years)
Ruillé	1821 to 1870 (49 years)
Ruillé (boarding school)	1824 to 1836 (12 years)
Saint-Cyr-en-Pail	1825 to 1833 (8 years)
Saint-Denis d'Anjou	1827 to 1878 (51 years)
Saint-Denis d'Orques	1821 to 1833 (12 years)
Saint-Germain-le-Guillaume	1822 to 1831 (9 years)
Saint-Hilaire-du-Harcouet	1827 to 1828 (1 year)

Saint-James	1826 to 1847 (21 years)
Saint-Lambert-des-Lecées	1827 to 1831 (4 years)
Saint-Martin-le-Beau	1827 to 1831 (4 years)
Sainte-Suzanne	1827 to 1830 (3 years)
Véretz	1827 to 1828 (1 year)
Vouvray	1825 to 1831 (6 years)
Yvré-l'Evêque	1822 to 1831 (9 years)

1828

Abondant	1826 to 1870 (44 years)
Aigné	1823 to 1850 (27 years)
Aubigné	1825 to 1830 (5 years)
Beaune-la-Rolande	1827 to 1835 (8 years)
Bierné	1823 to 1830 (7 years)
Bonnétable	1827 to 1832 (5 years)
Bouère	1826 to 1888 (62 years)
Brou	1826 to 1833 (7 years)
Champgénéteux	1826 to 1833 (7 years)
Cheverny	1826 to 1831 (5 years)
Contres	1825 to 1830 (5 years)
Craon	1827 to 1903 (76 years)
Dampierre	1827 to 1878 (51 years)
Daon	1824 to 1852 (28 years)
Ecommoy	1823 to 1836 (13 years)
Evron	1827 to 1831 (4 years)
Grez-en-Bouère	1826 to 1832 (6 years)
Hardanges	1825 to 1860 (35 years)
La Pooté	1827 to 1844 (17 years)
Larchamp	1821 to 1829 (8 years)
Loches	1825 to 1831 (6 years)
Logron	1828 to 1830 (2 years)
Maisoncelles	1828 to 1830 (2 years)
Mamers	1824 to 1833 (9 years)
Marcillé-la-Ville	1823 to 1841 (18 years)
Marçon	1822 to 1836 (14 years)
Mayenne	1825 to 1842 (17 years)

Milly-la-Forêt	1828 to 1865 (37 years)
Montmirail	1826 to 1846 (20 years)
Montourtier	1822 to 1835 (13 years)
Mortagne	1825 to 1830 (5 years)
Nogent-le-Bernard	1824 to 1831 (7 years)
Parcay-sous-Rillé	1827 to 1829 (2 years)
Rochecorbon	1825 to 1830 (5 years)
Ruillé	1821 to 1870 (49 years)
Ruillé (boarding school)	1824 to 1836 (12 years)
Saint-Cyr-en-Pail	1825 to 1833 (8 years)
Saint-Denis d'Anjou	1827 to 1878 (51 years)
Saint-Denis d'Orques	1821 to 1833 (12 years)
Sainte-Suzanne	1827 to 1830 (3 years)
Saint-Germain-le-Guillaume	1822 to 1831 (9 years)
Saint-Hilaire-du-Harcouet	1827 to 1828 (1 year)
Saint-Lambert-des-Lecées	1827 to 1831 (4 years)
Saint-Martin-le-Beau	1827 to 1831 (4 years)
Saint-James	1826 to 1847 (21 years)
Souligné-sous-Vallon	1828 to 1831 (3 years)
Vallon	1828 to 1845 (17 years)
Véretz	1827 to 1828 (1 year)
Viviers	1828 to 1830 (2 years)
Vouvray	1825 to 1831 (6 years)
Yvré-l'Evêque	1822 to 1831 (9 years)

1829

Abondant	1826 to 1870 (44 years)
Aigné	1823 to 1850 (27 years)
Aubigné	1825 to 1830 (5 years)
Beaune-la-Rolande	1827 to 1835 (8 years)
Bierné	1823 to 1830 (7 years)
Bonnétable	1827 to 1832 (5 years)
Bouère	1826 to 1888 (62 years)
Brou	1826 to 1833 (7 years)
Champgénéteux	1826 to 1833 (7 years)
Cheverny	1826 to 1831 (5 years)

Contres	1825 to 1830 (5 years)
Craon	1827 to 1903 (76 years)
Dampierre	1827 to 1878 (51 years)
Daon	1824 to 1852 (28 years)
Ecommoy	1823 to 1836 (13 years)
Evron	1827 to 1831 (4 years)
Grez-en-Bouère	1826 to 1832 (6 years)
Hardanges	1825 to 1860 (35 years)
La Pooté	1827 to 1844 (17 years)
Loches	1825 to 1831 (6 years)
Logron	1828 to 1830 (2 years)
Maisoncelles	1828 to 1830 (2 years)
Mamers	1824 to 1833 (9 years)
Marcillé-la-Ville	1823 to 1841 (18 years)
Marçon	1822 to 1836 (14 years)
Mayenne	1825 to 1842 (17 years)
Milly-la-Forêt	1828 to 1865 (37 years)
Montmirail	1826 to 1846 (20 years}
Montourtier	1822 to 1835 (13 years)
Mortagne	1825 to 1830 (5 years)
Nogent-le-Bernard	1824 to 1831 (7 years)
Rochecorbon	1825 to 1830 (5 years)
Rouessé-Vassé	1829 to 1835 (6 years)
Ruillé	1821 to 1870 (49 years)
Ruillé (boarding school)	1824 to 1836 (12 years)
Saint-Cyr-en-Pail	1825 to 1833 (8 years)
Saint-Denis d'Anjou	1827 to 1878 (51 years)
Saint-Denis d'Orques	1821 to 1833 (12 years)
Sainte-Suzanne	1827 to 1830 (3 years)
Saint-Germain-le-Guillaume	1822 to 1831 (9 years)
Saint-James	1826 to 1847 (21 years)
Saint-Lambert-des-Lecées	1827 to 1831 (4 years)
Saint-Martin-le-Beau	1827 to 1831 (4 years)
Souligné-sous-Vallon	1828 to 1831 (3 years)
Vallon	1828 to 1845 (17 years)
Viviers	1828 to 1830 (2 years)

Vouvray	1825 to 1831 (6 years)
Yvré-l'Evêque	1822 to 1831 (9 years)

1830

Abondant	1826 to 1870 (44 years)
Aigné	1823 to 1850 (27 years)
Beaune-la-Rolande	1827 to 1835 (8 years)
Bonnétable	1827 to 1832 (5 years)
Bouère	1826 to 1888 (62 years)
Brou	1826 to 1833 (7 years)
Champgénéteux	1826 to 1833 (7 years)
Cheverny	1826 to 1831 (5 years)
Craon	1827 to 1903 (76 years)
Dampierre	1827 to 1878 (51 years)
Daon	1824 to 1852 (28 years)
Ecommoy	1823 to 1836 (13 years)
Evron	1827 to 1831 (4 years)
Grez-en-Bouère	1826 to 1832 (6 years)
Hardanges	1825 to 1860 (35 years)
La Pooté	1827 to 1844 (17 years)
Loches	1825 to 1831 (6 years)
Mamers	1824 to 1833 (9 years)
Marcillé-la-Ville	1823 to 1841 (18 years)
Marçon	1822 to 1836 (14 years)
Mayenne	1825 to 1842 (17 years)
Milly-la-Forêt	1828 to 1865 (37 years)
Montmirail	1826 to 1846 (20 years)
Montourtier	1822 to 1835 (13 years)
Nogent-le-Bernard	1824 to 1831 (7 years)
Rouessé-Vassé	1829 to 1835 (6 years)
Ruillé	1821 to 1870 (49 years)
Ruillé (boarding school)	1824 to 1836 (12 years)
Sablé	1830 to 1846 (16 years)
Saint-Cyr-en-Pail	1825 to 1833 (8 years)
Saint-Denis d'Anjou	1827 to 1878 (51 years)

Saint-Denis d'Orques	1821 to 1833 (12 years)
Saint-Germain-le-Guillaume	1822 to 1831 (9 years)
Saint-James	1826 to 1847 (21 years)
Saint-Lambert-des-Lecées	1827 to 1831 (4 years)
Saint-Martin-le-Beau	1827 to 1831 (4 years)
Souligné-sous-Vallon	1828 to 1831 (3 years)
Vallon	1828 to 1845 (17 years)
Vouvray	1825 to 1831 (6 years)
Yvré-l'Evêque	1822 to 1831 (9 years)

1831

Abondant	1826 to 1870 (44 years)
Aigné	1823 to 1850 (27 years)
Beaune-la-Rolande	1827 to 1835 (8 years)
Bonnétable	1827 to 1832 (5 years)
Bouère	1826 to 1888 (62 years)
Brou	1826 to 1833 (7 years)
Champgénéteux	1826 to 1833 (7 years)
Choisel	1830 to 1835 (5 years)
Craon	1827 to 1903 (76 years)
Dampierre	1827 to 1878 (51 years)
Daon	1824 to 1852 (28 years)
Ecommoy	1823 to 1836 (13 years)
Grez-en-Bouère	1826 to 1832 (6 years)
Hardanges	1825 to 1860 (35 years)
Lhomme	1831 to 1831 (months)
La Pooté	1827 to 1844 (17 years)
Mamers	1824 to 1833 (9 years)
Marcillé-la-Ville	1823 to 1841 (18 years)
Marçon	1822 to 1836 (14 years)
Mayenne	1825 to 1842 (17 years)
Milly-la-Forêt	1828 to 1865 (37 years)
Montmirail	1826 to 1846 (20 years)
Montourtier	1822 to 1835 (13 years)
Rouessé-Vassé	1829 to 1835 (6 years)
Ruillé	1821 to 1870 (49 years)

Ruillé (boarding school)	1824 to 1836 (12 years)
Sablé	1830 to 1846 (16 years)
Saint-Cyr-en-Pail	1825 to 1833 (8 years)
Saint-Denis d'Anjou	1827 to 1878 (51 years)
Saint-Denis d'Orques	1821 to 1833 (12 years)
Saint-James	1826 to 1847 (21 years)
Vallon	1828 to 1845 (17 years)

1832

Abondant	1826 to 1870 (44 years)
Aigné	1823 to 1850 (27 years)
Beaune-la-Rolande	1827 to 1835 (8 years)
Bouère	1826 to 1888 (62 years)
Brou	1826 to 1833 (7 years)
Champgénéteux	1826 to 1833 (7 years)
Choisel	1830 to 1835 (5 years)
Craon	1827 to 1903 (76 years)
Dampierre	1827 to 1878 (51 years)
Daon	1824 to 1852 (28 years)
Ecommoy	1823 to 1836 (13 years)
Hardanges	1825 to 1860 (35 years)
Laigné-Chéripeau	1832 to 1834 (2 years)
La Pooté	1827 to 1844 (17 years)
Mamers	1824 to 1833 (9 years)
Marcillé-la-Ville	1823 to 1841 (18 years)
Marçon	1822 to 1836 (14 years)
Mayenne	1825 to 1842 (17 years)
Milly-la-Forêt	1828 to 1865 (37 years)
Montmirail	1826 to 1846 (20 years)
Montourtier	1822 to 1835 (13 years)
Rouessé-Vassé	1829 to 1835 (6 years)
Ruillé	1821 to 1870 (49 years)
Ruillé (boarding school)	1824 to 1836 (12 years)
Sablé	1830 to 1846 (16 years)
Saint-Cyr-en-Pail	1825 to 1833 (8 years)
Saint-Denis d'Anjou	1827 to 1878 (51 years)

Saint-Denis d'Orques	1821 to 1833 (12 years)
Saint-James	1826 to 1847 (21 years)
Vallon	1828 to 1845 (17 years)

1833

Abondant	1826 to 1870 (44 years)
Aigné	1823 to 1850 (27 years)
Beaune-la-Rolande	1827 to 1835 (8 years)
Bouère	1826 to 1888 (62 years)
Chéméré-le-Roi	1833 to 1860 (27 years)
Choisel	1830 to 1835 (5 years)
Craon	1827 to 1903 (76 years)
Dampierre	1827 to 1878 (51 years)
Daon	1824 to 1852 (28 years)
Ecommoy	1823 to 1836 (13 years)
Hardanges	1825 to 1860 (35 years)
Laigné-Chéripeau	1832 to 1834 (2 years)
La Pooté	1827 to 1844 (17 years)
Marcillé-la-Ville	1823 to 1841 (18 years)
Marçon	1822 to 1836 (14 years)
Mayenne	1825 to 1842 (17 years)
Milly-la-Forêt	1828 to 1865 (37 years)
Montmirail	1826 to 1846 (20 years)
Montourtier	1822 to 1835 (13 years)
Rouessé-Vassé	1829 to 1835 (6 years)
Ruillé	1821 to 1870 (49 years)
Ruillé (boarding school)	1824 to 1836 (12 years)
Sablé	1830 to 1846 (16 years)
Saint-Denis d'Anjou	1827 to 1878 (51 years)
Saint-James	1826 to 1847 (21 years)
Saint-Symphorian	1833 to 1834 (1 year)
Vallon	1828 to 1845 (17 years)

1834

| Abondant | 1826 to 1870 (44 years) |
| Ahuillé | 1834 to 1837 (3 years) |

Aigné	1823 to 1850 (27 years)
Beaune-la-Rolande	1827 to 1835 (8 years)
Bouère	1826 to 1888 (62 years)
Chémeré-le-Roi	1833 to 1860 (27 years)
Choisel	1830 to 1835 (5 years)
Craon	1827 to 1903 (76 years)
Dampierre	1827 to 1878 (51 years)
Daon	1824 to 1852 (28 years)
Ecommoy	1823 to 1836 (13 years)
Hardanges	1825 to 1860 (35 years)
La Pooté	1827 to 1844 (17 years)
Marcillé-la-Ville	1823 to 1841 (18 years)
Marçon	1822 to 1836 (14 years)
Mayenne	1825 to 1842 (17 years)
Milly-la-Forêt	1828 to 1865 (37 years)
Montmirail	1826 to 1846 (20 years)
Montourtier	1822 to 1835 (13 years)
Poncé	1834 to 1860 (26 years)
Préaux	1834 to 1878 (44 years)
Rouessé-Vassé	1829 to 1835 (6 years)
Ruillé	1821 to 1870 (49 years)
Ruillé (boarding school)	1824 to 1836 (12 years)
Sablé	1830 to 1846 (16 years)
Saint-Denis d'Anjou	1827 to 1878 (51 years)
Saint-James	1826 to 1847 (21 years)
Vallon	1828 to 1845 (17 years)

1835

Abondant	1826 to 1870 (44 years)
Ahuillé	1834 to 1837 (3 years)
Aigné	1823 to 1850 (27 years)
Bouère	1826 to 1888 (62 years)
Chémeré-le-Roi	1833 to 1860 (27 years)
Craon	1827 to 1903 (76 years)
Dampierre	1827 to 1878 (51 years)
Daon	1824 to 1852 (28 years)

Ecommoy	1823 to 1836 (13 years)
Hardanges	1825 to 1860 (35 years)
La Pooté	1827 to 1844 (17 years)
Marcillé-la-Ville	1823 to 1841 (18 years)
Marçon	1822 to 1836 (14 years)
Mayenne	1825 to 1842 (17 years)
Milly-la-Forêt	1828 to 1865 (37 years)
Montmirail	1826 to 1846 (20 years)
Neau	1835 to 1835 (months)
Poncé	1834 to 1860 (26 years)
Préaux	1834 to 1878 (44 years)
Ruillé	1821 to 1870 (49 years)
Ruillé (boarding school)	1824 to 1836 (12 years)
Sablé	1830 to 1846 (16 years)
Saint-Denis d'Anjou	1827 to 1878 (51 years)
Saint-James	1826 to 1847 (21 years)
Vallon	1828 to 1845 (17 years)

1836

Abondant	1826 to 1870 (44 years)
Ahuillé	1834 to 1837 (3 years)
Aigné	1823 to 1850 (27 years)
Bouère	1826 to 1888 (62 years)
Chéméré-le-Roi	1833 to 1860 (27 years)
Craon	1827 to 1903 (76 years)
Dampierre	1827 to 1878 (51 years)
Daon	1824 to 1852 (28 years)
Grand-Oisseau	1836 to 1888 (52 years)
Hardanges	1825 to 1860 (35 years)
La Pooté	1827 to 1844 (17 years)
Marcillé-la-Ville	1823 to 1841 (18 years)
Mayenne	1825 to 1842 (17 years)
Milly-la-Forêt	1828 to 1865 (37 years)
Montmirail	1826 to 1846 (20 years)
Poncé	1834 to 1860 (26 years)
Préaux	1834 to 1878 (44 years)

Ruillé	1821 to 1870 (49 years)
Ruillé-Froidfond	1836 to 1845 (9 years)
Ruillé-le-Gravelais	1836 to 1878 (42 years)
Sablé	1830 to 1846 (16 years)
Saint-Denis d'Anjou	1827 to 1878 (51 years)
Saint-James	1826 to 1847 (21 years)
Vallon	1828 to 1845 (17 years)
Vallon	1836 to 1845 (9 years)

1837

Abondant	1826 to 1870 (44 years)
Aigné	1823 to 1850 (27 years)
Allonnes	1837 to 1838 (1 year)
Bouère	1826 to 1888 (62 years)
Chéméré-le-Roi	1833 to 1860 (27 years)
Craon	1827 to 1903 (76 years)
Dampierre	1827 to 1878 (51 years)
Daon	1824 to 1852 (28 years)
Gennes	1837 to 1878 (41 years)
Grand-Oisseau	1836 to 1888 (52 years)
Hardanges	1825 to 1860 (35 years)
La Pooté	1827 to 1844 (17 years)
Le Buret	1837 to 1847 (10 years)
Le Tréport	1837 to 1876 (39 years)
Marcillé-la-Ville	1823 to 1841 (18 years)
Mayenne	1825 to 1842 (17 years)
Milly-la-Forêt	1828 to 1865 (37 years)
Montmirail	1826 to 1846 (20 years)
Poncé	1834 to 1860 (26 years)
Préaux	1834 to 1878 (44 years)
Ruillé	1821 to 1870 (49 years)
Ruillé-Froidfond	1836 to 1845 (9 years)
Ruillé-le-Gravelais	1836 to 1878 (42 years)
Sablé	1830 to 1846 (16 years)
Saint-Berthevin	1837 to 1860 (23 years)
Saint-Denis d'Anjou	1827 to 1878 (51 years)

Saint-James	1826 to 1847 (21 years)
Vallon	1828 to 1845 (17 years)
Vallon	1836 to 1845 (9 years)

1838

Abondant	1826 to 1870 (44 years)
Aigné	1823 to 1850 (27 years)
Alexain	1838 to 1840 (2 years)
Bierné	1838 to 1860 (22 years)
Bouère	1826 to 1888 (62 years)
Brûlon	1838 to 1903 (65 years)
Chéméré-le-Roi	1833 to 1860 (27 years)
Craon	1827 to 1903 (76 years)
Dampierre	1827 to 1878 (51 years)
Daon	1824 to 1852 (28 years)
Ernée	1838 to 1903 (65 years)
Gennes	1837 to 1878 (41 years)
Grand-Oisseau	1836 to 1888 (52 years)
Hardanges	1825 to 1860 (35 years)
Issoudu	1838 to 1846 (8 years)
La Pooté	1827 to 1844 (17 years)
Le Buret	1837 to 1847 (10 years)
Le Tréport	1837 to 1876 (39 years)
Marcillé-la-Ville	1823 to 1841 (18 years)
Mayenne	1825 to 1842 (17 years)
Milly-la-Forêt	1828 to 1865 (37 years)
Montmirail	1826 to 1846 (20 years)
Poncé	1834 to 1860 (26 years)
Pont-Aucemer	1838 to 1894 (56 years)
Préaux	1834 to 1878 (44 years)
Rânes	1838 to 1891 (53 years)
Ruillé	1821 to 1870 (49 years)
Ruillé-Froidfond	1836 to 1845 (9 years)
Ruillé-le-Gravelais	1836 to 1878 (42 years)
Sablé	1830 to 1846 (16 years)
Saint-Berthevin	1837 to 1860 (23 years)

Saint-Denis d'Anjou	1827 to 1878 (51 years)
Saint-Denis de Gastines	1838 to 1838 (months)
Sainte-Croix	1838 to 1868 (30 years)
Saint-James	1826 to 1847 (21 years)
Vallon	1828 to 1845 (17 years)
Vallon	1836 to 1845 (9 years)

1839

Abondant	1826 to 1870 (44 years)
Aigné	1823 to 1850 (27 years)
Alexain	1838 to 1840 (2 years)
Bierné	1838 to 1860 (22 years)
Bouère	1826 to 1888 (62 years)
Brûlon	1838 to 1903 (65 years)
Chéméré-le-Roi	1833 to 1860 (27 years)
Craon	1827 to 1903 (76 years)
Dampierre	1827 to 1878 (51 years)
Daon	1824 to 1852 (28 years)
Ernée	1838 to 1903 (65 years)
Gennes	1837 to 1878 (41 years)
Goron	1839 to 1840 (1 year)
Grand-Oisseau	1836 to 1888 (52 years)
Hardanges	1825 to 1860 (35 years)
Issoudu	1838 to 1846 (8 years)
La Pooté	1827 to 1844 (17 years)
Le Buret	1837 to 1847 (10 years)
Le Tréport	1837 to 1876 (39 years)
Mansigré	1839 to 1860 (21 years)
Marcillé-la-Ville	1823 to 1841 (18 years)
Mayenne	1825 to 1842 (17 years)
Milly-la-Forêt	1828 to 1865 (37 years)
Montmirail	1826 to 1846 (20 years)
Poncé	1834 to 1860 (26 years)
Pont-Aucemer	1838 to 1894 (56 years)
Préaux	1834 to 1878 (44 years)
Rânes	1838 to 1891 (53 years)

Ruillé	1821 to 1870 (49 years)
Ruillé-Froidfond	1836 to 1845 (9 years)
Ruillé-le-Gravelais	1836 to 1878 (42 years)
Sablé	1830 to 1846 (16 years)
Saint-Berthevin	1837 to 1860 (23 years)
Saint-Denis d'Anjou	1827 to 1878 (51 years)
Sainte-Croix	1838 to 1868 (30 years)
Saint-James	1826 to 1847 (21 years)
Vallon	1828 to 1845 (17 years)
Vallon	1836 to 1845 (9 years)
Vandoeuvres	1839 to 1857 (18 years)
Vendôme	1839 to 1860 (21 years)

1840

Abondant	1826 to 1870 (44 years)
Aigné	1823 to 1850 (27 years)
Bierné	1838 to 1860 (22 years)
Bouère	1826 to 1888 (62 years)
Brûlon	1838 to 1903 (65 years)
Chéméré-le-Roi	1833 to 1860 (27 years)
Craon	1827 to 1903 (76 years)
Dampierre	1827 to 1878 (51 years)
Daon	1824 to 1852 (28 years)
Ernée	1838 to 1903 (65 years)
Gennes	1837 to 1878 (41 years)
Grand-Oisseau	1836 to 1888 (52 years)
Hardanges	1825 to 1860 (35 years)
Issoudu	1838 to 1846 (8 years)
La Pooté	1827 to 1844 (17 years)
Le Buret	1837 to 1847 (10 years)
Le Tréport	1837 to 1876 (39 years)
Mansigré	1839 to 1860 (21 years)
Marcillé-la-Ville	1823 to 1841 (18 years)
Mayenne	1825 to 1842 (17 years)
Milly-la-Forêt	1828 to 1865 (37 years)
Montmirail	1826 to 1846 (20 years)

Poncé	1834 to 1860 (26 years)
Pont-Aucemer	1838 to 1894 (56 years)
Préaux	1834 to 1878 (44 years)
Précioré	1840 to 1881 (41 years)
Rânes	1838 to 1891 (53 years)
Ruillé	1821 to 1870 (49 years)
Ruillé-Froidfond	1836 to 1845 (9 years)
Ruillé-le-Gravelais	1836 to 1878 (42 years)
Sablé	1830 to 1846 (16 years)
Saint-Berthevin	1837 to 1860 (23 years)
Saint-Denis d'Anjou	1827 to 1878 (51 years)
Sainte-Croix	1838 to 1868 (30 years)
Saint-James	1826 to 1847 (21 years)
Vallon	1828 to 1845 (17 years)
Vallon	1836 to 1845 (9 years)
Vandoeuvres	1839 to 1857 (18 years)
Vendôme	1839 to 1860 (21 years)

APPENDIX VI

Early Schools of the Brothers of St. Joseph: Openings

(Adapted from *Sainte-Croix en France*.)

1821

Larchamp	1821 to 1829 (8 years)
Ruillé	1821 to 1870 (49 years)
Saint-Denis d'Orques	1821 to 1833 (12 years)

1822

Les Autels-Saint-Eloi	1822 to 1826 (4 years)
Marçon	1822 to 1836 (14 years)
Ménil	1822 to 1824 (2 years)
Montourtier	1822 to 1835 (13 years)
Saint-Germain-le-Guillaume	1822 to 1831 (9 years)
Saint-Pierre de Chevillé	1822 to 1823 (1 year)
Yvré-l'Evêque	1822 to 1831 (9 years)

1823

Aigné	1823 to 1850 (27 years)
Ardenay	1823 to 1828 (5 years)
Bierné	1823 to 1830 (7 years)
Ecommoy	1823 to 1836 (13 years)
Ernée	1823 to 1824 (1 year)

Laval (orphanage)	1823 to 1827 (4 years)
Marcillé-la-Ville	1823 to 1841 (18 years)
Meslay	1823 to 1870 (47 years)
Saint-Mars-la-Brière	1823 to 1827 (4 years)
Saint-Vincent-du-Lourouer	1823 to 1825 (2 years)

1824

Beaulieu	1824 to 1828 (4 years)
Daon	1824 to 1852 (28 years)
Désertines	1824 to 1828 (4 years)
Le Breil	1824 to 1826 (2 years)
Mamers	1824 to 1833 (9 years)
Meung-sur-Loire	1824 to 1827 (3 years)
Nogent-le-Bernard	1824 to 1831 (7 years)
Romorantin	1824 to 1827 (3 years)
Ruillé (boarding school)	1824 to 1836 (12 years)
Saint-Martin-du-Eois	1824 to 1827 (3 years)

1825

Aubigné	1825 to 1830 (5 years)
Channay	1825 to 1828 (3 years)
Contres	1825 to 1830 (5 years)
Cré-sur-Loir	1825 to 1827 (2 years)
Genneteil	1825 to 1828 (3 years)
Hardanges	1825 to 1860 (35 years)
Lignières-la-Doucelle	1825 to 1826 (1 year)
Loches	1825 to 1831 (6 years)
Mayenne	1825 to 1842 (17 years)
Mortagne	1825 to 1830 (5 years)
Preuilly	1825 to 1826 (1 year)
Rochecorbon	1825 to 1830 (5 years)
Saint-Cyr-en-Pail	1825 to 1833 (8 years)
Souday	1825 to 1827 (2 years)
Vouvray	1825 to 1831 (6 years)

1826

Abondant	1826 to 1870 (44 years)
Authon	1826 to 1828 (2 years)
Bouère	1826 to 1888 (62 years)
Brou	1826 to 1833 (7 years)
Champgénéteux	1826 to 1833 (7 years)
Cheverny	1826 to 1831 (5 years)
Grez-en-Bouère	1826 to 1832 (6 years)
La Loupe	1826 to 1828 (2 years)
Montmirail	1826 to 1846 (20 years)
Saint-James	1826 to 1847 (21 years)

1827

Beaune-la-Rolande	1827 to 1835 (8 years)
Bonnétable	1827 to 1832 (5 years)
Craon	1827 to 1903 (76 years)
Dampierre	1827 to 1878 (51 years)
Evron	1827 to 1831 (4 years)
La Pooté	1827 to 1844 (17 years)
Parcay-sous-Rillé	1827 to 1829 (2 years)
Saint-Denis d'Anjou	1827 to 1878 (51 years)
Saint-Hilaire-du-Harcouet	1827 to 1828 (1 year)
Saint-Lambert-des-Lecées	1827 to 1831 (4 years)
Saint-Martin-le-Beau	1827 to 1831 (4 years)
Sainte-Suzanne	1827 to 1830 (3 years)
Véretz	1827 to 1828 (1 year)

1828

Logron	1828 to 1830 (2 years)
Maisoncelles	1828 to 1830 (2 years)
Milly-la-Forêt	1828 to 1865 (37 years)
Souligné-sous-Vallon	1828 to 1831 (3 years)
Vallon	1828 to 1845 (17 years)
Viviers	1828 to 1830 (2 years)

1829

Rouessé-Vassé	1829 to 1835 (6 years)

1830

Choisel	1830 to 1835 (5 years)
Sablé	1830 to 1846 (16 years)

1831

Lhomme	1831 to 1831 (months)

1832

Laigné-Chéripeau	1832 to 1834 (2 years)

1833

Chéméré-le-Roi	1833 to 1860 (27 years)
Saint-Symphorian	1833 to 1834 (1 year)

1834

Ahuillé	1834 to 1837 (3 years)
Poncé	1834 to 1860 (26 years)
Préaux	1834 to 1878 (44 years)

1835

Neau	1835 to 1835 (months)

1836

Grand-Oisseau	1836 to 1888 (52 years)
Ruillé-Froidfond	1836 to 1845 (9 years)
Ruillé-le-Gravelais	1836 to 1878 (42 years)
Vallon	1836 to 1845 (9 years)

1837

Allonnes	1837 to 1838 (1 year)
Gennes	1837 to 1878 (41 years)
Le Buret	1837 to 1847 (10 years)
Le Tréport	1837 to 1876 (39 years)

Saint-Berthevin	1837 to 1860 (23 years)

1838

Alexain	1838 to 1840 (2 years)
Bierné	1838 to 1860 (22 years)
Brûlon	1838 to 1903 (65 years)
Ernée	1838 to 1903 (65 years)
Issoudu	1838 to 1846 (8 years)
Pont-Aucemer	1838 to 1894 (56 years)
Rânes	1838 to 1891 (53 years)
Saint-Denis de Gastines	1838 to 1838 (months)
Sainte-Croix	1838 to 1868 (30 years)

1839

Goron	1839 to 1840 (1 year)
Mansigré	1839 to 1860 (21 years)
Vandoeuvres	1839 to 1857 (18 years)
Vendôme	1839 to 1860 (21 years)

1840

Précioré	1840 to 1881 (41 years)

Schools in the order they were opened with first Brother assigned:

1821

	Ruillé	Andre Mottais
1	Saint-Denis d'Orques	Stephen Gauffe
2	Larchamp	Louis Duchêne

1822

3	Marçon	Basile Derouet
4	Montourtier	Baptiste Verger
5	Les Autels-St-Eloi	François Blanchet
6	Yvré-l'Evêque	Jean Vayer
7	Ménil	Victor Loupil
8	St.-Pierre de Chevillé	?

1823

10	Ernée	Martin Verger
11	Marcillé-la-Ville	Bernard Bonneau
12	St.-Vincent-du-Lourouer	Denis Touti
	Aigné	Marin Bulanger
	Ardenay	Augustin Riet
	Bierné	Michel Jouseau
	Ecommoy	Anthony Jousse → Martin Verger
	Laval	Joseph Bourdon & Charles Fairbault
	Meslay	Pierre Oger
	St-Mars-la-Brière	Julien Neveu

APPENDIX VII

Early Schools of the Brothers of St. Joseph: Closings

(Adapted from *Sainte-Croix en France*.)

1823

Saint-Pierre de Chevillé	1822 to 1823 (1 year)

1824

Ernée	1823 to 1824 (1 year)
Ménil	1822 to 1824 (2 years)

1825

Saint-Vincent-du-Lourouer	1823 to 1825 (2 years)

1826

Le Breil	1824 to 1826 (2 years)
Les Autels-Saint-Eloi	1822 to 1826 (4 years)
Lignières-la-Doucelle	1825 to 1826 (1 year)
Preuilly	1825 to 1826 (1 year)

1827

Cré-sur-Loir	1825 to 1827 (2 years)
Laval	1823 to 1827 (4 years)
Meung-sur-Loire	1824 to 1827 (3 years)

Romorantin	1824 to 1827 (3 years)
Saint-Mars-la-Brière	1823 to 1827 (4 years)
Saint-Martin-du-Eois	1824 to 1827 (3 years)
Souday	1825 to 1827 (2 years)

1828

Ardenay	1823 to 1828 (5 years)
Authon	1826 to 1828 (2 years)
Beaulieu	1824 to 1828 (4 years)
Channay	1825 to 1828 (3 years)
Désertines	1824 to 1828 (4 years)
Genneteil	1825 to 1828 (3 years)
La Loupe	1826 to 1828 (2 years)
Saint-Hilaire-du-Harcouet	1827 to 1828 (1 year)
Véretz	1827 to 1828 (1 year)

1829

| Larchamp | 1821 to 1829 (8 years) |
| Parcay-sous-Rillé | 1827 to 1829 (2 years) |

1830

Aubigné	1825 to 1830 (5 years)
Bierné	1823 to 1830 (7 years)
Contres	1825 to 1830 (5 years)
Logron	1828 to 1830 (2 years)
Maisoncelles	1828 to 1830 (2 years)
Mortagne	1825 to 1830 (5 years)
Rochecorbon	1825 to 1830 (5 years)
Sainte-Suzanne	1827 to 1830 (3 years)
Viviers	1828 to 1830 (2 years)

1831

Cheverny	1826 to 1831 (5 years)
Evron	1827 to 1831 (4 years)
Lhomme	1831 to 1831 (months)
Loches	1825 to 1831 (6 years)

Nogent-le-Bernard	1824 to 1831 (7 years)
Saint-Germain-le-Guillaume	1822 to 1831 (9 years)
Saint-Lambert-des-Lecées	1827 to 1831 (4 years)
Saint-Martin-le-Beau	1827 to 1831 (4 years)
Souligné-sous-Vallon	1828 to 1831 (3 years)
Vouvray	1825 to 1831 (6 years)
Yvré-l'Evêque	1822 to 1831 (9 years)

1832

| Bonnétable | 1827 to 1832 (5 years) |
| Grez-en-Bouère | 1826 to 1832 (6 years) |

1833

Brou	1826 to 1833 (7 years)
Champgénéteux	1826 to 1833 (7 years)
Mamers	1824 to 1833 (9 years)
Saint-Cyr-en-Pail	1825 to 1833 (8 years)
Saint-Denis d'Orques	1821 to 1833 (12 years)

1834

| Laigné-Chéripeau | 1832 to 1834 (2 years) |
| Saint-Symphorian | 1833 to 1834 (1 year) |

1835

Beaune-la-Rolande	1827 to 1835 (8 years)
Choisel	1830 to 1835 (5 years)
Montourtier	1822 to 1835 (13 years)
Neau	1835 to 1835 (months)
Rouessé-Vassé	1829 to 1835 (6 years)

1836

Ecommoy	1823 to 1836 (13 years)
Marçon	1822 to 1836 (14 years)
Ruillé (boarding school)	1824 to 1836 (12 years)

1837

Ahuillé	1834 to 1837 (3 years)

1838

Allonnes	1837 to 1838 (1 year)
Saint-Denis de Gastines	1838 to 1838 (months)

1839

1840

Alexain	1838 to 1840 (2 years)
Goron	1839 to 1840 (1 year)

APPENDIX VIII

Early Schools of the Brothers of St. Joseph 1821 - 1903 Alphabetical Order

(Adapted from *Sainte-Croix en France*)

Abondant	1826 to 1870 (44 years)
Ahuillé	1834 to 1837 (3 years)
Aigné	1823 to 1850 (27 years)
Alexain	1838 to 1840 (2 years)
Allonnes	1837 to 1838 (1 year)
Ardenay	1823 to 1828 (5 years)
Aubigné	1825 to 1830 (5 years)
Authon	1826 to 1828 (2 years)
Beaulieu	1824 to 1828 (4 years)
Beaune-la-Rolande	1827 to 1835 (8 years)
Bierné	1823 to 1830 (7 years)
Bierné	1838 to 1860 (22 years)
Bonnétable	1827 to 1832 (5 years)
Bouère	1826 to 1888 (62 years)
Brou	1826 to 1833 (7 years)
Brûlon	1838 to 1903 (65 years)
Champgénéteux	1826 to 1833 (7 years)
Channay	1825 to 1828 (3 years)

Chéméré-le-Roi	1833 to 1860 (27 years)
Cheverny	1826 to 1831 (5 years)
Choisel	1830 to 1835 (5 years)
Contres	1825 to 1830 (5 years)
Craon	1827 to 1903 (76 years)
Cré-sur-Loir	1825 to 1827 (2 years)
Daon	1824 to 1852 (28 years)
Dampierre	1827 to 1878 (51 years)
Désertines	1824 to 1828 (4 years)
Ecommoy	1823 to 1836 (13 years)
Ernée	1823 to 1824 (1 year)
Ernée	1838 to 1903 (65 years)
Evron	1827 to 1831 (4 years)
Gennes	1837 to 1878 (41 years)
Genneteil	1825 to 1828 (3 years)
Goron	1839 to 1840 (1 year)
Grand-Oisseau	1836 to 1888 (52 years)
Grez-en-Bouère	1826 to 1832 (6 years)
Hardanges	1825 to 1860 (35 years)
Issoudu	1838 to 1846 (8 years)
Laigné-Chéripeau	1832 to 1834 (2 years)
La Loupe	1826 to 1828 (2 years)
La Pooté	1827 to 1844 (17 years)
Larchamp	1821 to 1829 (8 years)
Laval	1823 to 1827 (4 years)
Le Breil	1824 to 1826 (2 years)
Le Buret	1837 to 1847 (10 years)
Les Autels-Saint-Eloi	1822 to 1826 (4 years)
Le Tréport	1837 to 1876 (39 years)
Lhomme	1831 to 1831 (months)

Lignières-la-Doucelle	1825 to 1826 (1 year)
Loches	1825 to 1831 (6 years)
Logron	1828 to 1830 (2 years)
Maisoncelles	1828 to 1830 (2 years)
Mamers	1824 to 1833 (9 years)
Mansigré	1839 to 1860 (21 years)
Marcillé-la-Ville	1823 to 1841 (18 years)
Marçon	1822 to 1836 (14 years)
Mayenne	1825 to 1842 (17 years)
Ménil	1822 to 1824 (2 years)
Meslay	1823 to 1870 (47 years)
Meung-sur-Loire	1824 to 1827 (3 years)
Milly-la-Forêt	1828 to 1865 (37 years)
Montmirail	1826 to 1846 (20 years)
Montourtier	1822 to 1835 (13 years)
Mortagne	1825 to 1830 (5 years)
Neau	1835 to 1835 (months)
Nogent-le-Bernard	1824 to 1831 (7 years)
Parcay-sous-Rillé	1827 to 1829 (2 years)
Poncé	1834 to 1860 (26 years)
Pont-Aucemer	1838 to 1894 (56 years)
Préaux	1834 to 1878 (44 years)
Précioré	1840 to 1881 (41 years)
Preuilly	1825 to 1826 (1 year)
Rânes	1838 to 1891 (53 years)
Rochecorbon	1825 to 1830 (5 years)
Romorantin	1824 to 1827 (3 years)
Rouessé-Vassé	1829 to 1835 (6 years)
Ruillé	1821 to 1870 (49 years)
Ruillé (boarding school)	1824 to 1836 (12 years)
Ruillé-Froidfond	1836 to 1845 (9 years)
Ruillé-le-Gravelais	1836 to 1878 (42 years)

Sablé	1830 to 1846 (16 years)
Saint-Berthevin	1837 to 1860 (23 years)
Saint-Cyr-en-Pail	1825 to 1833 (8 years)
Saint-Denis d'Anjou	1827 to 1878 (51 years)
Saint-Denis de Gastines	1838 to 1838 (months)
Saint-Denis d'Orques	1821 to 1833 (12 years)
Sainte-Croix	1838 to 1868 (30 years)
Saint-Germain-le-Guillaume	1822 to 1831 (9 years)
Saint-James	1826 to 1847 (21 years)
Saint-Hilaire-du-Harcouet	1827 to 1828 (1 year)
Saint-Lambert-des-Lecées	1827 to 1831 (4 years)
Saint-Mars-la-Brière	1823 to 1827 (4 years)
Saint-Martin-du-Eois	1824 to 1827 (3 years)
Saint-Martin-le-Beau	1827 to 1831 (4 years)
Saint-Pierre de Cheville	1822 to 1823 (1 year)
Sainte-Suzanne	1827 to 1830 (3 years)
Saint-Symphorian	1833 to 1834 (1 year)
Saint-Vincent-du-Lourouer	1823 to 1825 (2 years)
Souday	1825 to 1827 (2 years)
Souligné-sous-Vallon	1828 to 1831 (3 years)
Vallon	1828 to 1845 (17 years)
Vallon	1836 to 1845 (9 years)
Vandoeuvres	1839 to 1857 (18 years)
Vendôme	1839 to 1860 (21 years)
Véretz	1827 to 1828 (1 year)
Viviers	1828 to 1830 (2 years)
Vouvray	1825 to 1831 (6 years)
Yvré-l'Evêque	1822 to 1831 (9 years)

APPENDIX IX

Brothers of St. Joseph Receiving a Teaching Certificate in France

Number after the date = rank in General Matricule

1822	Feb 16	#4 Andre Mottais
	May 18	#5 Stephen Gauffre

1823	Oct 7	#14 Pierre Oger
	Nov 2	#18 Vincent Pieau
	Dec 3	#13 Augustine Riet

1825	Mar 16	#17 Dominic Gautier
	June	#50 Mary Joseph Duval
	Sept 5	#97 Bruno Bouilly
	Sept 13	#78 John of God Duportail, #82 Vincent de Paul Plat
	Sept 25	#92 Athanasius Tarault
	Dec 5	#88 Stanislaus Derve

1826	May 31	#104 Mark Galinand, #111 Ireneus Trassard-Deslandes
	June 3	#85 Vital Breton

1827	Sept 5	#134 Casimir Bardou

1828	Oct 7	#20 Martin Verger, #30 Marin Bulanger, #79 Rémi Mérianne,

		#164 Onesimus Pillard, #178 Bernard Lecavorain
	Oct 21	#61 Arsène Bouvet
1829	Feb 12	#112 Matthew Plumard
	Oct 2	#193 Elisée Réau, #195 Lucian Dagoreau
182_	Apr 30	#42 Romain Bouvier
1830	Oct 2	#215 Donatian Nail, #219 Abel Guyon, #227 Macaire Chauvin
		#228 Theodosius Prieul, #241 Leopold Putiot
1835	Sept 2	#170 Celestine Forton, #245 Dositheus Leblanc
1837	Mar 1	#106 Leonard Guittoger
	Sept	#260 Paul Tessier, #316 Théophile Hervé
	Sept 5	#64 Alexis Chabrun
1838	Mar 3	#314 Zachary Cognet
	Sept	#308 Louis Gonzaga Galmard
1839	Mar	#311 Basil Gary
	Sept 3	#286 Hyacinth Côme
1840	Sept	#180 Raphael Forton, #369 Théotime Salmon
1841	Aug 22	#446 John Baptist Soutif
	Aug 31	#325 Gustave Rose, #381 Anatole Lecoq
1842	Mar 31	#283, #323 Isidore Garnier
	Sept	#289 Gregory of Nazianzan Leroy, #313 Theodore Feau
1843	Apr	#344 Heliodorus Leblanc, #414 Chrysostom Maillard,
		#423 Robert Boyer
	Apr 3	#339 Eugene Leroux
	May 11	#345 Leon Cotin

1844	Apr 16	#367 Sylvain Gareau
	Apr 17	#368 Francis Xavier Ménand
	Apr 22	#280 Narcissus Hulot
	Sept 4	#352 Bernard Legras, #386 Charles Perrotel
1845	Apr	#346 Hippolytus Pieau
1846	Apr 28	#353 Dositheus Foret
1848	May 11	#413 Adolph Blot
1852	Mar	#443 Leander Faverie
1855	Mar 29	#340 Edmond Marteau

APPENDIX X

Date of death for Brothers of Saint Joseph who entered before the 1837 Fundamental Act of Union and died in the Community

(Age in italics. Rank after year of death.)

Jan 7	*Alexis (Jean-Pierre Chabrun) 61*	**1871**	**64**
Jan 8	*Thomas d'Aquin (Alexandre Meleux-Laperriere) 20*	**1836**	**205**
Jan 10	*Casimir (Julien Bardou) 29*	**1841**	**134**
Jan 10	*Romain (François Bouvier) 69*	**1870**	**42**
Jan 21	*Léon (Norbert-Auguste Cotin) 74*	**1894**	**345**
Feb 8	*Maxime (François Boisramé) 26*	**1832**	**66**
Feb 8	*Dosithée (François Leblanc) 21*	**1838**	**245**
Feb 8	*Elisée (Félix-Hippolyte Réau) 81*	**1894**	**193**
Feb 12	*Rémi (Etienne Mérianne) 79*	**1888**	**79**
Feb 12	*Louis de Gonzague (Pierre Galmard) 76*	**1893**	**308**
Feb 16	*Flavien (Louis-Victor Manceau) 21*	**1830**	**176**
Feb 19	*Théophile (Jean Fréard) 19*	**1832**	**135**
Feb 24	*Athanase (Michel-Etienne Tarault) 72*	**1873**	**92**
Feb 27	*Donatien (André-Louis-Paul Nail) 80*	**1886**	**215**
Mar 4	*Anaclet (Joseph Hallier) 26*	**1833**	**203**
Mar 4	*Julien (Julien Henry) 22*	**1836**	**247**

Mar 12	Jean-Marie (Jean-Marie Gauchet) 27	1826	58
Mar 16	André (André Pierre Mottais) 44	1844	4
Mar 24	François d'Assise (François-Marie Tulou) 55	1853	166
Mar 25	Irénée (Joseph-Almire Trassard-Deslandes) 44	1852	111
Apr 1	Dorothée (Joseph Bigot) 70	1873	98
Apr 14	Adrien (Louis Legeai) 70	1873	76
April 17	Eugène (Constant-Julien Leroux) 79	1913	339
Apr 28	Jean-Climaque (Jean-Baptiste Contamin) 68	1866	101
May 7	Zacharie (Jean-Baptiste Cognet) 79	1897	314
May 9	Stanislas (Louis-Joseph-Grégoire Derve) 84	1888	88
May 10	Bonaventure (Pierre Tulou) 59	1856	165
May 12	Matthieu (Pierre Plumard) 79	1888	112
May 24	Martin (Jean Verger) 66	1865	20
May 25	Jérôme (René Porcheré) 26	1826	52
May 29	Sylvain (Victor-Ephrem-Marie Gareau) 81	1904	367
June 1	Marin (Michel Bulanger) 64	1860	30
June 4	Lucien (Alphonse-François Dagoreau) 77	1889	195
June 5	Macaire (Guillaume-Michel Chauvin) 70	1880	227
June 9	Léonard (Pierre-François Guittoger) 84	1887	106
June 25	Théodule (François Barbé) 45	1853	347
June 28	François d'Assise (Nicolas-Pierre Drouin) 19	1837	285
June 30	Vital (Auguste-Casimir Breton) 77	1886	85
July 5	Jean-Marie (Toussaint-Julien Gigon) 65	1851	284
July 8	Marc (François-Charles-Marthe Galinand) 77	1879	104
July 17	Elie (Auguste-Nicholas-Patrice Pérony) 51	1867	338
July 23	Vincent (Jean Pieau) 93	1890	18
Aug 4	Patrice (Thomas Brière) 65	1875	249
Aug 12	Onésime (Mathurin-Pierre-François Pillard) 79	1876	164
Aug 22	Vincent-de-Paul (Jean-Baptiste Vincent Plat) 67	1873	82
Aug 24	Philippe de Néri (Jean-Baptiste Bougault) 40	1841	38
Aug 25	Baptiste (Baptiste Verger) 61	1859	8

Aug 30	*Bernard (Adolphe-Jean Legras) 57*	**1881**	**352**
Aug 31	*Grégoire de Nazianze (Henri Leroy) 77*	**1900**	**289**
Sept 2	*Clément (François Deschamps) 42*	**1851**	**287**
Sept 6	*Ignace (Louis Boissé) 17*	**1835**	**254**
Sept 6	*Etienne (Etienne Gauffre) 58*	**1851**	**5**
Sept 13	*Célestin (Louis Forton) 27*	**1841**	**170**
Sept 15	*Pierre (Pierre Oger) 64*	**1869**	**14**
Sept 21	*Céleste (François Boissé) 21*	**1835**	**255**
Oct 4	*Abraham (Joseph-Louis Veaufleury) 27*	**1834**	**105**
Oct 15	*Hilarion (Louis Ferton) 32*	**1849**	**315**
Oct 31	*Arsène (Louis-Pierre Bouvet) 78*	**1883**	**61**
Nov 6	*Placide (Urbain Alard) 38*	**1850**	**351**
Nov 13	*Léopold (Pierre-Nicholas Putiot) 59*	**1864**	**241**
Nov 21	*Siméon (Charles Bouvier) 23*	**1830**	**49**
Nov 21	*Hilaire (Pierre Beaury 81*	**1890**	**282**
Nov 24	*Julien (François Corbin), 76*	**1892**	**350**
Dec 2	*Antonin (Pierre Lefèbvre) 77*	**1882**	**189**
Dec 3	*Augustin (Jean-Baptiste Riet) 60*	**1860**	**13**
Dec 13	*Basile (Michel Gary) 76*	**1888**	**311**
Dec 18	*Valéry (Jean Bruneau) 65*	**1883**	**307**
Dec 20	*Justin (Louis Gautier) 69*	**1870**	**373**
Dec 23	*François-Xavier (Joseph Ménand) 64*	**1888**	**368**
Dec 29	*Narcisse (Jean-François Hulot) 70*	**1887**	**280**

APPENDIX XI

Brothers of St. Joseph deaths of men who entered by 1840

(Age at time of death given after legal name.)

1826

58. Jean-Marie   Jean-Marie Gauchet 27   March 12

52. Jérôme   René Porcheré 26   May 25

1830

21. Flavien   Louis-Victor Manceau 21   February 16

49. Siméon   Charles Bouvier 23   November 21

1832

66. Maxime   François Boisramé 26   February 8

135. Théophile   Jean Fréard 19   February 19

1833

26. Anaclet   Joseph Hallier 26   March 4

1834

105. Abraham   Joseph-Louis Veaufleury 27   October 4

1835

254. Ignace   Louis Boissé 17   September 6

| 255. Céleste | François Boissé 21 | September 21 |

1836

| 205. Thomas d'Aquin | Alexandre Meleux-Laperrière 20 | January 8 |
| 247. Julien | Julien Henry 22 | March 4 |

1837

| 285. François d'Assise | Nicolas-Pierre Drouin 19 | June 28 |

1838

| 245. Dosithée | François Leblanc 21 | February 8 |

APPENDIX XII

Register of Brothers of Saint Joseph who entered before the 1837 Fundamental Act of Union and died in the Community

(Number at the end of each entry is rank from Matricule Générale.)

1826

Mar 12   *Jean-Marie (Jean-Marie Gauchet) 27, dies (#58)*

May 25   *Jérôme (René Porcheré) 26, dies (#52)*

1830

Feb 16   *Flavien (Louis-Victor Manceau) 21, dies (#176)*

Nov 21   *Siméon (Charles Bouvier) 23, dies (#49)*

1832

Feb 8   *Maxime (François Boisramé) 26, dies (#66)*

Feb 19   *Théophile (Jean Fréard) 19, dies (#135)*

1833

Mar 4   *Anaclet (Joseph Hallier) 26, dies (203)*

1834

Oct 4   *Abraham (Joseph-Louis Veaufleury) 27, dies (105)*

1835

Sept 6   *Ignace (Louis Boissé) 17, dies (254)*

Sept 21   *Céleste (François Boissé) 21, dies (255)*

1836

Jan 8   *Thomas d'Aquin (Alexandre Meleux-Laperriere) 20, dies (205)*

Mar 4   *Julien (Julien Henry) 22, dies (247)*

1837

June 28   *François d'Assise (Nicolas-Pierre Drouin) 19, dies (285)*

1838

Feb 8   *Dosithée (François Leblanc) 21, dies (245)*

1841

Jan 10   *Casimir (Julien Bardou) 29, dies (134)*

Aug 24   *Philippe de Néri (Jean-Baptiste Bougault) 40, dies (38)*

Sept 13   *Célestin (Louis Forton) 27, dies (170)*

1844

Mar 16   *André (André Pierre Mottais) 44, dies (4)*

1849

Oct 15   *Hilarion (Louis Ferton) 32, dies (315)*

1850

Nov 6   *Placide (Urbain Alard) 38, dies (351)*

1851

Apr 1 [?]   *Dorothée (Joseph Bigot) 70, dies (98)*

Sept 2   *Clément (François Deschamps) 42, dies (287)*

Sept 6   *Etienne (Etienne Gauffre) 58, dies (5)*

July 5   *Jean-Marie (Toussaint-Julien Gigon) 65, dies (284)*

1852

Mar 25   *Irénée (Joseph-Almire Trassard-Deslandes) 44, dies (111)*

1853

Mar 24   *François d'Assise (François-Marie Tulou) 55, dies (166)*

June 25   *Théodule (François Barbé) 45, dies (347)*

1856

May 10   *Bonaventure (Pierre Tulou) 59, dies (165)*

1859

Aug 25   *Baptiste (Baptiste Verger) 61, dies (8)*

1860

June 1   *Marin (Michel Bulanger) 64, dies (30)*

Dec 3   *Augustin (Jean-Baptiste Riet) 60, dies (13)*

1864

Nov 13   *Léopold (Pierre-Nicholas Putiot) 59, dies (241)*

1865

May 24   *Martin (Jean Verger) 66, dies (20)*

1866

Apr 28   *Jean-Climaque (Jean-Baptiste Contamin) 68, dies (101)*

1867

June 21   *Ernest (Joseph Nicolas Fournier) 53, dies (337)*

1869

Sept 15   *Pierre (Pierre Oger) 64, dies (14)*

1870

Jan 10   *Romain (François Bouvier) 69, dies (42)*

Dec 20   *Justin (Louis Gautier) 69, dies (373)*

1871

Jan 7   *Alexis (Jean-Pierre Chabrun) 61, dies (64)*

1873

Feb 24	*Athanase (Michel-Etienne Tarault) 72, dies (92)*
Apr 1	*Dorothée (Joseph Bigot) 70, dies (98)*
Apr 14	*Adrien (Louis Legeai) 70, dies (76)*
Aug 22	*Vincent-de-Paul (Jean-Baptiste Vincent Plat) 67, dies (82)*

1875

Aug 4	*Patrice (Thomas Brière) 65, dies (249)*

1876

Aug 12	*Onésime (Mathurin-Pierre-François Pillard) 79, dies (164)*

1879

July 8	*Marc (François-Charles-Marthe Galinand) 77, dies (104)*

1880

June 5	*Macaire (Guillaume-Michel Chauvin) dies (227)*

1881

Aug 30	*Bernard (Adolphe-Jean Legras) 57, dies (352)*

1882

Dec 2	*Antonin (Pierre Lefèbvre) 77, dies (189)*

1883

Oct 31	*Arsène (Louis-Pierre Bouvet) 78, dies (61)*
Dec 18	*Valéry (Jean Bruneau) 65, dies (307)*

1886

Feb 27	*Donatien (André-Louis-Paul Nail) 80, dies (215)*
June 30	*Vital (Auguste-Casimir Breton) 77, dies (85)*

1887

June 9	*Léonard (Pierre-François Guittoger) 84, dies (106)*
Dec 29	*Narcisse (Jean-François Hulot) 70, dies (280)*

1888

Feb 12	*Rémi (Etienne Mérianne) 79, dies (79)*
May 9	*Stanislas (Louis-Joseph-Grégoire Derve) 84, dies (88)*
May 12	*Matthieu (Pierre Plumard) 79, dies (112)*
Dec 13	*Basile (Michel Gary) 76, dies (311)*
Dec 23	*François-Xavier (Joseph Ménand) 64, dies (368)*

1889

June 4	*Lucien (Alphonse-François Dagoreau) 77, dies (195)*

1890

July 23	*Vincent (Jean Pieau) 93, dies (18)*
Nov 21	*Hilaire (Pierre Beaury 81, dies (282)*

1892

Nov 24	*Julien (François Corbin), 76, dies (350)*

1893

Feb 12	*Louis de Gonzague (Pierre Galmard) 76, dies (308)*

1894

Jan 21	*Léon (Norbert-Auguste Cotin) 74, dies (345)*
Feb 8	*Elisée (Félix-Hippolyte Réau) 81, dies (193)*

1897

May 7	*Zacharie (Jean-Baptiste Cognet) 79, dies (314)*

1900

Aug 31	*Grégoire de Nazianze (Henri Leroy) 77, dies (289)*

1904

May 29	*Sylvain (Victor-Ephrem-Marie Gareau) 81, dies (367)*

1913

April 17	*Eugène (Constant-Julien Leroux) 79, dies (339)*

APPENDIX XIII

Brothers of St. Joseph: Perseverance 1820 to 1837

Statistics based on data from General Matricule

YEAR(S)	ENTERED	LEFT/ DISMISSED	PERSEVERE	% BY YEAR PERSEVERE	% TOTAL PERSEVERE
1820	4	2	2	2/4 = 50%	2/4 = 50%
1820-1821	6 + 4 = 10	5 + 2 = 7	1 + 2 = 3	1/6 = 17%	3/10 = 30%
1820-1822	15 + 10 = 25	11 + 7 =18	4 + 3 = 7	4/15 = 27%	7/25 = 28%
1820-1823	19 + 25 = 44	16 + 18 = 34	3 + 7 = 10	3/19 = 16%	10/44 = 23%
1820-1824	29 + 44 = 73	23 + 34 = 57	6 + 10 = 16	6/29 = 21%	16/73 = 22%
1820-1825	42 + 73 = 115	29 + 57 = 86	13 + 16 = 29	13/42 = 31%	29/115 = 25%
1820-1826	38 + 115 = 153	36 + 86 = 122	2 + 29 = 31	2/38 = 5%	31/153 = 20%
1820-1827	27 + 153 = 180	22 + 122 = 144	5 + 31 = 36	5/27 = 19%	36/180 = 20%
1820-1828	31 + 180 = 211	25 + 144 = 169	6 + 36 = 42	6/31 = 19%	42/211 = 20%
1820-1829	22 + 211 = 233	20 + 169 = 189	2 + 42 = 44	2/22 = 9%	44/233 = 19%
1820-1830	7 + 233 = 240	6 + 189 = 195	1 + 44 = 45	1/7 = 14%	45/240 = 19%
1820-1831	3 + 240 = 243	3 + 195 = 198	0 + 45 = 45	0/3 = 0%	45/243 = 19%
1820-1832	1 + 243 = 244	0 + 198 = 198	1 + 45 = 46	1/1 = 100%	46/244 = 19%
1820-1833	14 + 244 = 258	10 + 198 = 208	4 + 46 = 50	4/14 = 29%	50/258 = 19%
1820-1834	12 + 258 = 270	12 + 208 = 220	0 + 50 = 50	0/12 = 0%	50/270 = 19%
1820-1835	0 + 270 = 270	0 + 220 = 220	0 + 50 = 50	0/0 = 0%	50/270 = 19%
1820-1836	28 + 270 = 298	20 + 220 = 240	8 + 50 = 58	8/28 = 29%	58/298 = 20%
1820-1837	7 + 298 = 305	4 + 240 = 244	3 + 58 = 61	3/7 = 43%	61/305 = 20%

APPENDIX XIV

Brothers of St. Joseph: Entrance at Ruillé 1820-1835, Le Mans 1836-1838

Numbers from the General Matricule

YEAR	ENTERING	LEAVING	DISMISSED	DECEASED	TOTAL
1820	4				4
1821	6	1			9
1822	15				24
1823	19	1	4		38
1824	38	4	3		61
1825	43	11	8		85
1826	40	9	11	2	101
1827	27	13	10		105
1828	34	29	7		103
1829	22	18	7		100
1830	12	23	8	2	79
1831	3	10	3		69
1832	1	8	1	2	55
1833	15	3	3	1	67
1834	12	7	4	3	65
1835	7	3	3	2	64
1836	17	8	8	2	63
1837	15	5	3	1	69
1838	48	19	1	1	96

APPENDIX XV

Obediences given to Brothers of St. Joseph by the Bishop of Le Mans at their annual retreat September 8, 1834

(1830 Mottais Accounts Book, page 95)

Aboudaun	Br. Benjamin, Br. Patrick
Aigné	Br. Marin
Ahuille	Br. Julian
Baume la Aolande	Br. Jerome
Bouëre	Br. [?], Br. Lucian
Craon	Br. Bruno, Br. Arsene, Br. Macaire
Chemeré-le-roi	Br. Servier [?], Br. Stephen
Choisel	Br. Alphonse
Daon	Br. Matthew
Dampierre	Br. Athanasius
Ecommoy	Br. Martin
Esclinous	[no one listed]
Hardanges	Br. Adrian
Lapôté	Br. Abraham
Marçon	Br. Basil, Br. Gatian
Marcille la Ville	Br. Dominic
Mayenne	Br. Bernard, Br. John Chrysostom, Br. Eustache, Br. Darthe [?]
Meslay	Br. Pierre

Milly	Br. Baptist, Br. Gervais
Montmirail	Br. Mary-Joseph
Montcurtier	Br. Vital
Pensionnas	Br. Vincent, Br. Louis Gazagne
Poncé	Br. Rémi
Préaux	Br. Rouraiss
Rouchessé-Passé	Br.Casimir
Ruillé (école)	Br. Vincent de Paul
St.Yarnes	Br. Alexis, Br. Césaire
St. Denis d'Anjou	Br. Mark, Br. Donatian
Sablé	Br. Abel, Br. Theodore
Vallon	Br. Leopold, Br. Raphael

APPENDIX XVI

Obediences given to Brothers of St. Joseph at their annual retreat August 25, 1836

(1830 Mottais Accounts Book page 165)

Abondant	Br. Casimir, Br. August (this last one from Sept. 12)
Aigné	Br. Marin
Ahuille	Br. Gatian
Bouëre	Br. Irenée, Br. Luician
Chemeré-le-roi	Br. Vital
Craon	Br. Bruno, Br. Arsene, Br. Patrick
Dampierre	Br. Athanasius
Daon	Br. Matthew
Ecommoy	[no one listed]
Hardanges	Br. Adrian
Lapôté	Br. Theodore
Marcille la Ville	Br. Dominic
Mayenne	Brs. Alexis, Phillip, Celestine, Joseph, Vincent de Paul
Meslay	Br. Pierre
Milly	Br. Baptist, Br. Jerome, Br. Gervais
Montmirail	Br. Mary-Joseph, Br. Ignatius
Préaux	Br. Martin
Ruillé le Grardais	Br. Macaire
St. Denis d'Anjou	Br. Mark, Br. Hyacinth, Br. Ambrose
Sablé	Br. Abel, Br. Felix, Br. Onézime

Vallon	Br. Leopold, Br. Raphael
St. James	Br. Stanislaus, Br. Césaire
Poncé	Br. Rémi
Auille-Froid-Fond	Br. Dorothée
Oisseau (le Grand)	Br. Dosithée, Br. Alexander
Gennes near Chateau-Gontier	Br. Donatian Sept. 4, 1836

Br. Agathange sent to Craon Dec. 15, 1836

Br. Thomas Aquinas sent to Bouëre January 3, 1837

APPENDIX XVII
Religious Profession of Final Vows

Brothers of St. Joseph

Brackets around rank number indicate that the member entered not at Ruillé but rather at Le Mans where he would have been under the direction of Basil Moreau, who assumed directorship of the Brothers in August 1835 and who himself professed vows in 1840. Of the first 100 men to join the Brothers of St. Joseph (1820 to 1825), only 18 took final vows (one as late as 1867), and 4 died before taking final vows.

Date of Profession	Religious Name	Rank	Entrance	Death/ Departure
1836 August 25	Andre Mottais	#4	1820	d. 1844
1837 August 30	Vincent Pieau	#18	1822	d. 1890
	Martin Verger	#20	1822	d. 1865
	Philip Neri Bougault	#38	1823	d. 1842
	Francis of Assisi Tulou	#166	1827	d. 1853
	Abel Guyon	#219	1829	left 1842
	Gervais Guibon	#220	1829	left 1842
	John Mary Gigon	[#284]	1835	d. 1851
1838 February 8	Dositheus Leblanc	#245	1832	d. 1838
August 19	Baptist Verger	#8	1821	d. 1859
	Augustine Riet	#13	1822	d. 1860

	Rémi Mérianne	#79	1825	d. 1888
	Athanasius Tarault	#92	1825	d. 1873
	John Climacus Contamin	#101	1825	d. 1866
	Leonard Guittoger	#106	1825	d. 1887
	Iraneus Deslandes	#111	1825	d. 1852
	Matthew Plumard	#112	1825	d. 1888
	Casimir Bardou	#134	1826	d. 1841
	Bonaventure Tulou	#165	1827	d. 1856
	Parick Brière	#249	1833	d. 1875
	Basil Gary	[#311]	1837	d. 1888
1839 August 22	Alexis Chabrun	#64	1824	d. 1871
	Adrian Legeai	#76	1825	d. 1873
	Onesimus Pillard	#164	1827	d. 1876
	Antonin Lafèbvre	#189	1828	d. 1882
1840 May 17	Louis Marchand	[#385]	1839	d. 1841
August 15	Rev. Basil Moreau	[#272]	1835	d. 1873
	Rev. Edward Sorin	[#374]	1839	d. 1893
	Rev. Paul Célier	[#303]	1836	left. 1842
	Rev. Pierre Chappé	[#318]	1837	d. 1880
	Rev. Augustin Saunier	[#334]	1838	left 1848
August 22	Justin Gautier	[#373]	1838	d. 1870
August 23	Hilaire Beaury	[#282]	1835	d. 1890
	Clement Deschamps	[#287]	1836	d. 1851
1841 July 25	Lawrence Ménage	[#403]	1840	d. 1873
	Francis Xavier Patoy	[#420]	1840	d. 1896
	Joachim André	[#437]	1841	d. 1844
August 15	Rev. Isidore Hiron	[#300]	1835	left 1848
	Rev. Philbert Sargeuil	[#407]	1840	left 1846
	Rev. Theodore Davy	[#408]	1840	d. 1871

	Rev. Louis Vérité	[#411]	1839	d. 1859
	Rev. Louis Champeau	[#416]	1840	d. 1880
August 22	Stanislaus Derve	#88	1825	d. 1888
	Louis Gonzaga Galmard	[#308]	1836	d. 1893
	Hilarion Ferton	[#315]	1837	d. 1849
1842 August 15	Rev. Victor Haudebourg	[#389]	1840	left 1851
	Rev. Joseph Rézé	[#410]	1840	d. 1899
	Rev. Francis Pattou	[#449]	1841	d. 1858
August 23	Stephen Gauffre	#5	1820	d. 1851
	Leopold Patiot	#241	1820	d. 1864
	Zachary Cognet	[#314]	1837	d. 1897
1843 August 15	Rev. Julian Hupier	[#273]	1835	d. 1873
	Rev. Victor Drouelle	[#348]	1837	d. 1875
August 27	Joseph Rother	[#451]	1841	left 1850
1844 August 22	Vincent de Paul Plat	#82	1825	d. 1873
	Theodulus Barbé	[#347]	1838	d. 1853
	Placidus Alard	[#351]	1838	d. 1850
	Ignatius Feron	[#387]	1839	left 1857
1845 August 22	Julian Corbin	[#350]	1838	d. 1892
1846 August 23	Pierre Oger	#14	1822	d. 1869
	Alexander Theule	[#391]	1838	left 1869
	Pascal Desprez	[#406]	1840	left 1868
	Adolph Blot	[#413]	1840	d. 1883
1847 August 22	Arsène Bouvet	#61	1824	d. 1883
	Vital Breton	#85	1825	d. 1886
	Elisée Réau	#193	1828	d. 1894
	Lucian Dagoreau	#195	1828	d. 1889

	Gregory Leroy	[#289]	1836	d. 1900
1848 August 22	Bernard Legras	[#352]	1838	d. 1881
	Ephrem Gillet	[#422]	1840	left 1857
Novem 22	August Pongnant	[#371]	1839	d. 1900
1850 August 15	Rev. Théotime Salmon	[#369]	1839	d. 1854
August 22	Macaire Chauvin	#227	1829	d. 1880
	Eugene Leroux	[#339]	1838	d. 1913
1851 August 28	Hyacinth Côme	[#286]	1836	left 1862
	John Baptist Soutif	[#446]	1841	d. 1908
1852 August 25	Mark Galinard	#104	1825	d. 1879
	Emmanuel Guyon	[#341]	1838	left 1865
	Francis Xavier Ménand	[#368]	1838	d. 1888
1854 August 24	Charles Perrotel	[#386]	1839	d. 1888
1858 August 22	Basilide Portayt	[#421]	1840	d. 1859
1859 August 15	Rev. Silvin DeMarseul	[#302]	1835	left 1868
1860 May 31	Marin Bulanger	#30	1823	d. 1860
1867 August 15	Romain Bouvier	#42	1823	d. 1870
1872 August 15	Narcissus Hulot	[#280]	1835	d. 1887
1881 August 15	Sylvain Gareau	[#367]	1838	d. 1904
1888 August 18	Leon Cotin	[#345]	1838	d. 1894
	Dennis Lebossé	[#447]	1841	d. 1900

APPENDIX XVIII

Brothers of St. Joseph who died before taking final vows in the Community

(considered novices in spite of number of years in the Community)

Rank	Name	Entered	Died	Age at Death
#49	Siméon (Charles Bouvier)	1824	1830	23
#52	Jerome (Rene Porcheré)	1824	1826	26
#58	Jean-Marie (Jean-Marie Gauchet)	1824	1826	26
#66	Maxime (François Boisramé)	1824	1832	26
#98	Dorothée (Joseph Bigot)	1825	1873	70
#105	Abraham (Joseph-Louis Veaufleury)	1825	1834	27
#135	Théophile (Jean Fréard)	1826	1832	19
#170	Célestin (Louis Forton)	1827	1842	15
#176	Flavien (Louis-Victor Manceau)	1827	1830	21
#203	Anaclet (Joseph Hallier)	1828	1833	26
#205	Thomas d'Aquin (Alexandre Meleux-Laperrière)	1828	1836	20
#215	Donatien (André-Louis-Paul Nail)	1829	1886	80
#247	Julien (Julien Henry)	1833	1836	22
#254	Ignace (Louis Boissé)	1833	1835	17
#255	Céleste (François Boissé)	1833	1835	23
#285	François d'Assise (Nicholas Pierre Drouin)	1836	1837	19
#307	Valéry (Jean Bruneau)	1836	1883	65
#443	Léandre (Jean-Jacques-Victor Faverie)	1841	1882	56

APPENDIX XIX

Brothers who signed the September 1, 1831 "Declaration."

Number from the *Matricule Générale* is given before the name.
Family name, if not part of the signature, is given after the name.

8	Baptiste Jean Verger	[died in 1859]
4	Andre Pierre Mottais 1st Director	[died in 1844]
18	Vincent Ferier Jean Pieau	[died in 1890]
42	Romain François Bouvier	[died in 1870]
X	Michel Coupine	[not in the *Matricule*]
36	Henry [Taupin] 3rd Director	[dismissed in 1834]
106	Leonard Guittoger 2nd Director	[died in 1887]
88	Stanislaus Joseph Grégoire Derve	[died in 1888]
166	François Marie Tulou	[died in 1853]
101	Jean Climaque J.B. Contamin	[died in 1866]
164	Onézime Mathurin Pilard	[died in 1876]
20	Martin Jean Verger	[died in 1865]
79	Rémi E. Merianne	[died in 1888]
5	Etienne Gaufre	[died in 1851]
189	Antonin Pierre Lefèbvre	[died in 1882]
82	Vincent de Paul Jean Baptiste Vincent Plat	[died in 1873]
50	Marie Joseph Pierre René Duval	[dismissed in 1851]

Brothers who signed the promise formula on September 5, 1831

4	André [Mottais]	[died in 1844]
106	Léonard Guittoger	[died in 1887]
36	Henry Taupin	[dismissed in 1834]
79	Rémi Merianne	[died in 1888]
85	Vital Breton	[died in 1886]
18	Vincent [Pieau]	[died in 1890]
20	Martin [Jean Verger]	[died in 1865]
88	Stanislaus [Joseph Grégoire Derve]	[died in 1888]
101	J. Climaque [Jean-Baptiste Contamin]	[died in 1866]
5	Etienne [Gaufre]	[died in 1851]
164	Onézime [Mathurin Pilard]	[died in 1876]
13	Augustin [Jean-Baptiste Riet]	[died in 1860]
61	Arsène [Louis-Pierre Bouvet]	[died in 1883]
221	Louis De Gonzague [Louis-Michel] Gondard [dismissed in 1835]	
220	Gervais [Jean Guibon]	[left in 1842]
166	François d'Assise [François-Marie Tulou]	[died in 1853]
42	Romain [François Bouvier]	[died in 1870]
111	Irénée [Joseph-Almire Trassard-Deslandes] [died in 1852]	

Signatures on the Fundamental Act of Union, March 1, 1837
(Taken from Vanier 522)
Following each name is the *General Matricule* number.

Vincent	18	[died 1890]
Léonard	106	[died 1887]
André	4	[died 1844]
Baptiste	8	[died 1859]
Pierre	14	[died 1869]
Martin	20	[died 1865]
Rémi	79	[died 1888]
Philippe	38	[died 1842]
Stanislaus	88	[died 1888]
Arsène	23	[died 1883]

Etienne	5	[died 1851]
Lucien	195	[died 1889]
Alexis	64	[died 1871]
Marc	104	[died 1879]
Irénée	111	[died 1852]
Marie-Joseph	50	[dismissed 1851]
Célestin	170	[died 1842]
Dosithée	245	[died 1838]
Hyacinthe	286	[left 1862]
Matthieu	112	[died 1888]
Vital	85	[died 1886]
Ignace	254	[died 1835?]
Athanase	92	[died 1873]
Raphaël	180	[left 1850]
Donatien	215	[died 1886]
Agathange	296	[left 1844]
Léopold	241	[died 1864]
Elisée	193	[died 1894]
Abel	219	[left 1842]
Marin	30	[died 1860]
Narcisse	280	[died 1887]
Jérôme	299	[left 1839]
Bruno	97	[dismissed 1838]
Théodule	223?	[dismissed 1833?]
Paul	260	[dismissed 1844]
Gervais	220	[left 1842]
Patrice	249	[died 1875]
Ambroise	144?	[dismissed 1827?]
Adrien	76	[died 1873]
Macaire	227	[died 1880]
Dorothée	98	[died 1873]
Jean-Climaque	101	[died 1866]
Casimir	134	[died 1841]
Vincent-de-Paul	82	[died 1873]
Antonin	189	[died 1882]
Alphonse-Rodriguez	252?	[dismissed 1836?]

Dominique	17	[dismissed 1841]
Julien	247?	[died 1836?]
Aldric	304	[left 1839]
Basile	311	[died 1888]
Clément	287	[died 1851]
Valéry	307	[died 1883]
Louis-de-Gonzague	308	[died 1893]
Romain	42	[died 1870]
J.N. Hupier	273	[died 1893]
R. Moriceau	275	[left 1841]
[S] de Marseul	302	[left 1868]
V. Drouelle	348	[died 1875]
P. Chappé	318	[died 1880]
P. Celier	303	[left 1842]
A. Saunier	334	[left 1848]
B. Moreau	272	[died 1873]

APPENDIX XX

Letters by Brother Andre Mottais

(Letters listed in bold type were discovered in 2018.)

1. December 5, 1820	**to family**
2. July 25, 1821	**to family**
3. August 28, 1821	**to family**
4. December 23, 1821	**to family**
5. May 29, 1822	**to family**
6. October 11, 1825	to Brother Adrien
7. December 23, 1825	**to family**
8. March 13, 1826	to family
8. June 22, 1826	to Brother Adrien
9. March 13, 1826	**to family**
10. July 27, 1826	to all the Brothers
11. June 27, 1827	**to family**
12. Dec. 18, 1827	to Brother Adrian
13. September 1, 1828	**to family**
14. May 7, 1829	Inventory at Milly
15. September 15, 1829	**to family**
16. Sept. 23, 1829	to Brother Adrian
17. Nov. 11, 1829	Notes on Milly
18. Sept, 1830	Report to Brother Stanislaus
19. April 19, 1831	Account of visit by Bishop Carron
20. April 21, 1831	Report on State of the Congregation
21. July 20, 1831	to Brother Adrian
22. Sept. 1831	Alliance Formula

23. Sept. 1831	Vow Formula
24. Dec. 14, 1831	List of Benefactors
25. Jan. 17, 1832	Memo
26. May 12, 1832	**to family**
27. June 20, 1832	Report
28. September 9, 1832	**to family**
29. Feb. 4, 1833	Memoir of Father Lamare
30. Aug. 20, 1833	to Sisters of Providence
31. Oct. 21, 1833	to Sisters of Providence
32. Nov. 4, 1833	to Sisters of Providence
33. Feb. 5, 1834	to Sisters of Providence
34. Aug. 18, 1834	to Bishop Bouvier
35. Oct. 17, 1834	to Brothers of St. Joseph
36. Nov. 14, 1834	to Bishop Bouvier
37. Apr. 8, 1835	to Bishop Bouvier
38. April 30, 1835	Affidavit
39. May 5, 1835	to Father Lottin
40. June 28, 1835	Memo
41. September 9, 1837	**to family**
42. Feb. 17, 1838	Memoir of Father Dujarie
43. May 6, 1838	**to family**
44. May 18, 1840	to Brother Vincent Pieau
45. July 11, 1840	to Mottais family
46. Aug. 1, 1840	to Basil Moreau
47. Dec. 1, 1841	to Basil Moreau
48. October 3, 1842	**to family**
49. October 14, 1842	**to family**
50. May 25, 1843	to Brother Vincent Pieau
51. May 26, 1843	to Brother Vincent Pieau

TIMELINE
Including Brothers who entered before 1841 and remained to death

Number after a Brother's name is his rank in the General Matricule.

1773

July 21	Clement XIV suppresses the Jesuits

1774

May 10	Louis XV dies; succeeded by grandson Louis XVI
September 22	Death of Pope Clement XIV

1775

February 15	Accession of Pope Pius VI

1778

February	France recognizes United States as independent

1780

August 19	Birth of Pierre-Jean de Béranger, poet
September 8	Birth of Jean-Marie de Lamennais

1782

June 19	Birth of Félicité De La Mennais, philospher

1786

January 10   Birth of Brother Jean-Marie Gigon (284)

1787

August 1   Death of St. Alphonsus Liguori

1789

July 14   Fall of the Bastille
August 27   Declaration of the Rights of Man

1790

February 20   Death of Emperor Joseph II

1791

March 10   Pope Pius VI condemns the French Revolution
June 20   Royal family flees Paris
December 6   Death of Mozart

1792

March 1   Death of Emperor Leopold II
May 13   Birth of Giovanni Mastai-Ferreti (Pius IX)
May 29   Birth of Brother Henri Taupin (36)
August 4   Order suppressing religious houses (except hospitals)
August 18   Order suppressing all religious congregations
August 26   All refractory priests ordered into exile
September 8   Birth of Brother Stephen Gauffre (5)

1793

January 21   Execution of Louis XVI
July 13   Assassination of Marat by Charlotte Corday
September 17   Reign of Terror begins
October 16   Execution of Marie Antoinette
November 10   Feast of Liberty, Goddess of Reason, in Paris

1794

June 8   Festival of the Supreme Being

July 28	Execution of Robespierre

1795

May 24	Last Paris uprising
July 17	Birth of Brother Marin Bulanger (30)
September 23	New Constitution approved
December 26	James Dujarié ordained

1796

October 3	Birth of Brother Onesimus Pillard (164)
August 5	Birth of Brother Bonaventure Tulou (165)

1797

February 15	Birth of Brother Vincent Pieau (18)
December 1	Birth of Brother Baptiste Verger (8)

1798

February 20	Pope Pius VI leaves Papal States
March 3	Birth of Brother John Climacus Contamin (101)
March 7	French invade Papal States
April 26	Birth of Eugène Delacroix
July 24	Napoleon occupies Cairo
August 27	Death of Louis Watteau

1799

February 7	Birth of Brother Martin Verger (20)
February 7	Birth of Brother Jean-Marie Gauchet (58)
February 11	Birth of Basil Moreau (272)
August 29	Death of Pope Pius VI
October 9	Napoleon returns to France
November 10	Napoleon disbands French Directory government
November 22	Napoleon forms new government

1800

January 1	Birth of Brother Jerome Porcheré (52)
February 21	Birth of Brother Andre Mottais (4)

February 24	Birth of Brother Augustin Riet (13)
March 14	Accession of Pope Pius VII
May 15	Napoleon invades Italy
July 8	Birth of Brother Romain Bouvier (42)
?	Birth of Augustin Noury (276)

1801

January 19	Birth of Brother Athanasius Tarault (92)
February 9	Birth of Brother Justin Gautier (373)
July 15	Concordat signed by Napoleon and Pius VII
October 5	Birth of Brother Mark Galinand (104)

1802

February 26	Birth of Victor Hugo
May 12	Birth of Jean-Baptiste Lacordaire, journalist preacher
May 20	Napoleon reinstates slavery in the colonies
July 13	Birth of Brother Leonard Guittoger (106)
July 26	Birth of Brother Dorothée Bigot (98)
July 31	Birth of Brother Philip Neri Bougault (38)
August 31	Birth of Theodore Davy (408)

1803

January 1	James Dujarié named pastor of Ruillé
February 26	Birth of Brother Adrien Legeai (76)
April 30	Louisiana Purchase
December 11	Birth of Hector Berlioz

1804

March 21	Napoleonic Code goes into effect
March 30	Birth of Brother Stanislaus Derve (88)
May 14	Napoleon given title of emperor
May 18	First French Empire established
November 19	Birth of Brother Pierre Oger (14)
December 2	Napoleon crowns himself emperor
?	Birth of Brother Basilide Portayt (421)

1805

January 19	Birth of Brother Arsène Bouvet (61)
March 20	Birth of Brother Maxime Boisramé (66)
April 26	Birth of Brother Leopold Putiot (241)
May 13	Birth of Brother Antonin Lefèbvre (189)

1806

	Foundation of La Petite Providence
January 25	Birth of Brother Donatien Nail (215)
March 4	Birth of Brother Vincent de Paul Plat (82)
March 19	Birth of Brother Anaclet Hallier (203)
July 12	Napoleon dissolves Holy Roman Empire
August 22	Death of Fragonard
November 30	Napoleon captures Warsaw

1807

January 17	Birth of Brother Abraham Veaufleury (105)
February 14	Birth of Brother Simeon Bouvier (49)
May 6	Birth of Brother Irénée Trassard-Deslandes (111)

1808

February 2	French troops occupy Papal States
March 17	Christian Brothers invited back into France
April 20	Birth of Napoleon III
October 21	Birth of Brother Vital Breton (85)

1809

January 12	Birth of Brother Flavian Manceau (176)
February 1	Birth of Brother Matthew Plumard (112)
February 10	Birth of Brother Rémi Mérianne (79)
February 13	Birth of Brother Clement Deschamps (287)
March 19	Birth of Brother Alexis Chabrun (64)
May 17	Papal States annexed by France
June 3	Birth of Brother Joachim André (437)
November 3	Birth of Pierre Chappé (318)
December 14	Napoleon divorces Josephine

1810

February 17	Birth of Brother Macaire Chauvin (227)
March 13	Birth of Julien-Narcissee
March 13	Birth of Charles Montalembert, liberal Catholic
April 9	Birth of Brother Patrick Brière (249)
September 23	Birth of Brother Camillus Delalande (425)

1811

December 21	Birth of Brother Lucian Dagoreau (195)

1812

February 2	Birth of Brother Placide Alard (351)
March 12	Birth of Brother Casimir Bardou (134)
August 9	Birth of Victor Drouelle (348)
August 29	Birth of Brother Theophilus Fréard (135)
September 14	Napoleon arrives in Moscow
September 20	Birth of Brother Basil Gary (311)
November 12	Birth of Brother Elisée Réau (193)
November?	Birth of Brother Louis Marchand (385)

1813

June 29	Birth of Brother Julian Henry (247)
December 12	Birth of Brother Céleste Boisée (255)

1814

February 6	Birth of Edward Sorin (374)
February 23	Birth of Joseph-Peter Rézé (410)
March 31	Paris occupied by Austrian troops
April 4	Napoleon abdicates; Louis XVIII restored
May 4	Napoleon exiled to Elba
October	Law allowing ecclesiastical schools (petits séminaries)

1815

January 21	Louis XVI and Marie Antoinette buried at St. Denis
February 26	Napoleon escapes from Elba

February 28	Birth of Brother Célestin Forton (170)
March 12	Birth of Brother Lawrence Ménage (403)
June 15	Birth of Brother Thomas Aquinas (205)
June 18	Napoleon defeated at Waterloo
July 7	Louis XVIII restored again
October 11	Birth of Louis Vérité (411)
October 16	Napoleon exiled to St. Helena
October 23	Birth of Brother Elie Pérony (338)

1816

January 17	Birth of Brother Julian Corbin (350)
February 29	School openings allowed by communes or individuals
March 11	Birth of Brother Dosithée Leblanc (245)

1817

February 10	Birth of Brother Hilaire Beaury (282)
February 24	Birth of Brother Hilarion Ferton (315)
May 12	Birth of Brother Brother Zachary Cognet (314)
June 11	Concordat with Holy See
June 13	Birth of Brother Louis Gonzaga Galmard (308)
July 14	Death of Madame de Staël
August 21	Birth of Brother Francis of Assisi Drouin (285)
October 3	Birth of Brother Narcisse Hulot (280)
December 5	Birth of Louis Champeau (416)
?	Marianists founded by Guillaume Chaminade

1818

January 20	Birth of Brother Théotime Salmon (369)
February 20	Birth of Brother Theodulus Barbé (347)
April 28	Birth of Brother Ignatius Boissé (254)
June 3	Birth of Brother Valéry Bruneau (307)
July	Zoé du Roscoät arrives at Ruillé

1819

| March 26 | Birth of Brother Leon Cotin (345) |
| May 17 | Law supporting morality and religion |

| June 6 | Agreement signed by de Lamennais and Deshayes |
| November 26 | Le Mans Bishop de Pidoll dies |

1820

February 13	Duc de Berry murdered
May 20	Bishop de la Myre consecrated for Le Mans
July 15	Pierre Hureau (Brother Ignace) enters (first Brother)
July 27	Birth of Brother Marie (Francis Xavier) Patoy (420)
August 20	Louis Duchêne (Brother Louis) enters (second Brother)
October 20	Birth of Brother Charles Perrotel (386)
October 22	Andre Mottais (Brother Andre) enters (third Brother)
November 16	Etienne Gauffre (Bro. Etienne) enters (fourth Brother)

1821

February	Brother Andre opens a school in Ruillé
May 5	Death of Napoleon
May 20	Bishop de la Myre consecrated for Le Mans
June	Pierre Hureau leaves Brothers of St. Joseph
June	Andre Mottais sent to Le Mans for five months
November	Andre Mottais returns to Ruillé
December	Andre Mottais sent to Paris for six months
	Brother Etienne opens a school at St. Denis d'Orques
	Brother Louis opens a school at Larchamp

1822

June 13	Birth of Brother Gregory Nazianzus Leroy (289)
June 24	Mother Marie-Madelaine dies
July 14	Birth of Brother Adolph Blot (413)
?	First habits: Andre Mottais and Stephen Gauffre
October 9	Jean Pieau (Brother Vincent) enters

1823

March 18	Birth of Charles Moreau (461)
April	France invades Spain
July 20	Michel Taupin (Brother Henry) enters
August 20	Death of Pope Pius VII
September 4	Birth of Brother Bernard Legras (352)

September 28	Accession of Pope Leo XII
October 7	Birth of Brother Eugene Leroux (339)
December 8	Birth of Brother Sylvain Gareau (367)

1824

February 2	Birth of Brother Francis Xavier Ménand (368)
April 15	Pierre Hureau (Brother Ignace) re-enters
July 20	Birth of Brother Auguste Pongnant (371)
August 20	Schools put under the bishops
September 16	Death of Louis XVIII
November 11	Opening of the Grand St.-Joseph

1825

January 8	Etienne Mérianne (Brother Rémi) enters
March 19	Birth of Brother Anselm Caillot (395)
April 10	Death of Paul Louis Courier, journalist
April 20	Law against sacrilege
May 7	Death of Antonio Salieri, composer
May 24	Law to enhance congregations of sisters
May 25	Anointing of Charles X
September 15	Pierre Guittoger (Brother Leonard) enters

1826

March 12	Death of Brother Jean-Marie Gauchet (58) at Mayenne
April 3	Birth of Brother Gatian Monsimer (396)
May 25	Death of Brother Jerome Porcheré (52) at Ruillé

1828

February 8	Birth of Jules Verne
November	Boarding school opens in Ruillë

1829

February 10	Death of Pope Leo XII
March 31	Accession of Pope Pius VIII

1830

February 16	Death of Brother Flavian Manceau (176) at Larchamp
July 5	French invasion of Algeria
July 25	Riots in Paris against Charles X
July 27-29	July Revolution; Charles X flees Paris
August 2	Abdication of Charles X
August 9	Duke of Orleans becomes King Louis Philippe
November 21	Death of Brother Simeon Bouvier (49) at Ruillé
November 30	Death of Pope Pius VIII

1831

| February 2 | Accession of Pope Gregory XVI |
| April 21 | Sisters and Brothers separate finances in Ruillé |

1832

February 8	Death of Brother Maxime Boisramé (66) at Ruillé
February 19	Death of Brother Theophilus Fréard (135) at Mayenne
June 5	Worker rebellion in Paris

1833

March 4	Death of Brother Anaclet Hallier (203) at Ruillé
May 20	Pledge of union: Angers and Le Mans Good Shepherd
August 27	Death of Bishop Carron in Le Mans

1834

| October 2 | Dismissal of Brother Henry Taupin |
| October 4 | Death of Brother Abraham Veaufleury (105) at La Pôoté |

1835

March 2	Death of Francis I, Emperor of Austria
July 28	Attempted assassination of King Louis-Phillipe
August 31	Transfer of Brothers from Ruillé to Le Mans
September 6	Death of Brother Ignatius Boissé (254) at Ruillé
September 21	Death of Brother Celeste Boissé (255) at Ruillé
November	Brother Leonard goes to Ploërmel

1836

January 8	Death of Brother Thomas Aquinas (205) at Le Mans
March 4	Death of Brother Julian Henry (247) at Ahuillé
June 4	Death of Augustin Noury (276) at Le Mans
August 25	Brother Andre Mottais makes perpetual vows
August 31	Sale of the Grand St.-Joseph

1837

March 1	The Fundamental Pact
June 28	Death of Brother Francis of Assisi (285) at St. Aignan

1839

March 9	France withdraws from Mexico

1841

December 28	Death of Abbé Gabriel Deshayes

1844

March 16	Death of Brother Andre Mottais

1846

June 1	Death of Pope Gregory XVI
June 16	Accession of Pope Pius IX

1848

February 24	Revolution forces Louis-Phillipe to abdicate
December 2	Emperor Ferdinand I of Austria abdicates

BIBLIOGRAPHY

Bernoville, Gaëtan. *Basile Moreau et la Congrégation de Sainte-Croix.* Paris: Grasset, 1952.

Blain, Jean-Baptiste. *The Life of John Baptist de La Salle.* Trans. Richard Armandy, FSC. 2 vols. Landover, MD: Lasallian Pub., 2000.

Burtchaell, CSC, James T. *One Congregation, Two Societies: How Much Fellowship?* Notre Dame: Holy Cross History Association, 2003.

Catta, Etienne, and Tony Catta. *Basil Anthony Mary Moreau.* Trans. Edward L. Heston, CSC. 2 vols. Milwaukee: Bruce, 1955.

Catta, Tony. *Jacques Dujarié.* Trans. Edward L. Heston. Milwaukee: Bruce, 1960.

Cavanaugh, CSC, John. *The Priests of Holy Cross.* Notre Dame: University Press, n.d.

Chronicles, Congregation of Holy Cross. Notre Dame: Holy Cross General Archives.

Connolly, James, CSC. "Charism: Origins and History." In Costin. Vol. 1.

Connolly, James, CSC. "In the Beginning There were Two: The Fundamental Act of Union and the Origins of the Congregation of Holy Cross." Notre Dame: Indiana Province Archives, 1987.

Costin, CSC, Georgia. *Fruits of the Tree, Sequicentennial Chronicles, Sisters of the Holy Cross.* 2 vols. Notre Dame: Sisters of the Holy Cross, 1991.

Dansette, Adrien. *Religious History of Modern France.* Trans. John Dingle. 2 vols. New York: Herder, 1948.

de La Salle, John Baptist. *The Spirituality of Christian Education.* Ed. Carl Koch, Jeffrey Calligan, FSC, and Jeffrey Gros, FSC. New York: Paulist Press, 2004.

De Liguori, St. Alphonsus. *The Great Means of Salvation and of Perfection.* Vol. 3 in *Complete Works.* 17 vols. Ed. Eugene Grimm. 3rd ed. New York: Benziger Brothers, 1886.

Deville, Raymond. *The French School of Spirituality: An Introduction and Reader.* Trans. Agnes Cunningham. Pittsburgh: Duquesne University Press, 1994.

Dionne, CSC, Gerard. "Brothers and Priests in Holy Cross: Two Ways of Living the Same Vocation to Religious Life." Privately printed monograph: 1994.

Dionne, Gerard, CSC. "Book Review" of Thomas Maddix, CSC, *Naming the Options: A Study of the Mission of the Brothers of Holy Cross During a Period of Comfort and Discomfort.* Rpr. Klawitter, *Mottais,* 84-101.

Gervais, CSC, Bernard. *General Matricule.* Notre Dame, IN: Midwest Province Archives, 1944.

Heston, Edward, CSC. "The Cross Our Only Hope." *The Annals of Our Lady of Lourdes.* Notre Dame: Moreau Seminary Library. Typescript.

Klawitter, George, CSC. *Adapted to the Lake: Letters by the Brother Founders of Notre Dame, 1841-1849.* New York: Peter Lang, 1993.

Klawitter, George, CSC. *After Holy Cross, Only Notre Dame.* New York: iUniverse, 2003.

Klawitter, George, CSC, ed. *Brother André Mottais, Pioneer of Holy Cross: "Remove my name every time it appears."* Austin: St. Edward's University, 2001.

Klawitter, CSC, George. *Holy Cross in Algeria: The Early Years, 1840-1849.* New York: iUniverse, 2007.

Maddix, Thomas, CSC. "Breaking the Historical Amnesia: A Fresh Look at the Originating Vision of the Brothers of St. Joseph." In *Naming the Options.* Rpr. Klawitter, *Mottais.* 67-83.

Maddix, Thomas, CSC. *Naming the Options: A Study of the Mission of the Brothers of Holy Cross During a Period of Comfort and Discomfort.* Diss. The Pacific School of Religion, 1989.

Mérianne, Rémi, CSC. *Recueil Documentaire.* Ed. Philéas Vanier, CSC. Notre Dame: Holy Cross Archives.

Moreau, Basil Anthony Mary. *Circular Letters.* Trans. Edward L. Heston, CSC. 2 vols. n.c.: n.p., 1943.

Moreau, Charles. *Le Très Révérend Père Basile-Antoine Moreau, Prêtre du Mans, et ses Oeuvres.* 2 vols. Paris: Firmin-Didot, 1899.

Morin, CSC, Garnier. *From France to Notre Dame.* Notre Dame: Dujarie Press, 1952.

Mottais, CSC, André. *Comptes et Inventoires.* (1830 – 1836). Vol. 2. CSCG 161. University of Notre Dame: General Archives.

O'Dwyer, Ephrem, CSC. *The Curé of Ruillé.* Notre Dame: Ave Maria Press, 1941.

Smith, Charles Edward, CSC. *Documentation for Preserving the Memory of Canon James François Dujarie.* Private printing: 2003.
Vanier, Philéas, CSC. *Le Chanoine Dujarié, 1767-1838.* Montréal: Fides, 1948.

Printed in the United States
By Bookmasters